HIGH WIRE

PETER GOSSELIN

HIGH WIRE

*The Precarious Financial Lives
of American Families*

BASIC
BOOKS

A Member of the Perseus Books Group
New York

Books published by Basic Books are available at special discounts for bulk purchases in the United States by corporations, institutions, and other organizations. For more information, please contact the Special Markets Department at the Perseus Books Group, 2300 Chestnut Street, Suite 200, Philadelphia, PA 19103, call (800) 810-4145, ext. 5000, or e-mail special.markets@perseusbooks.com.

Designed by Jeff Williams
Set in 11.5 point Minion

Library of Congress Cataloging-in-Publication Data
    Gosselin, Peter.
    High wire : the precarious financial lives of American families / Peter Gosselin.
        p.   cm.
    Includes bibliographical references and index.
    ISBN 978-0-465-00225-2 (hardcover : alk. paper)
1. United States—Economic policy. 2. United States—Social policy.
3. Economic security—United States. 4. Households—Economic aspects—United States. 5. Family—Economic aspects—United States.
I. Title. II. Title: Precarious financial lives of American families.
HC106.83.G67 2008
330.973—dc22   2008003962

10 9 8 7 6 5 4 3 2 1

To Nora and Jacob, and to Robin.

CONTENTS

PREFACE

As this book went to press in early 2008, the U.S. economy had landed itself in trouble. Employment, which had been expanding, contracted. Growth, which had been rising, slipped. Consumer spending, which had been strengthening, weakened. House prices tumbled. Energy prices rocketed. Blindsided by the subprime mortgage mess, financial markets came close to clutching in a way that left much of the nation and a good deal of the world on edge. Before the year is out, America may be in a full-blown recession.

Recessions matter to more of us than Wall Street traders and corporate executives. They raise the risk that you or your spouse may lose your job. They cause the value of your savings and your biggest investment, your home, to shrink. They threaten your most carefully laid plans for protecting your family and covering such big costs as college education, medical care, and retirement. If accompanied by price hikes for food and fuel, they can make it more expensive to get through a week. That's why everybody with any power—from the Federal Reserve to President George W. Bush and the Congress—began scrambling to get growth going again.

But let me be clear: This book is not about the transitory ups and downs of the economy. The threats to you and your family that I describe are intensifying during this period of economic weakness, but they are not a product of that weakness. Unless something big changes, they will still be at work and intensifying when the economy has regained its strength and gone back to booming.

That's why interest rate cuts, fiscal stimulus, and other efforts to revive growth—while they may help in the immediate future—are not front and center here. What you'll read in these pages, and in the stories of the people whom you'll meet there, is not a view of the economy from 30,000 feet, but rather as it appears from out your front door. The central question that I'll be asking is not how the economy is doing but how you are doing within it, and how that has changed over time.

My answer is not the standard answer about how this is a prosperous nation that may have been sidetracked by recession but is ready to return to doling out affluence to most of its citizens. And it is not the almost-as-common one that this is a prosperous nation that directs most of its benefits to a lucky handful of people. My view is that Americans, from the working poor to the reasonably rich, are in danger of taking steep financial falls from which they have a terrible time recovering; that the fraction of Americans facing this danger is on the rise and now constitutes a majority; and that the size of the falls we may take is also growing. All but the wealthiest among us are operating on a high wire, compelled to keep our balance, largely on our own. And we must do so while buffeted by financial forces far beyond our control, sometimes even beyond our knowledge.

There is one more point as well: Living and working in this country has not always been like this and does not have to be like this now. We can decide whether this is what we mean America to be.

1

INTRODUCTION

THIS IS A BOOK ABOUT EARNING A LIVING, affording a family, and making it through a work life in America today, and it begins with two seemingly irreconcilable facts.

The first is that for most of the past quarter century, the United States has enjoyed the return of a resilient and growing prosperity that once seemed lost. The economy has doubled in size. The gross domestic product, the broadest measure of annual output, has climbed from just over $7 trillion to almost $14 trillion.

Employment has remained high, inflation low. And unlike the prosperity immediately following World War II, which seemed largely the product of the United States being the last nation standing after the conflict, and which, in any case, unexpectedly began to falter after 1970, the recent growth has been no onetime windfall. Instead, it seems to have sprung from a new enthusiasm for technology, a wide-ranging policy decision to get out of the way of free markets, and a willingness on the part of many Americans to plunge into the global economy with an optimism unmatched by most of our overseas competitors.

The second fact is that many of us, even the affluent among us—those with family incomes running into the hundreds of thousands of dollars—have arrived at the new century increasingly uneasy, with a gnawing sense that our circumstances are changing in ways that leave us less secure. This apprehension has little to do with terrorism or nuclear proliferation or even the Iraq war, much as these issues matter to people. It has not emerged from worry over religious or moral values, or the erosion of constitutional freedoms, or political ideology. Indeed, it has not been public events that sometimes awaken us and leave us tossing in bed. Instead, fleetingly, but recurrently, we have been night-stalked by questions about our private lives: What will happen to my job? Can I pay the doctor? How will I cope if I can't work or my spouse can't? Could I replace my house if it caught fire or was hit by a flood? How will I pay for my children's education? Will my kids do as well as I have done? And behind these questions is a broader concern that, for all of the recent economic growth, the rules by which the world now runs are no longer moving with us, but against us.

Is this a case of needless anxiety in an age of rapid, but generally positive, change? Faced with too much new technology, new competition, new immigration, new social mores—too much "new" in our lives—are we hyperventilating on a continental scale? Do we simply need to get a grip? Or could it be, is it just possible, that millions of Americans have glimpsed an uncomfortable new reality—that the progress of the overall economy is being purchased at a price of diminished security for our families and ourselves? Could it be that the world of work no longer offers the old promise of material progress and security in exchange for diligence and prudent living? At a time when any serious injury or illness may bring ruinous medical bills, can we still count on full protection from those health insurance policies that cost us more each year? Have unrecognized loopholes crept into our homeowners insurance? Does more education really shield us from the inroads of global competition, as our leaders tell us? Most of all, in terms of our personal lives, does America still mean what we always thought it meant?

To begin to understand this paradox—how the United States as a whole could have grown richer while individuals and families have become financially less secure—and to begin to see whether the American promise endures, it is useful to look to the past, in this case to the distant past, New England in 1620. In that year, as the small sailing ship the *Mayflower* rode at anchor off the coast of Cape Cod, William Bradford and his fellow Pilgrims faced a crisis: Winter was coming on. Blown off course by storms, they would have to settle far north of their intended destination. And they faced the unexpected prospect of mutiny. Although most of us think of the *Mayflower* colonists as a tight-knit band of religious dissenters, in fact many on the ship did not share the Pilgrims' religious views; they had been recruited only to help finance the voyage. Now, some of these "Strangers," as the Pilgrims called them, muttered about going their own way, threatening a potentially fatal schism. So Bradford called a meeting. The result was the Mayflower Compact, a terse but unequivocal agreement to "combine ourselves together into a civil body politic" that would create such laws and regulations "as shall be thought most meet and convenient for the general good of the Colony, unto which we promise all due submission and obedience." Forty-one of fifty men on board signed on behalf of themselves, their wives, and their children.

The colonists who founded Plymouth Plantation were in the New World for all sorts of reasons—some to pursue religious beliefs, others to seek fortune, still others to enhance what fortunes they already had. And they were a people not much given to compromise. Yet under the pressure of brutal necessity—as many as half would die within a year—they agreed to yield some part of their individual autonomy to the group. More important, they agreed to a certain mutual responsibility for the well-being of one another, even if meeting that responsibility might sometimes clash with their private interests.

This implicit bargain lay at the heart of virtually everything that followed. The Revolution, the Constitution, the rise of a huge and diverse nation, all rested upon a common understanding: The new society would be dedicated to individual, not collective, dreams, but everyone would nevertheless accept some responsibility for each other and for the common good.

Strangely, however, over the past twenty-five years or so, the bargain struck aboard the *Mayflower* and extended forward through almost four hundred years of often turbulent history has begun to unravel. The basic social contract on which American society has always rested—no matter how imperfectly—has begun to change. The inherent balancing of competing interests that lay at the heart of the bargain has been upset. And it is something about this change that stirs the uneasiness so many Americans feel in their private lives.

As we shall see in the coming chapters, the specific elements of the change have come with surprisingly little public attention. What noisy political debates there have been—for instance, over welfare reform and Social Security—have involved comparatively small numbers of people or have ended in draws that have left the status quo intact. In fact, the main business of change has occurred not in the glare of the public arena but in the relative obscurity of the private sector. But there, the results have been remarkable. The old idea that, even as we pursue our personal destinies, we owe an obligation to each other, to a "civil body politic," and to a "general good," has been shunted aside. In its place, wrapped in the economic doctrine of free markets and the moral precept of personal responsibility, stands a new first principle: Each of us is now expected to forge our own future, free to rise or fall as our talents and luck may dictate. And we are expected to do so with little or no assurance that if, through hard work, we succeed, we can hang on to what we have achieved. At the heart of this credo is the belief that free markets can solve problems—even social problems—better than government or, for that matter, almost any other institution. Whatever the challenge, the best approach is to get out of the way and let the market define the path to a solution. Indeed, it is argued, any attempt to do otherwise through "social engineering"—whether it be via a government guarantee of medical care or a business corporation's guarantee of pension benefits—will not only fail but make matters worse.

Instead of joining together to solve problems that affect the whole society, the heralds of the new approach say, more responsibility should be placed on individuals and families alone. Only when people themselves bear the consequences of financial reversal will they take the steps necessary to protect themselves. As we shall see, the logic of this last position has proved surprisingly appealing. It keeps cropping up in unlikely corners of the remade economy.

And as these new ideas have spread, they have sharply eroded the old idea that the bounty of America should be broadly shared and that those who worked hard and played by the rules should be able to count on some minimum level of protection against bad times and personal misfortune. Small wonder, then, that so many people have felt like they are living on a high wire without a net to soften a fall.

MOST ECONOMISTS scoff at the notion that the recent prosperity has come at an offsetting cost of greater peril for many, perhaps most, Americans. For them, the story line of the past twenty-five years has been almost entirely positive. America ended the 1970s with skyrocketing inflation, stagnating output, and stalling productivity. There were fistfights at the gas pump and President Jimmy Carter on television deploring a national malaise. A new generation of leaders—most prominently Ronald Reagan—set about remaking the economy in the image of its frontier predecessor, deregulating industries, reeling in social benefits, and railing against government. Both they and their Democratic successor, Bill Clinton, embraced free trade. They welcomed competition from developing countries that had lower wages and production costs—including Asia, where millions of workers possessed education and technical training at least equal to those of their U.S. counterparts. And almost everybody applauded the unfettered spread of new technology, including, at long last, the integration of computers into almost every aspect of daily life.

The new prescription seemed to work. As surprisingly as it had stalled, productivity—the output per worker that's widely accepted as the chief determinant of living standards—resumed its upward trajectory. And the American economy returned to growing in such long, steady strides, with low inflation and high output, that policymakers such as Federal Reserve chairman Ben Bernanke have dubbed the change from the 1970s the "Great Moderation."

ONLY THE PAST TWENTY-FIVE YEARS have *not* been a "Great Moderation" for many Americans, including Richard Coss Jr. I first met Coss, then forty-eight, in the fall of 2002. Until six months earlier, he had been a vice president with Pittsburgh's giant PNC Bank, making nearly a six-figure salary in current dollars (well over that amount in constant 2007 dollars), with a wife and three children. I was interviewing him for a story for the *Los Angeles Times,* where I work, about the changing nature of unemployment.

As Coss—tall, taciturn, with short-cropped, almost military, hair—recounted what it was like to go from earning several thousand dollars a week to collecting a few hundred in unemployment benefits, from seeing his savings balloon to watching them shrivel, from helping his retired parents financially to relying on them for gifts, I found myself struggling to maintain my professional distance. But the parallels between the two of us kept piling up. We both had MBAs, his from Duke, mine from Columbia. We'd both spent our careers in businesses rocked by change, in his case banking, in mine journalism. Our daughters were about the same age. *"This could be me!"* I thought. *"This could be my family!"*

Most people—myself included—flee from such a conclusion. And for years, we've been aided in this dodge by the burst of growth that lifted the material lives of millions of Americans, making the Cosses look like the unfortunate but atypical few who get left behind. As I listened to Coss and his wife, Janet, however, I began to realize that their experience carried a larger meaning. One of the most praised aspects of the Great Moderation has been a substantial drop in the nation's unemployment rate. If you're in the workforce today, your chances of losing your job are lower on average than in the past. But what the Cosses' experience said was that this improvement had come with an unpleasant side effect: Although you might be less likely to lose your job, if you do lose it, the damage is likely to be much, much greater. That's because the unemployment safety net has not kept pace with changing economic realities, and the new personnel strategies of most businesses make rehiring a much slower and less reliable process than it used to be, especially for white-collar professionals.

ECONOMISTS AND POLICYMAKERS usually react to stories such as the Cosses' by acknowledging some transitional choppiness en route to today's success. They agree that not everything has worked out swimmingly for everyone. But they generally discount the experience of folks like the Coss family as isolated—the difficulties of a particular industry (autos) or region (the Rust Belt) or class of workers (older ones, blue-collar ones, superfluous middle managers). That, or the unfortunate but inevitable exception to an otherwise positive development.

To the extent the experts do try to square the aggregate economy's strong performance with the insecurity of many of those who depend on it for their livelihoods, they generally don't focus on problems such as the Cosses'. Instead, they point to income inequality, the growing gulf between the rich and the rest of us that some commentators fear may dissolve the social glue that has held the nation together. Indeed, in the past twenty-five years, the top 1 percent of Americans have gone from claiming less than 10 percent of the fruits of the economy to claiming almost 20 percent. But focusing on income inequality turns out to be a not very useful way to try to understand how people assess their own situations. That's because although Americans can get exercised about the enormous incomes of those at the pinnacle of the economy, few worry too much about them. Indeed, far from being a cause for alarm, the country's income numbers leave most people figuring they've dodged a bullet. So long as their incomes are a reasonable distance from the bottom, they don't think that the widening divide greatly threatens their personal well-being.

This book will not be about income inequality. Whether inequality contributes to people's insecurity or not, I believe there is another more immediate cause for that insecurity, however dimly perceived or imperfectly understood: an increase in the risk that Americans must bear as they provide for their families, pay for their houses, save for their retirements, and grab for the good life. The increased risk is the product of a shift of economic dangers from the broad shoulders of business and government, which once helped us handle them, to the backs of working families. And the shift has not just affected the working poor and those in the great statistical middle, but has reached households long thought immune to dislocation, those with six-figure incomes, comfortable houses, and most of the trimmings of affluence.

A wide array of protections that families such as the Cosses—and most likely yours—could once rely on to shield them from direct blasts of the market economy have been scaled back or effectively eliminated, things such as stable jobs, affordable health coverage, guaranteed pensions, short unemployment spells, long-lasting unemployment benefits, and a near-certain payoff for earning a college degree. Equalizing institutions that used to ensure that the benefits of growth and rising productivity were broadly shared—among them quality public education and labor unions—have broken down. Even such simple self-protective mechanisms as bought-and-paid-for home and auto insurance have been altered in ways that leave you bearing more of the burden. The combination of changes doesn't mean that people can't prosper. They can and do; just look around. But the changes do mean that if you take a fall, the resulting losses can include career, house, saving, pension, and the ability to provide educational and other opportunities for your children. And almost no one—from the underclass to the affluent—is immune from these life-rattling plunges.

For all of the seeming promise of the Great Moderation, "for all of the progress of the past twenty-five years, we haven't reduced economic risks," said Robert A. Moffitt, a Johns Hopkins University economist and editor in chief of the *American Economic Review,* the economics profession's premier academic journal. "We've increased them for individuals and households. We've left many Americans leading economically riskier lives than they did a generation ago."

Besides the Cosses, some of the other people you'll meet in these pages are Debra Potter, who provided her family with a plush life as one of Virginia's top insurance agents until she was struck by disease and jilted by one of the very insurers whose products she'd been selling. You'll meet Ron Burtless, an Indiana steel company electrician with a nice suburban home until an industrial accident left him injured and the business and government safety nets that were supposed to protect him left him on the verge of bankruptcy. You'll meet Bruce Meyer and Allan Hess, who lived the executive high life in boomtown Atlanta of the 1990s, but, try as they might, seem unable to get back on top of their game during the rocky 2000s. You'll meet Elvira Rojas, who thought she'd provided for her immigrant family with a unionized dishwashing job at a Los Angeles hotel until the hotel went nonunion. You'll meet Julie and Terry Tunnell, who thought that with all of their business knowledge they'd purchased plenty of insurance for their San Diego home, only to discover the insurance didn't cover half of what they'd expected when the house was consumed by wildfire. You'll meet Laurie Vignaud, a big bank executive and housing specialist who's having to decide on her own whether to rebuild in the ruined stretches of suburban New Orleans. You'll meet Leah Bryner of Salt Lake City, who earned the college degree we tell young people they must have but then found herself in a series of internships and temp jobs that got her to the doorstep of adulthood, but never quite over the threshold. And you'll meet my family.

It is important to be clear about what's being said with these people's stories and the accompanying arguments and what is not. Too often journalists are prosperity deniers. They try to convince their audiences that what may look like growth and feel like growth isn't really growth at all, but something false or hollow. I am making no such argument. The prosperity of the past twenty-five years has been real and, especially that of the late 1990s, has helped improve the lives of millions of Americans, period. Separately, some who seek to describe a new trend may engage in overstatement. They may claim, for example, that the mass of working Americans is at imminent risk of being struck down by a pervasive and never-before-identified threat. But in some sense, my point is the opposite. In the chapters that follow I will show that the *incidence* of many kinds of income-threatening events—such as unemployment in the Cosses' case—has declined. But I will also show that the economy has changed in ways that have pushed up—way up—the *consequence* should you be struck by one of these events. And in the calculus of how often a bad thing can happen and how bad it is if it does, the result has been to leave you and your family at much greater risk.

Some readers will react to this claim by conceding that families do face greater risks. But they'll quickly add that many of these same families also face the possibility of greater reward. That was the purpose of the market-driven public policy, they will say, and it's a trade-off they are willing to make. My answer, which will come up in one way or another repeatedly, is that most Americans are not clamoring for trade-offs, certainly not when it comes to their personal lives. They assume that hard work and responsible behavior are required to achieve a decent living standard, but they believe the rewards should include not only opportunity but also reasonable security for themselves and their families. Yes, they'll sometimes take chances to improve their situations. But most are not in the business of flitting from one living arrangement to another in search of the best "deal." Much as some may enjoy visiting Las Vegas, buying a lottery ticket, or watching *Deal or No Deal,* most of us are much more concerned about protecting what we have built for ourselves over our working lives than about getting a chance to hit life's jackpot.

So where do these new dangers land? Especially after the nation's long run of prosperity, the sidewalks of most neighborhoods aren't littered with economic casualties. So who is being hit by them? How do they show up in people's lives? To begin answering these questions requires a quick tour of the building blocks of most families' finances.

To listen to those whose business it is to offer personal finance advise, you'd think that a family's economic circumstances depend on figuring out what some distant trend like the trade balance means for them, and cashing in on it. But from the doorstep of most working American households, the struts that hold up all but the richest of Americans are pretty much what they have been for generations. And it is around these struts that trouble is now gathering.

Presuming they are in good health, the first cornerstones of most people's economic lives are their jobs, their paychecks, and, in today's world, those of their spouses. Although many Americans have learned to stretch their resources and thus their lifestyles by borrowing, this goes only so far. To a considerable extent, the income that families can amass, much of it from earnings, sets the outer limits for how they can live and what they can aspire to. Of course, jobs and paychecks aren't static. What may matter as much as what a position pays now is how long it will last, and whether it will open up to better

jobs either with the same employer or with others. And at least traditionally, much of what has determined whether these kinds of improvements come one's way has been a person's education, especially
college education.

But jobs and the job market are changing in ways that leave many
families, even many that haven't taken a fall, further out on the economic limb. Paychecks for many Americans are not keeping pace
with inflation or productivity at a time in the economic cycle when
they typically do. The improvements in women's wages, which once
helped offset the income reverses of their male spouses, are no longer
providing as much of a cushion. And that means the downside aspects of two-earner households are coming to the fore. To be sure, as
women have become bigger economic forces, they have helped boost
their families' finances. But they've also boosted the chances—and
the consequences—of a serious reversal. There are two earners instead of one who can lose a job, two instead of one who can suffer a
pay cut. And since most families peg their lifestyles—including such
bedrock items as house and car payments and the educational costs
of children—to the combined incomes of both workers, the impact
of losing one of the incomes can be quick and drastic. Many jobs are
not lasting as long as they used to, leaving the families that depended
on those jobs less stable than they once were. Moreover, for a growing number of people who either lose jobs or can't land them in the
first place, the results are long stays in the netherworld of consulting,
temp work, and, for young workers just starting out, internships.
Finally, as we shall see, college is no longer providing the bulwark
against economic tumult that it once did.

For most working people, jobs are the source of another crucial
cornerstone of economic life besides income: the benefits that employers provide—the health and disability insurance, pensions
and 401(k)s, training, and severance, as well as the bevy of tax
break–heavy savings accounts for everything from child care to commuting costs. Although these seem inconsequential to many people,

especially young people, because they don't show up in a paycheck and often go untapped, they essentially *are* working Americans' backstop against economic trouble, their personal safety nets. Nothing that Washington provides comes anywhere close to matching their scale. But here, too, or perhaps here especially, changes have occurred that are leaving people less securely protected. Fewer employers are providing benefits, and those that do are providing fewer of them. In addition, decades of court rulings have produced a quiet revolution in the federal law that governs benefits. As a result, employers and the companies they hire to administer their programs have increasingly wide latitude over whether to provide benefits and under what conditions. They face comparatively few—and much delayed—penalties if benefit coverage is wrongly denied.

Investments, accumulated home equity, and borrowing also contribute to the financial underpinnings of individuals and their families. Americans' infatuation with investment took off with the early 1980s, at the start of a bull market in stocks that lasted nearly twenty years. After the stock bust of 2000, much of this popular enthusiasm switched to housing, and now even that is being tested. Economists argue that people's new familiarity with markets and investments gives them the tools to smooth out the ups and downs of their economic lives through personal savings and debt. President George W. Bush, among others, has elaborated this idea into a vision of an "Ownership Society" in which families operate on their own financially, borrowing their way across bad times. People no longer need the employer- or government-provided safety nets on which workers traditionally depended, so this vision goes. But the improvements in most families' finances—though real—simply are nowhere near large enough to support the burdens they are being asked to bear. The latest figures from the Federal Reserve's Survey of Consumer Finances, our only real source of information about household wealth, show that the net worth (that is, excess of assets over debt) for the median family at dead center of the economy had

increased by one-third since the late 1980s, to about $102,000. That
may sound like a lot of money for an average family, but remember
that it includes home equity, savings, and other assets that are not
available in times of trouble without great sacrifice, such as selling
your house. And if this full amount was available to you at retirement to buy an annuity—a guaranteed stream of income for the rest
of your life—that total would only get you a monthly payment of
$650. This certainly would help, but $650 is not enough to live com-
fortably on even with Social Security. Estimates for those nearer
but not at the top of the economy show larger increases, but still
not enough to cope with a major illness, a long layoff, or any of a
dozen other mishaps that regularly befall people over the course of
a work life.

Finally, mixed in among all of the other items that families count
on in their own economic lives, there's insurance—the life, health,
auto, and homeowner policies that people purchase to protect
against the "what ifs" of death, disease, and disaster. It's something
most of us seldom think about except on those relatively rare occasions when we must file a claim. Yet purely in terms of what is protecting most of us against financial calamity, the value of our
personal insurance policies is actually far larger than the value of all
our other assets put together—almost twice as large, by my estimate.
It's a bit of a math game, but it illustrates how important, if unappre-
ciated, plain-vanilla insurance is to almost all of us: If you add up all
the accumulated value of all the stocks Americans own, plus all the
accumulated value in the equity of our houses, you get about $27.6
trillion. The face value—that is, the amount of protection all Americans own through health, auto, and homeowner insurance—adds up
to some $51.5 trillion.

That total, enormous though it is, does not begin to capture the
awesome benefits of the basic idea that underlies insurance—the
idea of pooling risk by having a lot of people kick in a little in order
that no one has to pay a lot in the form of steep losses. In some sense,

that idea is the same as the one at the core of the Mayflower Compact: Sharing some risks and burdens broadly makes it possible for individuals to pursue their personal goals more freely and safely. "All insurance, indeed all of modern finance, comes down to this," said Yale finance theorist Robert J. Shiller, "that various forms of human disappointment and economic suffering are risks to which probabilities can be attached and that arrangements can be made to reduce these disappointments and blunt their impact on individuals by dispersing their effects among large numbers of people."

As with jobs, benefits, and investments, however, many kinds of insurance are changing in ways that leave more burdens on policyholders and fewer on the companies. Many insurers are devising increasingly sophisticated techniques to measure the risk of providing everything from health to homeowners' coverage, for instance, or to predict whether a potential policyholder will file a claim. They are using these techniques to raise the premiums they charge, limit the dangers that they will insure, or get out of covering some people altogether. That leaves many families to go without coverage or to try to do the nearly impossible given the potential costs involved: save enough to handle the cost of a major illness or injury, or the destruction of their own house or cars on their own.

Beyond the struts or foundation stones that people or their employers provide, the federal and state governments also operate programs that undergird Americans' economic lives. These include unemployment compensation in case of job loss, workers' compensation in case of on-the-job injury, Medicaid, Social Security Disability, the earned-income tax credit for the working poor, and some cash welfare for those who are destitute or disabled during their working years. Social Security and Medicare remain the most important bulwarks in old age for the majority of Americans. In addition, during the past twenty-five years, Washington greatly expanded its promise to help people and regions in case of natural disaster, at least in part on the theory that the nation is now a single integrated economy so that damage to any part must be repaired in order to make the whole operate smoothly. But for most of the two-plus years since Hurricane Katrina struck New Orleans in 2005, those promises have appeared alternately empty or ineffective, and most home and business owners in that unfortunate region have been left to find their own ways back to a functioning society.

Taken together, these foundation stones—public and private— have been the key to what America has become. Far from making people complacent, as some social philosophers feared in the past and many economists continue to worry about, they have unleashed society's productive energies. Far from fostering sloth, the record shows that making the foundations of people's lives more secure has encouraged millions of people to push their personal prospects to the utmost—to the resounding benefit of themselves and the country.

Given the size of these benefits and their comparatively modest cost, it seems surprising that these pillars of the modern nation should have come under attack in recent years. Yet these attacks have enjoyed considerable success. The evidence is that, although much of what's driving recent changes in the economy and in working Americans' circumstances is almost certainly powerful and impersonal forces like technological innovation and globalization, much of the adjustment to these forces appears to have been left to individuals and their families to handle. It is almost as if the Mayflower Compact had been flipped on its head: Where the new arrivals in this country agreed to certain minimal obligations to each other and to society and could otherwise go their own way, the current generation of working Americans has been assigned the all-consuming task of being society's first responder to forces well beyond anyone's ability to control or even fully understand. Both these external forces and the fact that workers must now cope with them largely on their own leave people increasingly open to steep financial falls.

To ALL APPEARANCES, Richard Coss Jr. is a textbook case of the kind of multigenerational upward mobility that Americans have always treasured. There's just one problem: Today, his name is on the economic casualty list.

His life had an American Dream beginning. His father, Richard Coss Sr., seventy-six, got a job right out of high school as a grinder at Landis Machine Company in Waynesboro, Pennsylvania. Except for two years as an infantryman in Korea during the early 1950s, the elder Coss worked continuously for thirty years. He changed jobs only once, to move to Mack Truck in Hagerstown, Maryland, where he joined the United Auto Workers (UAW) Union, Local 171. His wife, Iolene, was a secretary for the assistant superintendent of schools in nearby Smithburg, Maryland. Their combined salary, which never topped $60,000 in current dollars, together with some state scholarship money, put three sons through college. "Go to college, get a better-paying job, and live a better life than I had," Coss Sr. remembers telling his son. Rick Coss heeded the advice. He went to nearby Western Maryland College for an undergraduate degree, then on to the tree-lined campus of Duke for an MBA.

Rick Coss had a head for numbers, and the first ten years of his career went almost exactly as planned. Straight out of Duke in the late 1970s, he landed a $21,500-a-year job with Mellon Financial Corporation, the mainstay of the Mellon family fortune and a pillar of the Pittsburgh economy. Mellon Financial had never had a major layoff in its 118-year history. Coss climbed steadily from one position to another, each time for more money. By his thirtieth birthday, he was earning as much as his father had in his best year. And the younger Coss's household income was helped when he married Janet Rathke, a fellow Mellon employee. By 1983, the couple was making more than $65,000, the equivalent of about $140,000 in 2007 dollars, and had purchased their first house. By 1984, the first of their three daughters, Lisa, had arrived. It was in 1987, while they were expecting their second child, Amy, that the trouble began.

In the wake of the 1970s oil crisis, when energy prices seemed to have no place to go but up, Mellon had lent heavily to the Texas oil industry. The high prices encouraged development of new oil fields, however, as well as energy saving by consumers. So instead of going up, oil prices reversed direction and started down. The about-face left Mellon stuck with half a billion dollars in bad loans. The company responded by doing the unthinkable: It laid off 2,000 employees, among them Richard Coss Jr. At the time, Coss had thought he was only months away from being named a "calling officer," essentially one of Mellon's prestigious ambassadors to the business world. The layoff caught him completely by surprise. Still, he scrambled and landed a spot with the much smaller Bryn Mawr Trust Company, helping it open a new consulting business.

For a few years, life settled back into its old order. But when Bryn Mawr Trust was walloped by real estate losses in the early 1990s, it eliminated the consulting business and, with it, Coss's job. This time, he was out of work for more than a year and had to dig into the family's savings. "We sort of prided ourselves that we had put that money away," Janet Coss said. "We'd been so prudent and proud, and now the money was going."

Eventually, Coss found a job at Pittsburgh's other big bank, PNC. During his eight years there, he rose to become a product-profitability director. That put him at the center of the institution's new strategy: It was moving away from traditional lending to focus on providing fee-based services such as back-office processing for other companies. But the new strategy proved a bust, and the bank reversed course. And once more, Coss found himself out of work.

Each time a job evaporated, Coss collected unemployment compensation from the state-federal unemployment insurance program that had been created way back in the Great Depression. And each time he filed a claim, the fraction of his lost wages that the government insurance payments covered got smaller. The state's payment formula, although among the most generous in the nation, had risen only modestly during the previous fifteen years; also, the maximum payment was capped, and Coss was making more with each job. As a result, the difference between his pay and the jobless benefit checks after he got laid off grew wider. Cutting out what few luxuries the Cosses enjoyed did not begin to close the gap.

It may be tempting to step around Richard Coss with a sympathetic nod. Perhaps he belongs to one of those isolated groups that economists love to talk about, in this case middle managers squeezed out as U.S. corporations have grown more efficient. In any case, how else should America treat someone like Coss? What's the alternative? Certainly, the United States is not going to adopt the expansive government benefits so favored in Europe. Still, the Cosses' experience is worth a closer look. And three things about it jump out.

First, Coss had all of the right educational credentials. And for years, he reaped the financial rewards that those credentials are supposed to ensure. Until his career began its downward slide, he and his family enjoyed incomes greater than those earned by close to 90 percent of working Americans. Moreover, Coss worked in one of the industries—financial services—that's commonly cited as having a substantial role in the nation's future. His was no backwater Rust Belt career.

Second, each job loss was the result not of his own failure to perform, but of his employer suffering reverses largely of its own making and certainly beyond his control: The banks made strategic mistakes. But instead of bearing the costs themselves, they were able to pass the consequences of their errors straight along to Coss and other employees. Then, while Coss struggled for survival, his former employers regrouped and prospered. Newly merged Mellon is now among the nation's largest banking companies. So is PNC. Even tiny Bryn Mawr rebounded.

Third, once unemployment caught up with Coss, it kept coming back. And each jobless spell was longer and financially more debilitating than its predecessor. This was true even though the nation's average unemployment rate trended downward during the two decades Coss kept running into trouble.

What these three points suggest is not an economy delivering unalloyed improvements such as higher pay for those who get more education or greater stability for workers who choose careers in growth sectors of the economy. Instead, Coss's experience suggests an economy in which the most powerful entities—in this case, major corporations—are able to shift the consequences of their mistakes onto loyal but defenseless employees. And there is little chance the companies will be asked to help care for the victims, in part because the strategy masks the severity of the damage: The layoffs let the banks make quick course corrections, return to profitability, and hire new—but usually different—workers, thus helping to hold down the average unemployment rate. So a rise in the risk of long-term, financially damaging joblessness has been covered up by a fall in the overall jobless rate. And that points to one more notable fact about Richard Coss's experience: Although he found a new job following each setback, the new jobs never quite equaled the old ones, certainly not in security. Like a bouncing ball that loses a little momentum with each bounce, he began losing economic altitude with each job change. Despite all the talk of greater opportunities, said MIT economist Paul Osterman, American workers have been offered a devil's deal. "In effect, what we've said to people is, 'We'll reduce your chances of becoming unemployed, but if you do lose a job, you'll have hell to pay.'"

Some readers, especially younger ones, may find it hard to imagine an economy that would operate in a way that spared Richard Coss Jr. and his family their troubles. Yet it is not necessary to imagine such an economy. Richard Coss Sr. lived in one. For that matter, he still does.

In his long career, there were slack periods when the workweek would shrink from fifty hours to forty hours to thirty hours. But thanks to the power of the UAW and the competitive strength of the company for which the older Coss worked most of his adult life, there were smaller paychecks but no layoffs. And even during slow times, Mack Truck kept delivering the negotiated benefits—the health insurance that paid for Iolene's diabetes care and the disability coverage that made up lost wages when Coss Sr. was out of work for two months recovering from a fall off the roof of his house. The economic dangers that the company did not cover, the family managed to take care of on its own, through insurance and the earnings from a Laundromat Coss Sr. operated as a side business. The parents never had a credit card, never borrowed against the house. In his top year, the elder Coss made less than $40,000, and his wife less than $20,000, about $100,000 in 2007 dollars. They had pensions with early retirement provisions that let them quit working at fifty-seven. And they got retiree health benefits through Mack and the UAW. The package means they have about $50,000 a year to live on now. That's enough to rent a small place near Cypress Gardens, Florida, every winter and to spend a few weeks at Emerald Isle, North Carolina, every summer.

THE MOST OBVIOUS DIFFERENCE between the working lives of Coss Jr. and Sr. centers on their respective employers and how they treated the people who worked for them. Mack Truck promised lifetime employment in a union contract and made good on it. The promise shielded the elder Coss from virtually all of the ups and downs of the economy, even during the tumultuous 1970s. Indeed, records show that once the elder Cosses were through the Korean War and had had their boys, the family's annual income didn't vary more than about 30 percent up or down for most of their work lives. The younger Coss was never offered such a deal and, thinking back, acknowledges that he probably would not have accepted it if it had been offered—not in the beginning, at least. The result is that he has been repeatedly toppled. Family records show that his income hit peaks in the early 1980s and again in the early and late 1990s, but it also took harrowing nosedives—for example, falling between 2001 and 2002 by more than 90 percent.

Economists examining the income histories of the two generations of Cosses are quick to say that the younger Coss should have saved more in his peak years to be ready for his trough ones, although they did, in fact, save, a move that put them a giant step ahead of most families in the United States. But if you ask these economists if they themselves have socked away enough to cope with a 90 percent income plunge, most will concede they have not. But even if it's not realistic to say the Cosses should have protected themselves through all-out saving, experts point out that the world in which American corporations operate has changed radically between the work lives of father and son. Not even the mighty autoworkers union can any longer provide its members with the deal it delivered for the elder Coss. Today, contract negotiations are more likely to center on givebacks than on gains. And corporate executives never tire of pointing out that generous benefit packages, including comprehensive health care and traditional pensions, raise their costs and make them less competitive against foreign rivals. All true. And it is

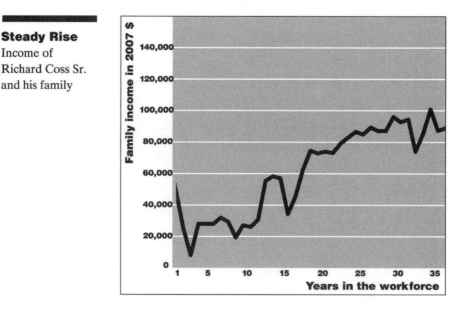

Steady Rise
Income of
Richard Coss Sr.
and his family

equally true that there is no practical way to return to the earlier era, when U.S. business corporations dominated the world economy like the Colossus.

But it is at precisely this point that discussions about the economy and the circumstances of working Americans usually take a peculiar turn. Having said that American employers are unlikely ever again to be able to provide their employees with the kind of protections that workers enjoyed as recently as twenty-five years ago, some analysts slide—almost as if they were not making a dramatically different point—into an argument that no social institution can or should provide working Americans any protections at all. This last step has tremendous significance, and, though little remarked on now, is likely to give rise to a great national debate. Stripped to its essence, the question to be decided is this: After four centuries of working out a humane and productive balance between the right of individuals and business corporations to pursue their private interests and their obligations to the common good, does America really intend to turn back the clock and become a "no-promise society"? Or will it instead find new ways to rebalance the old equation—retaining the energy

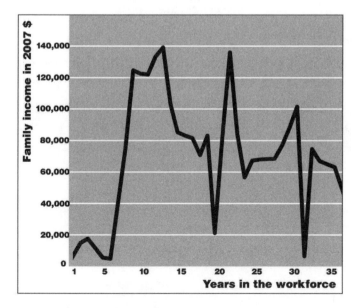

Wild Ride
Income of
Richard Coss Jr.
and his family

and entrepreneurial zeal of the present system while restoring some of the protections against misfortune, protections that not only encourage personal enterprise but also give real meaning to the phrase "Ownership Society"?

THERE IS ONE MORE LESSON to be derived from the different experiences of the older and younger Cosses: a clearer understanding of how it is possible that so little attention could have been paid to such drastic changes in what counts as a job, in what protections an employee can expect from an employer, and in the extent to which people must cope with economic setbacks on their own. How could such revolutionary changes have taken place with so little public discussion? Admittedly, both the union contract and the bank decisions to lay off workers reflected separate, quite different periods of history, and each reflected the era in which it occurred. But that does not explain how the country got from one set of realities to the other with hardly anyone saying a word about what the changes would mean.

To a large extent, the explanation is that the changes have occurred out of the public arena in the comparative isolation of the private sector—in decisions large and small made by individual employers and spread over thousands and thousands of individual workers. While Washington, the news media, and most of the pundit class were preoccupied with high-profile political battles between conservative ideologues and their often feckless liberal opponents, change was being imposed by corporate managers whose decisions were seldom monitored by anyone more concerned with the larger good than a stock analyst.

The financial protections that sheltered the elder Cosses were not created overnight. In their most direct form, they stemmed from a single contract between the labor union Coss Sr. belonged to and the company he worked for. But that contract represented the culmination of a long, complex struggle stretching back into the previous century. As the nation grappled with the problems that came with the transformation from a predominantly agrarian society to an urban, industrial society, it developed new institutions, new laws and policies, and new ways of looking at the relationship between workers and those who hired them. Looking back now, we may conclude that the rise of huge unions able to negotiate comprehensive contracts for good pay and long-term benefits was a relatively brief phenomenon. The idea behind it was neither new nor transitory, however. It was the old idea of seeking ways to make our society fairer and safer for all its citizens by recognizing a degree of mutual obligation. And the troubles that engulfed the younger Cosses reflected the breaking down of that process. Just as his father's lifelong security came from a single contract and a single employer, the younger Coss's slide into financial insecurity was almost entirely the result of layoffs that particular firms ordered in pursuit of their private business strategies. In addition, some of the most important changes were in the fine grain of companies' altered assumptions and practices, not in widely trumpeted corporate about-faces. Mack Truck, for example, downsized its payroll by reducing workers' hours during slack periods, but benefits remained intact. By contrast, Mellon Bank offered severance pay but few benefits to those it laid off. Finally, almost none of the changes that occurred between the two generations register in the standard statistics that Americans use to measure their economy. That means the changes have been almost invisible to policymakers and the public.

So what is the vision of those who not only say that key economic protections on which working families have relied are fading but say that they should fade? The early architects of the nation's quarter-century economic makeover offered vivid arguments on this point. Shifting risk from business and government to working families was crucial to reinvigorating the economy, they said, not so much because it would relieve institutions of troublesome burdens but because it would force people to be more active, earnest economic players. These advocates were adamant that no effort be made to spare people the consequences of this new approach, lest the process be short-circuited and the larger benefits lost. For example, George Gilder, whose 1981 book, *Wealth and Poverty*, became one of the guiding texts of the early Reagan administration, warned that any effort to shelter individuals by "diffusing, equalizing, concealing, shuffling, smoothing, evading, relegating and collectivizing, the real risks . . . of economic change" would backfire by weakening the economy. Taking the castor oil straight down was the ticket, Gilder suggested. The only hope he offered the patient was that "with more of the risks borne by individual citizens . . . and thus vigilantly appraised and treated . . . the overall system may be more stable."

In the years since these arguments were first made, the idea that working families should be more on the hook for their own economic fortunes has been a subtext in many of Washington's hottest domestic policy debates. Regular warnings that Social Security and Medicare—the nation's two biggest domestic programs—are financially unsustainable and must be "reformed" have been coupled with calls for cutbacks in federal spending. The largely unspoken message has been that government safety nets are luxuries the nation can no longer afford. Instead, working families must step up to provide more of their own retirement income, pay more of their own medical bills in old age, and bear more of their own economic risks.

As it has happened, the most prominent efforts to shift risk from government to working families have thus far failed. Presidents Reagan and George W. Bush both sought to change Social Security drastically, but the huge social insurance program remains essentially intact and continues to provide a floor against poverty in old age. In the case of the other great federal safety net program, Medicare, President Bush and congressional Republicans have created health savings accounts that would do for health insurance what 401(k)s have done for personal retirement: shift much of the cost and risk from employers to employees. But, at least to date, the new health arrangement has not caught on. In fact, legislation authorizing the accounts pushed in the opposite direction by including a huge expansion of the federal health insurance program—the addition of a prescription drug program. Yet these developments have done little to quiet conservative calls for working Americans to take on more responsibility for protecting themselves against setbacks.

Economists at conservative institutions like the University of Chicago and think tanks like the Heritage Foundation have contributed to the drumbeat for change by resurrecting an old concept called "moral hazard." That is the name given to the idea that people will act more responsibly and make a greater effort to do what they should if the cost of failing to do so falls on them, not someone else, and conversely, that they will act less responsibly and with less effort if they are relieved of the cost. Expressed in the current vernacular, it means that "having skin in the game" makes us focus on playing better. As economists have applied this idea to public policy and law, it suggests that any policy permitting a person to dodge the financial consequences of an event actually makes that event more likely to happen. In the extreme, the idea is that fire insurance promotes fires by reducing homeowners' incentive to prevent them; they know insurance companies will cover the losses. Expressed in this fashion, the idea may seem almost fanciful. But "moral hazard" has been applied to a wide array of business and government practices. For example, arguments have been advanced that welfare causes poverty, unemployment benefits promote unemployment, and health insurance encourages people to get unnecessary medical care. In each case, the proposed solution is to shift more of the consequences of bad events onto individuals and families. In theory, this would give people more incentive to make sure the bad events don't befall them. Of course, it's hard to see how Richard Coss Jr. could have done much to keep Mellon Financial from wrongly betting on ever-higher oil prices or PNC from picking what turned out to be a losing corporate strategy. But the idea is that he could shield himself and his family by keeping a more watchful eye on his employer, being ready to jump to a new employer at the first sign of trouble, and building up savings.

In the end, some of the most influential arguments for removing traditional protections and shifting risks to workers turn on a particular reading of both the nation's distant past and the years immediately preceding the economy's recent return to stable growth. Virtually all advocates of moral hazard and free-market social policy "hark back to some earlier time," according to economic historian David Moss, "when America was full of vigor and individualist spirit and when every citizen faced his own risks with a sense of stoic independence and pride." In reality, said Moss, no such idyllic time ever existed in the United States. "It's impossible to locate a moment in American history from the Constitution writing on forward when policymakers weren't providing some kinds of risk-sharing arrangements, first for business, then workers, the elderly, consumers . . . in the end for just about everybody in one form or another." And, not by accident, the country has grown steadily larger, richer, and stronger. But that has hardly weakened the political, almost spiritual, appeal of the notion of people—especially other people—standing on their own without a steadying hand from their employers or their government.

That attitude seemed all the more plausible because of how fast and seemingly effectively Americans—especially middle-class Americans—adapted to the economic turbulence of the 1970s. Of course, people have adapted at every other economic juncture, we are told—during the westward expansion and the industrialization of the nineteenth century, during the Great Depression and World War II and the great boom of the mid-twentieth century. But in the 1970s, ordinary Americans seemed to grab the financial reins with exceptional enthusiasm. In the process, they set off a money revolution.

When people saw that the productivity slump of the '70s was threatening their standard of living, they switched from being one-earner households to two-earner households. The fraction of families with two incomes jumped from one-third to nearly one-half in a decade and has now reached three-quarters. Similarly, for decades people had set aside money in bank savings accounts known as "passbook" accounts because of the small record books that passed back and forth between customers and bank tellers whenever a deposit was made. The interest rates on these accounts were low. When people realized that high inflation was eating up these rates and destroying the value of their money in the 1970s, they dumped the passbook accounts in favor of money market accounts, mutual funds, and stock portfolios. And when they realized that inflation was flipping the logic of thrift—making it smarter to borrow now and repay later with inflation-cheapened dollars—they flipped, too, beginning a romance with credit cards, mortgage refinancing, and home equity loans that endured beyond the Great Inflation and has yet to end. As early as 1980, analysts were marveling at Americans' ability to roll with the economic punches. "It turns out that people can scramble and keep up longer than you think they can," remarked economist Barry Bosworth.

When the Federal Reserve finally announced near the turn of the new century that more than half of households owned stock directly or indirectly, the revolution in how Americans managed their personal finances seemed well on its way to completion. Even ordinary Americans now seemed to be financial sophisticates able to borrow their way across bad times and smooth out the ups and downs of earnings with investment. "We've finally gotten a piece of the action" is how author Joseph Nocera put it in a mid-1990s book that was both a history and a manifesto of the money revolution. "If we have to pay attention now, if we have to come to grips with our own tolerance for risk," Nocera wrote, "if we're forced to spend a little time learning about which financial instruments make sense for us and which ones don't, that seems . . . an acceptable price to pay. Democracy always comes at some price," he said. "Even financial democracy."

The problem is that the piece of the action that most Americans have gotten during the past twenty-five years is not what optimists like Nocera had expected. Stock investments have turned out to be substantially riskier than many had thought. As important, stocks' elevated role in the economy has helped fuel the jittery corporate competitiveness that has loosened job ties, encouraged benefit cuts, and weakened, rather than strengthened, the finances of many families. Although homes have provided many families with substantial returns, they turn out not to be the only-up investments we've been repeatedly told they were. Their values are now in a steep swoon in many parts of the country. And most of the financial engineering applied to the household turns out to be just another avenue for borrowing.

More important, what Americans have done with their piece of the action suggests that most of us are not very good investors and thus not well suited to play our new risk-bearing roles. Until recently, more than one-quarter of people who are eligible for employer-provided 401(k)s had failed to sign up for them, according to the Federal Reserve. More than half of those who did sign up funneled their money into overly conservative or overly aggressive investments, according to the nonpartisan Employee Benefit Research Institute. Investors may demand more choices, but then they seem confused by the number of options and either make poor decisions or no decisions at all. One study found that the chief reason people don't take advantage of tax breaks or employer matches to put away money for retirement is that they're afraid they will have to pay government-imposed penalties if they need to get at their money quickly. So the authors looked at working people who'd reached age sixty when the penalties no longer apply. Even among this group, 40 percent failed to save.

Such mistakes are not the exclusive domain of less affluent or less educated people. When I interviewed recent Nobel Prize winners in economics, I discovered that many had made the very same sorts of mistakes, either by not paying attention to their investments or by making faulty decisions when they did.

In the end, households are not hedge funds. It's not that people couldn't learn to be investors or risk managers, just as it's not that most could not figure out how to program their VCRs to record television shows. It's that smart investment is a time-consuming practice and most people's time is consumed with activities that they consider more pressing and closer to the heart of their lives—raising their families, doing their jobs, participating in their communities, chasing their goals. "I would rather spend my time enjoying my income than bothering about investments," said Clive W. J. Granger, a 2003 Nobel Prize winner and emeritus professor at the University of California–San Diego. His is an understandable outlook, but one that makes Granger as well as less credentialed Americans poor candidates to shoulder the new responsibilities for their economic well-being that have been thrust upon them, regardless of how affluent and accomplished they may be. Like many early champions of the money revolution, Nocera, now a columnist for *The New York Times*, has had second thoughts about the changes he once hailed. In a recent column assessing the career of another longtime champion of the stock market for the masses, Louis Rukeyser, the longtime host of television's *Wall Street Week,* Nocera wrote that he had come to realize that "investing is a talent that most of us will never have." Looking back on Rukeyser's relentless flogging of the notion that almost anyone could be a successful investor, Nocera said he was reminded of an old book by a stockbroker who had become disillusioned with the brokerage industry's pushing of mass stock investment. The title of the book was *Where Are the Customers' Yachts?* For most Americans, there have been no yachts.

IN 1989, TWO ECONOMISTS, Richard Burkhauser and Greg Duncan, dug into the question of exactly what it is that knocks the pins out from under families who take steep financial falls. In doing so, they were picking up on the work of an earlier generation of academics who had asked: How did the Great Depression come to roost on working Americans? Exactly what was the path or mechanism that led from a macroeconomic collapse to the devastation of so many individuals? You might think the answer is obvious, but it turns out to be a surprise. It wasn't the stock market crash of 1929 that had hurt most people; relatively few Americans owned stock back then. And it wasn't unemployment alone, because 75 percent of breadwinners held on to their jobs, yet the families of many still suffered. What turned out to have tipped many people into the abyss was one or another of a handful of ordinary events that could happen to anybody under any circumstances in the course of a working life—an illness or injury, a divorce, the birth of an unplanned child, a cutback in a person's wages or hours. These ordinary events, occurring at a time of heightened vulnerability, let trouble come flooding into the victims' lives and swamp them.

When Burkhauser and Duncan looked at the same list of events for the tumultuous but more prosperous 1970s and 1980s, they found the same pattern. Burkhauser and Duncan concluded that "we need not look to the Great Depression . . . to find frequent instances of economic loss and hardship; the risk of sharp decreases in living standards is significant at virtually every stage of life."

And when I looked at the list for the still more prosperous years since the two economists completed their study, I found the pattern still held true—but with one important difference. The fraction of families that experienced one of these unfortunate events and then took a huge income hit had climbed by almost *50 percent*. This is not the rising-tide prosperity that has been widely heralded over the past twenty-five years. Instead, it is something more punctuated, more unpredictable, more difficult to plan a life and raise a family around. Of course, in any given month or year, relatively few people experience such an unsettling event. But the question readers must ask is this: Do I think I can make it across an entire work life without such a setback? How many people do I know who have been so lucky that they never lost a job, got sick or injured, went through a divorce, or saw the world in which they were building careers take an unexpected and unhelpful turn? The question is not whether we need safeguards against adversity, but rather, when we do need them, as eventually many of us will, how reliable and effective will they be?

When Richard Coss Sr. and Iolene speak about their son, they do so cautiously. They know that his setbacks have hurt him, and they want to cause no more pain. A few years ago, they gave Rick and his family $20,000 and a 1991 Chevrolet Lumina to help tide them over a jobless spell. And they recognize that times have changed. "I know things are different now," the elder Coss said in a recent conversation. "The white collar don't have the protection anymore."

For his part, after his 2001 layoff, Rick Coss Jr. decided he was fed up with banking and business for the time being. He became the chief financial officer of the Light of Life Rescue Mission, a shelter for the homeless in Pittsburgh. Although he makes only about half his old salaries, the job thus far has proved far more stable, and he has been able to improve the health benefits both for the people who work at the mission and for those who depend on its services. "At this point," he says, "this is about the best I can do."

IN THE CHAPTERS THAT FOLLOW, we will meet other families that have tried to make a similar peace with adversity. We will examine how when they got to similar points in their lives, the particular safety nets on which they were counting proved less reliable than they had expected, and what they did about it. In some cases, the problem will turn out to have been with a government program or something else in the public sector. In many others, however, both the problem and the hoped-for solution will be found in the private sector—often with protections that individuals had arranged for, even bought and paid for years in advance of needing them.

One thing will become clear from both the stories and the numbers I will provide: No matter what one's political views about individuals bearing more risks, very few Americans are in a position to cope with their added responsibilities right now. That's because most of the changes that have shifted new burdens to families and, in the process, moved people further out on the economic limb have occurred in ways that have masked the full dimensions of what has happened.

Many of the people whom you'll meet in the coming chapters are well educated. Many have made far more money than most of us and rightly consider themselves financially sophisticated. Like Coss, they took economic hits that they did not realize they were exposed to or thought they had taken adequate precautions against. Only afterward did they realize that what they thought protected them had somehow been weakened or removed.

It might be comforting to think that these people just blew it: that they didn't work enough, save enough, or insure enough, that they made mistakes we would never make. But as you read their stories and absorb the analysis, ask yourself this: Am I really so different? Would I really have prepared against the setbacks that befell these people? Have I done so?

Wherever you stand on the question of how much people should go it alone, whatever your views about how much protection, if any, working families should expect from their employers, their communities, and their government, one thing seems clear: Somebody must tell Americans a great deal more about the economic dangers that lie in wait for them. Somebody must tell them that their economic anxieties are well founded. Only then can they and the country begin to address the challenge of how the dangers should be handled.

2

BENEFITS

O n Labor Day, 1974, less than a month after he became president following the resignation of Richard Nixon, Gerald Ford held a White House ceremony to sign a new law that he boldly predicted would give working Americans "more benefits and rights . . . than almost anything in the history of this country." Called the Employee Retirement Income Security Act, or ERISA, the measure was intended to sweep aside a patchwork of state measures and provide uniform national protection for the benefits that Americans receive through their employers. First and foremost, it covered pensions, but it also extended federal protection to health care coverage, disability and life insurance, severance pay, and a host of other benefits. That made it the most important safety net against economic trouble most Americans could have during their working lives—more immediately important even than Social Security or Medicare. Indeed, one of the new law's chief architects, New York Republican senator Jacob Javits, called ERISA "the greatest development in the life of the American worker since Social Security."

On Labor Day, 1974, nineteen-year-old Debra May of Birmingham, Alabama, was preparing to drop out of nearby Auburn University and—defying her parents' wishes—marry her high school
boyfriend. In Haverhill, Massachusetts, twelve-year-old Diane Andrews was playing quietly in the office of her father's small insurance
agency while he used the traditional end-of-summer break to catch
up on paperwork. Twenty-eight-year-old J. D. Lind of Tulsa, Oklahoma, and the crew of his small but booming construction company
were celebrating by taking the day off; Lind was "riding bronco" at a
local rodeo. As for James LaRue of Jinotega, Nicaragua, who was two
weeks away from turning fifteen that Monday in September, he was
helping his American-born father show a group of medical mission-
aries from New Berlin, Wisconsin, around the family's coffee plantation; New Berlin was Jinotega's sister city, and within three years, the
LaRues would move back to the United States, to Fort Worth.

Debra May, Diane Andrews, J. D. Lind, and James LaRue never
met. Nor did they ever meet President Ford. But in time, each of
them encountered the law Ford signed that day. And far from protecting them, when they faced problems that threatened to over-
whelm them and their families, ERISA imposed so much additional
pain, anguish, and injustice that—even now—it's hard to compre-
hend how so much good intention could have gone so awry. Worse
yet, what happened to them has become commonplace.

Today, social policy experts and politicians are preoccupied with
the question of what to do about the many increasingly competitive
and unconstrained employers who seem intent on offering only the
most meager benefits or providing no benefits at all. The more than
100 million Americans who have benefits and assume they're securely provided for may listen to this discussion with a certain
smugness. They shouldn't. ERISA poses a serious threat to their
ability to collect on the very benefits that they're counting on to
cover them. From bureaucratic fights with insurance companies
over covering a drug to financially devastating denials of all health

coverage, they are much more defenseless in the event of trouble than they think they are—and much more unprotected than the authors of ERISA ever intended them to be. "People who try to claim their employer-sponsored benefits are worse off than they were two or three decades ago," said senior judge William Acker Jr., who was appointed by President Reagan to the U.S. District Court for the Northern District of Alabama in Birmingham. "The law that was supposed to protect them has been turned on its head; the chief beneficiaries are now the insurance companies and benefit providers."

Or as California's Democratic lieutenant governor and former insurance commissioner John Garamendi put it, "The safety nets designed to keep people from being run over by economic forces beyond their control have been shredded. People who think they're safe and sound because of those nice benefits that their employers send them notices about should look at the fine print."

WHEN MOST AMERICANS HEAR ABOUT "safety nets," they generally think of food stamps or welfare checks intended to help the poor stave off destitution, not the sorts of things on which able-bodied and employed people like themselves depend. The truth, however, is that Americans at all but the very top of the economic ladder rely on a long list of protections to keep them secure in the ordinary course of their lives. And although some parts of this middle-class "safety net" are provided directly by the government, most of it is anchored in people's jobs. Employer-sponsored health insurance, for instance, covers 150 million people—more than 70 percent of the nation's working-age population. Employer-sponsored disability insurance policies cover more than 50 million workers, many of them among the nation's top earners. To this day, employer-sponsored life insurance covers more people than the individual policies sold by agents who have offices on Main Street, USA, and come to your house to explain the wonders of cash value and compound interest. After Social

Security, employer-sponsored retirement plans are the single largest source of income for America's 37 million retirees. In virtually every case where employers do anything more than hand out a pamphlet and tell employees they can buy themselves some protection if they like, the benefits that employers themselves provide are subject to ERISA. And in 1974, Gerald Ford, Jacob Javits, and just about every public policy expert in the United States would have thought that was a good thing.

THE LONG DEBATE that preceded ERISA's passage reflected—and helped crystallize—a big change in how Americans looked at pensions, health insurance, and the host of other benefits people receive through their employers. And this change was part of a still-larger development, centuries in the making—a realization that there are some dangers that individuals simply cannot handle well on their own, dangers that, if left unhandled, hurt both the individuals and the national economy.

Until the 1960s, the noncash portion of people's pay was usually considered of no great consequence—hence the term *fringe* benefits—and, in any case, was basically nobody's business but employers' and unions'. But when Studebaker Corporation shut its South Bend, Indiana, auto plant in 1963, throwing 7,000 people out of work and leaving some forty-year veterans with as little as fifteen cents on the dollar of promised pensions, many people were outraged and demanded action to keep such a thing from ever happening again. Although companies countered with arguments similar to ones heard today—that regulation would mean fewer pensions and that even risky pensions were better than none at all—reformers insisted on action. The reformers' view was that "people needed some certainty to organize their lives, especially distant parts of it like retirement, and that providing pensions that ended up not paying off left them worse off than they would have been if they'd had no pension at all," said law professor and historian James Wooten. "Security of expectations is important to people and to society as a whole." Pensions and other employer-sponsored protections, although they had started out as fringe benefits, were coming to be seen as essential—not just to individual workers but to the economic health of the nation as a whole.

Behind this transition was a still-broader change of outlook, one dating back to the beginning of the country and indeed long before. The change was deceptively simple but profound: Whereas for thousands of years most people had accepted the idea that their lot in life was to be helpless pawns in the grip of fate or divine will, many gradually began to embrace the notion that they should be able to approach their lives with a reasonable degree of certainty about what the future would bring if they lived in certain ways—if they worked hard, strove to improve themselves through education or training, and generally conducted themselves in a responsible, prudent, and productive manner. In other words, they came to reject the notion put forth by seventeenth-century English philosopher Thomas Hobbes that for most of mankind, life is "solitary, poor, nasty, brutish, and short." The seemingly simple shift from viewing oneself as a pawn to seeing oneself as a predictor and thus to a considerable degree captain of one's own fate has been called the essential definition of what it means to belong to the modern world instead of the Middle Ages. And perhaps nowhere in the world did this idea become more deeply rooted than in America. According to author Peter L. Bernstein, one offshoot of this new way of looking at life, when combined with the development of the mathematics of probabilities and statistics, was one of the great inventions of the modern world—private insurance. Its roots go back all the way to the intellectual flowering of the Renaissance, though most of us, if we think about it at all, associate the creation of insurance with Benjamin Franklin, who is credited with starting the first successful mutual insurance company to protect against fire. In America, as in most of the developed world, it has also helped feed a steady stream of government programs to take up the slack where insurance failed to do the job.

During the past twenty-five years, most of the commentary on both government and private programs to protect individuals and families has suggested they are new, unaffordable, and damaging to America's independent spirit. But in his book on government risk policy, *When All Else Fails,* economic historian David Moss showed that measures to shift, spread, or reduce the dangers, especially the economic dangers, that Americans face have been around "at least since the dawn of the Republic." He made the case that neither U.S. society nor the economy would likely have emerged or prospered without such measures. Spreading risk turned out to be a powerful stimulator of economic activity and growth.

For most of the nineteenth century, when state and federal governments' chief focus was on strengthening the weak and fragmented nation by encouraging investment and trade, the chief beneficiaries of these measures were businesses. As the United States moved from an agricultural to an industrial economy, manufacturers needed to assemble large pools of investment money. But outside investors were reluctant to contribute to such enterprises if—as the law then held—they could be personally liable and thrown in debtors' prison for anything that went wrong. The result was laws permitting the formation of limited liability corporations in which shareholders could invest without facing unlimited financial exposure if the company later lost money. The risk of a corporation being unable to pay its debts was thus shared by the company's founders, by the company's creditors, and by others who might be hurt if a firm went belly-up. Spreading the risk, it was believed, encouraged investors to create the new economic ventures considered vital if the nascent country was to grow. Similarly, as markets grew and trade stretched beyond individual communities during the course of the nineteenth century, businesses and individuals needed a form of money they could depend on. The result, after much struggle, was government-printed currency that was intended to provide a stable medium of exchange and replace the motley collection of private bank scrip and other forms of currency that had contributed to recurrent financial crises. Finally, there was the development of new bankruptcy laws. One side effect of rapid economic growth and westward expansion was that many people tried but failed at business. Helping them get back on their feet, relieved of old debts that could keep them from launching new entrepreneurial ventures, was considered good for the country. The bankruptcy laws that were written took an extraordinarily friendly attitude toward debtors and shifted much of the cost of business failure to creditors.

By the beginning of the twentieth century, the United States had been remade into a land of huge corporations, continent-stretching railroads, and giant cities. And the legal and financial infrastructure created by the government had played a vital role in the change. Laws establishing limited liability, creation of a common currency, and debtor-friendly bankruptcy statutes and other such measures had created an environment that encouraged investors and entrepreneurs to join together in bigger and bigger ventures because they felt confident that the future would be more stable and predictable than it would otherwise have been. We may not often think of it this way, but the legal and policy infrastructure is just as important to the economy as such more visible benefits as the interstate highway system and modern communication networks.

Yet great as the benefits of the economic transformation of the country were, and much as they owed to the development of a supportive legal and policy framework, the new economy generated a whole new set of economic dangers. This was especially so for the swelling ranks of industrial workers and salaried employees. And in one way or another, the nation wrestled with those dangers for most of the twentieth century. In a nutshell, the problem was this: So long as people lived and worked in small communities surrounded by family and sympathetic neighbors, perhaps even in settings where they could grow their own food, fix their own vehicles, and repair their own roofs, traditional ideals of self-reliance made some sense. But as the economy became more national and then global, and people became more specialized in the work they did and less able to do everything for themselves, they became increasingly interdependent—benefiting from the economies of scale encouraged by specialization but also left more vulnerable if a problem developed.

Moss described the situation of industrial workers at the dawn of the twentieth century this way: "Although wages had increased substantially in the late nineteenth century, most workers' financial positions remained precarious," he wrote. "In the new industrial economy, the loss of a job—whether because of a workplace injury, illness, old age or an economic downtown—could easily land a worker and his family in poverty. Extensive family support networks had helped to spread individual risks in older agricultural communities, but rapid urbanization left those traditional safety nets in tatters."

More than three decades later, after the creation of Social Security in 1935, President Franklin D. Roosevelt defended the new social insurance program and the administration's other safety net programs by citing the same trends. In an age when most workers lived in big cities and worked for large corporations, Roosevelt told a radio audience that it had become "increasingly difficult for individuals to build their own security single-handed." Accordingly, he said, government "must now step in and help them lay the foundation stones, just as government in the past has helped lay the foundations of business and industry." As late as the 1970s, President Richard M. Nixon was using similar arguments to justify expanding government help for the unemployed, saying the nation must put its "finest principles into action—including effective compassion for our fellow citizens and supportive action to help keep our private enterprise system stable, healthy, just and humane."

The "risk management," or safety net, programs established to protect individuals during the twentieth century included mandatory on-the-job accident insurance for workers, unemployment compensation to make up income lost to layoffs, wage and hour laws and later workplace safety rules to reduce the danger of injury, and, of course, Social Security and Medicare. Growing up beside these programs was an increasingly rich array of employer-sponsored benefits—induced by tax breaks, pushed by unions, and, when problems with the benefits cropped up, regulated by ERISA.

From the outset, ERISA was about the broad middle of America. Only the steadiest, most reliable workers held the kinds of jobs that carried substantial fringe benefits; only those who showed up for work year after year and turned in solid performances decade after decade could hope to qualify for meaningful benefits. It was the great backbone of American society that ERISA was intended to protect.

DEBRA MAY (soon to be Potter) ended up more than simply another member of the middle class. Starting with almost nothing, she built for herself and her family the kind of affluence that gives the American Dream a good name. At first, her life moved in zigzags. After quitting Auburn and marrying her high school sweetheart, she worked variously as a teacher, a secretary at a Pepsi-Cola bottling plant, and the director of a Girl Scout camp. By 1982, she was divorced with two children under the age of six. Within a year, however, she was remarried—to a young Presbyterian minister named Ron Potter, who had a child of his own from a previous marriage. The melded family moved to the small northwestern Virginia town of Winchester when Ron was appointed pastor of the Sunnyside Presbyterian Church. The couple quickly had two children together and set about raising their family. Debra Potter settled in to what she thought would be her life's work—stay-at-home mom and preacher's wife.

By the late 1980s, however, it had become clear to the Potters that they'd never be able to do all the things they wanted to do for their kids, including send them to college, on Ron's $20,000-a-year salary. One night, as Debbie helped an elderly parishioner fill out insurance forms, the solution dawned on her: Why not get her state insurance license? "Here was something I was already doing anyway and that helped people, and it had to pay more than I was making at the time," she would remember years later.

In the insurance business, especially in a community such as Winchester, there had always been a clear pecking order. The retail business of selling individual policies to prosperous families has traditionally been men's work, requiring client cultivation, golf games, and evenings out with customers. Selling group insurance, by contrast, carries no similar glamour, involving as it does the grunt work of convincing one corporate human resource manager after another to offer an employer-sponsored benefit, then lugging pamphlets from one night meeting to the next to explain to employees what their new health plan would cover and what it wouldn't—and what in heaven's name was disability insurance? It was to this side of the business that Potter was headed.

After getting her state license, Potter landed a position with the old-line Winchester agency of J. V. Arthur, Inc. As the agency's junior member, she was assigned the job older heads had studiously avoided—launching the agency's group business. Her predecessor had failed at the task, and her new bosses assumed that she would, too. But they had not counted on two things. The first was that the numbers were with Potter. She entered the group insurance field just as it was lifting off. The second thing her bosses had not counted on was that Debra Potter *believed* in benefits. "Everybody needs safety nets, even people on top of the world, and that's what I was selling," she would say later. In a matter of only a few years during the late 1980s and early 1990s, she became one of J. V. Arthur's top producers, selling 230 group programs covering thousands of employees and generating more than three-quarters of a million dollars a year in commissions for the agency. In the process, she started making some serious money for herself.

The realization that the family's fortunes had changed dawned slowly at the Potter household. At Christmastime in 1994, Debbie bought her sports-crazed husband a forty-eight-inch TV to watch football, golf, and soccer. "I realized I could pay cash and not even feel it," she said. Within a few years, the family was taking Caribbean cruises and had moved his parents and her elderly mother into nearby housing. By 2001, she was one of the top sellers in the state of Virginia, earning more than $250,000 a year. So great were Potter's energy and faith in her product that when the J. V. Arthur agency got snapped up by southeastern financial services giant BB&T, she made sure that she and everybody else in the agency was covered by some of the very insurance she was selling—a policy with UnumProvident Corporation, now Unum Group, the nation's largest disability carrier.

In 1999 Potter experienced the first twinge of a health problem that would balloon into a major medical crisis. It would turn out she was suffering from multiple sclerosis. Within a few years, she would need that disability policy more than almost anything. It was then that she would discover that neither the policy nor the federal law governing it worked in anything like the fashion that she'd expected and that she'd been telling her clients for nearly a decade.

We will return to Potter's story in a minute, but to fully appreciate its significance, it is important to understand that the problems she was about to encounter and the federal court's interpretation of ERISA, which was at the root of many of those problems, are not just about such arcane corners of the benefit world as disability insurance, but go to the very heart of what most Americans expect from their employers, especially health coverage and retirement provisions. And they are not just the troubles of a single individual, but are a danger facing working men and women across the country.

As Potter's career was lifting off in the early 1990s, Diane Andrews's once-promising life was lurching downhill. The little girl who'd played on the floor of her father's insurance agency grew into a young woman, finished vocational-technical high school, and landed a solid job with an AT&T factory in North Andover, Massachusetts. The position paid about $25,000 a year in current dollars and came with generous health benefits through one of the country's most venerable insurers, the Travelers. And Andrews met her future husband, Richard Clarke.

Having come off of a bad relationship with another man, she found Clarke, an auto mechanic, a wonderful change. He was funny and caring. He liked to pick apples at Russell Orchards in Ipswich, eat lobster outdoors at Woodman's in Essex, hike the White Mountains in New Hampshire. Within a year of their meeting, they married and bought a white clapboard house with a picket fence in Haverhill. Richard Clarke had a son, Justin, from a previous marriage, and by 1994, Andrews-Clarke had presented her new husband with three daughters of their own, Deanna, Lacey, and Carly.

As it would turn out, however, going for the good life does not carry an exemption against misfortune. At about the time that the couple's youngest daughter was born, Richard Clarke began to develop a drinking problem. He was not abusive, but he quickly became a danger to himself and others. In April 1994, he fell down the cellar stairs drunk and broke two ribs. When he was admitted to St. Joseph Hospital in nearby Nashua, New Hampshire, the doctors ordered him into a detoxification program. Under the terms of Diane's employer-sponsored Travelers' health plan, which covered Richard, insurance should have paid for thirty days of in-patient treatment. But a utilization review company hired by the insurer would approve only five days of treatment, which did almost nothing for the problem. The following September, Clarke checked into a second hospital seeking help to stop drinking. This time, the reviewer agreed to eight days, which again made almost no difference. Soon afterward, Clarke's drinking landed him in trouble with the police and a court ordered thirty days of detoxification. This time, the reviewer refused to approve payment for any treatment at all, so he was sent to a maximum security prison to dry out.

In late October, as Richard emerged from prison, Diane told her husband that he could not return to a house full of children unless he remained sober. Three weeks later, Richard Clarke, forty-one years old and clutching a sixteen-ounce beer can, was found dead in a car with the engine running and a garden hose extending from the tailpipe to the passenger compartment.

At the age of thirty-two, Diane Andrews-Clarke was left to raise three daughters under the age of four and, for a time, the twelve-year-old son of her dead husband. Her single salary, by this time about $35,000 in current dollars, was barely enough to cover her mortgage and buy groceries. All of this because of a problem, alcoholism, that millions of Americans struggle with and many eventually surmount, and all of it, in Andrews-Clarke's view, because of an insurance safety net that promised to help families like hers, but failed. So the young widow set out to sue Travelers and the insurer's utilization reviewer, among others, arguing that Clarke's death was the direct result of improper refusal to pay for the alcoholism treatment that her health plan provided for and that the insurer was required by state law to offer.

That's when she met ERISA.

J. D. LIND'S CHILDHOOD was like a Willie Nelson song. And for much of his adult life, he looked and lived like a roughened Marlboro Man— a rugged sometime rodeo rider who worked outdoors and was his own boss. Lind was the son of an over-the-road truck driver, one of the modern-day nomads who spend their lives crisscrossing the country in the cab of an eighteen-wheeler; J. D. grew up riding with his father and sleeping in the bunk up behind the driver's seat. Later, he spent two years in the U.S. Navy—serving off the coast of Vietnam—and then learned the construction business, first as a hired hand, then as owner of his own company, Construction Services of Tulsa.

He made good money, too, though he'd apparently inherited some of his father's wanderlust. Instead of settling in one place, Lind spent more than thirty years on projects that took him all over the United States. He found a niche as a subcontractor for big companies with construction projects nationwide. Over the course of twenty of those years, he and his crews worked in Atlanta, Indianapolis, and Sacramento building nursing homes for Manor Care, one of the giants in the elder-care field. He spent another decade erecting cell towers and switching stations for Williams Communications and Black & Veatch. In an average year, he'd pull down $80,000 in current dollars, but with overtime he could make as much as $125,000.

By his own admission, Lind smoked heavily, drank a good bit, and loved a party. But he also became a family man. He met an insurance agent named Linda Stilwell at a country-western dance in Tulsa in 1996. Within two months, they were living together in Stilwell's house in Broken Arrow, a Tulsa suburb. A couple of years later, they were married. He was just back from a cell-tower job in Reno in 2001 and was getting ready for a Fourth of July party aboard their cigarette boat on a nearby lake when he collapsed.

At first, J. D. wrote the problem off to the heat. But when he went back out on the road, he discovered his energy was gone. "It used to be I couldn't keep my hands off of things, and here I was falling asleep in my pickup in the middle of the day," Lind said recently. After 9/11, when Black & Veatch temporarily suspended construction and he returned to Broken Arrow, Linda convinced him to see a doctor. One of her arguments: He was covered under the Aetna health plan provided through her employer, Southwest General Insurance Agency, so the appointment wouldn't cost anything.

The meeting with a doctor was inconclusive, and Lind returned to work. By the following August, however, the exhaustion and accompanying tremors had become so bad he couldn't continue. That's when Aetna referred him to Dr. Jorge Gonzalez, a board-certified neurologist who concluded that, like Potter, the Marlboro Man had multiple sclerosis, or MS. Gonzalez had spent years studying the disease and had achieved good results treating patients with a pharmaceutical cocktail of Copaxone, Provigil, and Klonopin. The drugs were expensive—J. D.'s cost $2,000 a month—but the results were spectacular. The shakes and exhaustion disappeared, and by early 2003 Lind was ready to go back to work. Three days before he was scheduled to head out for a project in Cleveland, Linda stopped by the Family Meds pharmacy in Broken Arrow to get J. D.'s Provigil prescription refilled. To her astonishment, the pharmacy told her that Aetna had decided it would no longer pay for the drug. Lind would have to try a less expensive medication, Ritalin, first.

Lind called Gonzalez, who called Aetna to warn that, in his experience, people who responded to Provigil tended not to respond to Ritalin, and that the insurer was making a mistake. But the health plan physician was adamant. Lind would have to switch to the cheaper drug, or pay for the Provigil himself. Gonzalez wrote Aetna saying that he was switching the prescriptions under protest and reassured Lind that they could go back to Provigil as soon as they showed that Ritalin didn't work. But the new drug did more than not work; it left Lind blind. Within a week, the Aetna physician who'd ordered the substitute drug had reversed herself, and the plan started paying for Provigil again. Instead of flying to Cleveland to start working again, Lind settled in at home to wait for his sight to come back. But it didn't. Then in April, Aetna refused to pay for another medication, this time the monthly injection of Copaxone, which cost $1,500 per shot. The company subsequently admitted the refusal was a clerical error and again resumed payment. But still there was little improvement in Lind's symptoms. As the couple consulted new specialists, their out-of-pocket medical expenses skyrocketed. Without J. D.'s income, those costs went right on the credit card and, through a home equity loan, onto Linda's house.

In May 2004, J. D. and Linda sued Aetna for malpractice and asked for compensatory and punitive damages. They, too, were about to discover that "the greatest development in the life of the American worker since Social Security" was not living up to its promises.

JAMES LARUE, now forty-seven, left his small hometown in Nicaragua at the age of seventeen. The transition to his new home in Fort Worth was rough. But new friends gradually helped him get his bearing on the important things—driving, football, girls. Within a year, he'd started college at Texas Christian University, majoring in economics with a minor in math. He made money on the side by doing computer programming for students. In the case of one customer, MBA student Shannon Robinett, it wasn't money he wanted, but a date. He got it, and married her. The couple eventually had four children.

Right out of college, LaRue sold television advertising. But by twenty-four, he'd moved on to become a business consultant. His specialty—first at Alexander Proudfoot LP and later at DeWolff, Boberg & Associates, Inc.—was operations, getting into the bowels of a manufacturing firm or telecommunications company and making changes aimed at improving performance. The job was especially important at DeWolff because the consulting firm's sales pitch was that it promised to give customers a certain minimum return on its proposals, so executing change successfully was crucial to the consultant's success.

The work meant LaRue was a road warrior, on the move and living out of hotels most weekday nights. But it proved extraordinarily lucrative for a time. In his top years, he was making about $400,000 a year. And after his move to DeWolff in 1988, he was given an ownership stake in the company and a senior management position. According to documents in a subsequent lawsuit, LaRue's clients accounted for fully one-quarter of the firm's total sales in 1998. By 2000, the company's senior management team had voted LaRue one of three to become the firm's next generation of top managers. But within a year, LaRue was out.

In itself, such a reversal of fortune is not particularly surprising. Consulting firms are delicate operations where working relationships can form and break up over almost nothing. And in LaRue's case, the

break came when the financial markets and the economy were sinking and the consulting business, which is especially sensitive to economic reversals, was shaky. What is surprising, though, is what
happened just before and after the break.

By 2000, LaRue had put away about $400,000 in DeWolff's
401(k)-like savings plan. As he watched the market sink that spring
and summer, he realized it spelled trouble for his savings, so in September he wrote the company's savings-plan administrator a letter
ordering the administrator to sell his stocks and move him into
Treasury bills. Only the administrator did not make the change. But
LaRue wasn't notified of the fact for nearly a year. He resigned from
DeWolff in August 2001 and after some legal wrangling managed to
negotiate a deal to sell back his stake in the company. But there was
still the matter of the savings-plan money.

On 9/11, aware that the terror attack on the Twin Towers would
send markets plunging, LaRue called and again wrote ordering that
his savings be moved from stocks to Treasuries. But still the administrator did nothing. In subsequent court papers, the company acknowledged that LaRue had sought some changes in his savings
plans, but asserted that he had subsequently rescinded his requests by
phone, something LaRue adamantly denies doing.

In the end, LaRue's wish that his savings be moved from stocks to
T-bills was not acted upon until DeWolff changed savings-plan administrators in 2004, four years after his initial order to make the
switch. LaRue figured that the delay cost him about $150,000, and
when DeWolff would not agree to make up the difference, he sued to
recover his loss. That's when—like Potter, Andrews-Clarke, and Lind
before him—he encountered the new reality of ERISA.

FOR MANY YEARS, from the end of World War II through the 1970s,
the U.S. economy seemed capable of steadily lifting the material
fortunes of a broad swath of working Americans, including the
likes of Potter, Andrews-Clarke, Lind, and LaRue. Despite periodic

fluctuations in the business cycle, wars in Korea and then Vietnam, civil rights protests, urban riots, and a succession of oil shocks that sent energy prices flying, the wages and benefits of most working people rose smartly—well ahead of inflation. Major corporations considered it part of their duty to share the economic bounty, both to help shield workers from setbacks and to expand the market for their products. Businesses must find ways "of protecting the individual against the most damaging effects of inevitable change," said Eugene Holman, president of Standard Oil of New Jersey, which subsequently became Exxon and then Exxon Mobil. "So far as the management of my own company is concerned," he told a late 1940s audience, "we have formed the habit of thinking in terms of . . . lifetime employment" and steadily expanding benefits.

BEGINNING SOMETIME in the late 1970s, however, corporate executives and public policy makers began to rethink this approach. They became convinced that the economy's lifting powers were more limited than previously thought, particularly when it came to benefits. Now, America's benefit system is in crisis, say these influential voices. Some trace the trouble to the 1950s, the overweening demands of a once-powerful labor movement, and the overgenerous promise-making of what are now decried as feckless corporate leaders. Others see the problem as stemming from the naive conviction that the nation could remain the world's dominant producer essentially forever and so hand out ever-higher wages and benefits. Now, these business leaders say, rising competition, especially from inexpensive foreign workers in places such as India and China, means their companies can no longer afford to deliver the benefits they once did. Still others argue that demography is destiny and that the soon-to-begin retirement of the baby boomers would swamp almost any benefit system. Some even argue that employee-benefit programs distract business corporations from their true mission—making money. Among other things, they say, traditional benefits encourage employee behavior that many firms no longer want—especially loyalty and expectations of staying with the same company for a long time.

The private-sector dialogue echoes a parallel debate under way in Washington over whether the nation can any longer afford Social Security, Medicare, and the other social insurance benefits it now provides. And the combination has fueled predictions that working Americans had better brace for a sharp new decline in the economic protections that they traditionally received, especially when it comes to increasingly expensive health insurance. "With costs through the roof and with the majority of health care dollars going to companies' sickest and therefore least-productive workers, it's hard to see how you can align employers' business goals with their provision of employee health benefits, which means it's hard to see how these benefits can last," said benefits expert Sylvester Scheiber.

Certainly, signs of benefit trouble seem to be all around us. The once-dominant steel and airline industries have declared that they can't pay $24 billion in accumulated pension promises. They have shunted these liabilities to a federal backup agency, the Pension Benefit Guaranty Corporation (PBGC), which raises the risk of their being dumped on the taxpayers. Hundreds of thousands of steel and airline retirees have also watched as their employer-promised health care benefits, for which there is no similar federal backup, simply vanished. Next up could be the stumbling U.S. auto industry. And the problems are not confined to the economy's troubled sectors. Healthy giants such as IBM and Alcoa have begun to freeze pensions and trim health insurance contributions, substantially cutting their future costs and employees' future coverage. Meanwhile, some of the giant companies that sprang from the blossoming of personal computers and the Internet, companies such as Google and Cisco, have taken the process a step further. They have provided workers with flashy extras like manicured campuses, haute cuisine cafeterias, and state-of-the-art gyms that have diverted attention from the fact that in most instances these firms' benefits are distinctly stingier than those of their corporate predecessors. Essentially, no New Economy firms offer pensions. In most cases, their health coverage is only for individual workers, not families, at least not without an employee contribution.

But is the situation really so bleak? Must people now begin to fashion their own safety nets even in cases, such as health care, where costs can so thoroughly outstrip the resources not just of middle-income families but of affluent ones as well that the building of such personal safety nets is effectively impossible? A close look at the facts suggests two things. Whatever the current problems with employer-provided benefits, such benefits are nowhere near vanishing. At the same time, however, the combination of benefit cutbacks over the past twenty-five years and the calls for still more cuts in the future has encouraged businesses to look for ways to reduce or shed their responsibilities for employee benefits. It is a temptation that some companies and some executives appear to have found irresistible, and one that they have been able to pursue with help from, of all things, ERISA.

On the issue of whether benefits are on the way to being eliminated, consider first the case of health care. Although analysts have been issuing warnings similar to Scheiber's for decades and reformers have been complaining about the shrinkage of employer coverage and the steady rise of the uninsured, more than 60 percent of working Americans and their families still receive their health care insurance through their employers. Yes, they pay more in premiums than they used to. Yes, some employers now require employees to contribute toward the cost of spouses and children. And yes, the system may undergo substantial change in the coming years. But the fact remains that most working people, or at least most above the very lowest-paid, consider getting health insurance so vital that they won't take a job unless an employer offers some kind of coverage. The result is that there has been no wholesale retreat from employer-sponsored health insurance.

Or consider the benefit that has taken the biggest hit in recent years: the traditional pension. Even before the 2000 stock market crash and subsequent run of record low interest rates took their full toll on pension investment portfolios, executives and some public policy analysts were warning that pensions work against American companies in their competition with the benefit-lean employers of Asia and elsewhere. "We . . . have done what government policy encouraged us to do: offer retirement benefits and health-care benefits to our employees," said General Motors chief executive Rick Wagoner. "That has turned out to be a disadvantage for the U.S. compared with [other] countries" where these protections are either provided by government or not provided at all.

Once the full impact of the stock bust and its aftermath became clear, predictions about what would happen were little short of cataclysmic. Big plans would collapse. Because of the existence of the federal backup agency, the government could get stuck with another bailout like the one following the savings and loan fiasco in the 1980s and early 1990s. And companies that weathered the crisis would react by winding down their plans and getting out of the pension business once and for all, the Jeremiahs warned. According to numbers prepared at the time by the Pension Benefit Guaranty Corporation and the consulting firm of Watson Wyatt, the overall private pension system—which had 125 percent of what it needed to meet its obligations at the height of the stock boom in 2000—had only 84 to 90 percent by 2003. The trend seemed especially frightening at GM; by standard accounting measures, the automaker's pension funds were underfunded to the tune of $17.8 billion. "We've got a hole on the pension side," Wagoner conceded. Numbers such as these helped the Republican-led Congress push through legislation that—some argue unwisely—made employers substantially increase their contributions to their pensions and raised the standard on how closely firms have to keep their pension assets and liabilities matched.

Largely unnoticed over the past couple of years, however, many of the problems that prompted the predictions of cataclysm have corrected themselves. The stock market recovery, rising interest rates, and smart decisions by some employers have pushed the overall private pension system's so-called funding ratio from 80 percent or 90 percent back to 100 percent. By the end of 2006, GM's pensions had swung around and were now $17.1 billion *overfunded*. To be sure, there are still some seriously troubled pensions, among them those of other U.S. automakers. But even PBGC's worst-case scenario of the costs that it could end up shouldering shows a 22 percent improvement between 2005 and 2007. "Recent predictions of the pension system's demise were much exaggerated," said actuarial expert Ron Gebhardtsbauer. "When you consider that the combination of a stock crash and low interest rates at the same time [was] almost as bad for pensions as the Great Depression, their recovery has been pretty impressive." A century in the making, pensions and, more generally, the nation's mixed system of public programs and employer-sponsored retirement benefits have proved remarkably durable.

Reassuring as these recent developments may be, they are not reflected in what has become the dominant opinion among American corporate leaders, many politicians, and—in some ways most significant of all—members of the federal judiciary. Instead of taking heart from the improvements, these leaders have become convinced that the country has gone too far in promising protection, thereby sapping individual initiative and limiting the economy's room to maneuver in the global economy. And they believe the nation can no longer afford a generous benefits system. These views are especially strong among the cadre of business executives, political leaders, and judges whose thinking was shaped during the administration of President Reagan. How quickly and effectively this group's outlook has changed traditional American attitudes toward benefits can be seen in the results of two opinion surveys conducted by the Conference Board, a business research group. In the 1980s, it found that 56 percent of major corporations surveyed still agreed that "employees who are loyal to the company and further its business goals deserve an assurance of continued employment." A decade later, the Conference Board found, that number had dropped to just 6 percent. The new thinking seems to have had a particularly strong effect on the U.S. Supreme Court and many of the federal appeals courts.

According to ERISA's preamble, its intent is to "protect . . . participants in employee benefit plans and their beneficiaries." But starting with a 1985 case, *Massachusetts Mutual Life Insurance Company v. Russell*, the Supreme Court began hemming in those protections and expanding the arguments open to employers and benefit plan administrators to limit or deny benefits. Doris Russell was a claims examiner for the insurance company who became disabled with a back ailment. Massachusetts Mutual initially paid her benefits, but then suspended the payments for nearly five months while it questioned whether she really was suffering from a problem. The suspension forced her disabled husband to cash out his retirement savings. Russell sued for damages. Although an appeals court said that the federal law allowed for such damages, the Supreme Court concluded in a split decision that it did not. It reasoned that "ERISA's interlocking, interrelated and interdependent remedial scheme" was so comprehensive that the measure's congressional authors must have intended only remedies expressly provided for in the law. That generally has meant no more than resumption of the disputed benefits—no matter how long the legal process to get the benefits turned back on is, how damaging the consequences of the delay are, or, in many cases, how high the employees' legal fees go. The high court has interpreted the law's provisions to deny employees the out-of-seeking damages through a state court jury trial, saying that when it comes to employer-provided benefits, ERISA "pre-empts" all state laws. And it has invited insurers and others who administer benefit plans—both of whom have incentives to keep benefit costs low—to grant themselves special legal status that makes most of their decisions legally unassailable, even if the facts suggest that the insurers' or plan administrators' decisions may have been grossly self-serving.

The insurance industry argues that the trend in the law has strengthened rather than weakened the employee-benefit system. "It has allowed companies and unions to operate plans without getting chewed up by lawsuits," said insurance industry lawyer Steven J. Sacher. "That means they're willing to offer employees more choice of benefits at better prices." But the decisions by both the Supreme Court and the appeals courts appear to have had another effect as well. They have allowed companies to pursue a no-promise strategy without slashing or eliminating benefit programs outright—something many firms would not or could not do because employees would object. In place of such an approach, they have provided firms with the means to discourage employees from filing benefit claims and provided firms, insurers, and plan administrators with new powers to reject claims, and make the rejections stick.

WITH THIS HISTORY IN MIND, let's return to Debra Potter, the Virginia insurance agent, and to some of the others whose experiences illustrate what has happened to ERISA.

At what was then Provident Corporation, the predecessor of UnumProvident and now Unum Group, which provided Potter with her disability coverage and whose policies she was selling to the public, the company began seeking to tighten its claims-handling system during the mid-1990s. According to documents that emerged in subsequent court proceedings, Provident sought to reduce payouts on benefits and, wherever possible, to use ERISA—as it had come to be interpreted by the courts—to shield itself from lawsuits by workers and their families.

The company acted after concluding that it had sold too many liberal policies—through employers, and also directly to individuals; the latter plans, on their face, were not covered by the federal benefits law since they were not job-related benefits, but they still cost the company. Now, the company decided, the time had come to begin scrutinizing policyholders' benefit claims more carefully with an eye to reducing payouts, and also to start interpreting as many policies as possible as coming under ERISA. In one 1995 memo, Ralph W. Mohney Jr., who was then a senior vice president at Provident and is still with the company in its current form, described the measures adopted to carry out the new strategy as the firm's "claim improvement initiatives." He said the goal was to move the company from "a claim-payment approach to a claim management approach." "Return on these claim improvement initiatives is expected to be substantial," he informed top executives. "A 1% decrease in benefit cost . . . translates into approximately $6 million in annual savings."

In another 1995 memo, Jeffrey G. McCall, then an assistant vice president at Provident, said the company had set up a task force to ensure that ERISA covered as many of the firm's policies as possible. "The advantages of ERISA coverage in litigious situations are enormous," McCall wrote. "There are no jury trials. There are no compensatory or punitive damages. Relief is usually limited." To drive home the point, McCall said that a company lawyer had recently picked a dozen cases where the firm had paid out a total of $7.8 million in benefits. "If these 12 cases had been covered by ERISA," McCall wrote, "our liability would have been between zero and $0.5 million."

Top Unum executives say that the company never deliberately denied claims to improve the insurer's financial performance. Besides, the executives said, the firm has drastically altered its claims practices since then. Although they do not emphasize it, one of the chief reasons for the subsequent changes was a series of well-publicized investigations by state regulators. Although ERISA prohibits states from intervening to help individuals in most disputes over employee benefits, state regulators do have the right to investigate insurers' overall conduct, penalize them if they find improper activity, and in some cases ban them from doing business in their states. In 2004, regulators representing all fifty states looked at a random sample of 375 Unum cases to see whether the company was engaged in "systemic unfair claim settlement practices." The investigation concluded that there was evidence of such practices "sufficient to merit further regulatory action." All but two of the fifty states decided to settle with the company. California was the major holdout. In a 2005 probe, California regulators uncovered state-law violations in nearly one-third of a random sample of about 1,000 cases. John Garamendi, then California's insurance commissioner, now its lieutenant governor, labeled Unum "an outlaw company."

AT TRAVELERS, which provided Diane Andrews-Clarke and her family with health care insurance, the cost-cutting ran, if anything, even deeper than at Provident. The insurance giant began the 1990s by losing $5 billion on bum real estate investments, then getting socked with hundreds of millions of dollars in property insurance claims when Hurricane Andrew struck Florida in 1992. Its health care operation was about as old-line as any in the business; most clients still received care from expensive fee-for-service providers rather than from managed-care programs. But all of that changed in 1993, the year before Richard Clarke's death. That's when financial turnaround maestro Sanford I. Weill, who would later gain control of giant Citigroup Inc., snapped up the insurer. Ultimately, Weill got the company out of health care altogether by rolling Travelers' health business in with Metropolitan Life Insurance Company's, then selling policies covering 10 million people to United Health Care. But that was not before Weill slashed employment at Travelers by 12,000 and ordered such draconian cost cuts that one senior executive reportedly had to rummage through company trash bins for salvageable file folders. Travelers reacted by, among other things, turning to ERISA and to "utilization review" firms to clamp down on the health claims the firm was paying. According to court papers in a subsequent lawsuit, it was one of those firms, TAO Inc., that decided that

Travelers would pay for only five days of detoxification treatment for Clarke despite the fact that the company policy covering the Massachusetts man provided for thirty days and state law required thirty. It was another review firm, Greenspring, that decided on two subsequent occasions that Travelers would pay for only eight days of treatment and then no treatment at all. According to the judge in the case, the reason the firms' decisions could not be challenged was ERISA as it had been interpreted by higher courts.

WHEN THE HISTORY of the period is written, the recasting of ERISA from a shield protecting workers to one protecting giant corporations will occupy a major chapter in the story of how the social compact between employers and their employees was recast. That's because job-related benefits remain critical to the security of most Americans, and also because the recasting applies not just to a limited number of blue-collar factory workers but also to a wide array of employees, including white-collar professionals, high-tech specialists, and business executives at all but the very highest level of corporations. The law has become one of the most powerful tools available to private employers, insurers, and health plans for getting out from under costly obligations to workers and their families while minimizing legal consequences to themselves. (Public employees are not covered by the measure.) Thus, it has become a crucial vehicle for shifting economic dangers that our employers once helped us manage onto our backs. How such a thoroughgoing transformation could have occurred seems to baffle even some members of the Supreme Court itself. Writing in one recent case, Justice Ruth Bader Ginsburg, quoting a lower-court opinion, said that she joined "the rising judicial chorus urging that Congress and [this] Court revisit what is an unjust and increasingly tangled ERISA regime."

The easiest explanation for what produced this "tangled regime"—and how it occurred with so little public notice—is that ERISA was radically reinterpreted—and weakened—by Ginsburg's conservative colleagues both at the Supreme Court and in the lower courts. But even though conservative jurists certainly played an important role, especially in the past few years, the way was paved for their actions by several key factors in the law's history and structure.

The first is that ERISA began life as a pension measure, not an overall employee-benefit bill. In the late 1950s, the Senate's Permanent Subcommittee on Investigations, chaired by Senator John L. McClellan (D-AR) and employing as its chief counsel Robert F. Kennedy, dug deep into corruption in union pension and benefit funds. The combination of the corruption probes and the Studebaker pension problem set Congress on a long road toward creating ERISA. The initial focus, however, was on the corrupt handling of pension funds, and the law that finally emerged was largely about pots of money—that is, the huge sums sitting in corporate and union plans—and about the fiduciary obligations of those who managed them. This focus made perfectly good sense in the early 1970s, when a pension plan was, in fact, a pot of money set aside to provide benefits for a group of retirees in their old age and employer-provided health insurance was essentially a pot of money to pay the medical bills of a group of workers. But the narrow focus made increasingly less sense as traditionally defined benefit pensions were replaced by 401(k) investment accounts and health insurance plans became active players in delivering services instead of just paying the bills submitted by workers. A 401(k) is an individual, not a group, account, and one that is largely up to the employee to manage. And the very essence of managed health care is that it is a means by which employers or their agents decide in advance what medical treatments individuals can and cannot receive under the plan.

The mismatch that developed between the structure of the law and the new generation of benefits might not have made much difference had it not been for a second step taken by ERISA's authors. As matters stood before the measure's passage, employees who landed in disputes with their employer-provided health insurer would likely already have received medical treatment and would only be haggling over who would pay—an important but hardly a life-or-death issue. Even if an employee was covered by one of the then-newly invented health maintenance organizations and was being denied some kind of treatment, he or she could sue in state court, a powerful incentive for the HMO and the patient to reach an accommodation.

But as House and Senate negotiators were working out the final details of the new law, which had been more than a decade in the making, California suddenly popped up with a stringent benefit-protection proposal of its own. Not to be outdone and in order to avoid a clash between state and federal laws, the congressional negotiators—at their last meeting before the last major vote on the bill—inserted a tiny new provision saying ERISA would preempt any state law that did so much as "relate to [an] employee benefit plan." As one senior congressional staffer explained at the time, the "relate to" language had the effect of "occupying the field completely so that no state can regulate a private pension plan in any manner whatsoever"—or, for that matter, most aspects of health plans, disability policies, group life insurance, 401(k)s, or almost any other benefit that working Americans receive through their employers—even those they themselves pay for entirely.

THAT IS WHERE MATTERS RESTED until 1985, when the Supreme Court handed down the *Russell* decision. Among other things, the court used the decision to zero in on the pot-of-money aspect of the law. Even though ERISA explicitly states that its chief purpose is to protect benefit-plan participants, the court said ERISA's congressional authors were—in the words of the 1985 decision—"primarily concerned with the possible misuse of plan assets and with remedies that would protect the entire plan, rather than with the rights of an individual beneficiary." As time went by, the focus on pots of money would produce some of the court's strangest ERISA decisions.

The justices did not rest with the 1985 decision. In subsequent rulings, they allowed companies to write language into their benefit plans that gives special legal status to their denials of their employees' claims. The special status has meant that lower courts generally have had to defer to the denials, even when the companies have a substantial stake in denial because of the money it saves them. The status also has meant that an employee trying to challenge a claim denial in court must prove not just that the denial was wrong but that the officials making the decision were acting in an "arbitrary and capricious" manner—a burden of proof that is nearly impossible to meet.

Taken together, the Supreme Court decisions have discouraged aggrieved employees from suing employers or insurers because the most they can win are their original benefits, no matter how long they go without the benefits or how much they spend on legal fees to get them. The decisions have discouraged lawyers from taking ERISA cases because there is little hope of winning big money awards and prospective clients are often so financially strapped because of the benefit cutoff that they are unable to pay the lawyers. The decisions have created a disincentive for employers and insurers to pay expensive claims or settle cases because the most they can lose is what they would have paid in the first place. Finally, the decisions have ensured that the law and the increasingly individualized benefits of 401(k)s and managed health care that the law is supposed to govern grow increasingly out of sync, resulting in an ever more surreal series of court rulings.

Among those who fell down the legal rabbit hole and found herself struggling through the Wonderland of ERISA as rewritten by the Supreme Court was Diane Andrews-Clarke.

AFTER HER HUSBAND'S DEATH, Andrews-Clarke sued Travelers, TAO, Greenspring, and others in state court, arguing that Richard Clarke died as a direct result of the companies' improper refusal to pay for the alcoholism treatment that he needed, that her health plan promised, and that state law required be provided. But the insurer and the other defendants got the case removed to federal court, arguing that ERISA preempted state law and did not provide for damages. Once in federal court, lawyers for the insurer argued that the merits of Andrews-Clarke's claim that denying treatment had led to her husband's death were irrelevant. Under ERISA, they said, she was not entitled to damages no matter what the factual circumstances, because the Supreme Court had held in effect that all beneficiaries are entitled to are the benefits denied them and Richard Clarke, being dead, was no longer available to receive the benefits. In any case, defense lawyers argued, the aim of the law was to protect the pots of money that stand behind benefits, not individual beneficiaries.

The result was a long, slow defeat for Andrews-Clarke and her family. At the last stop, in U.S. District Court in Boston, Judge William Young, a Reagan appointee who was subsequently elevated to chief judge, could barely contain his fury at the position he was forced to take. "Under traditional notions of justice," Young wrote, "the harms alleged—if true—should entitle Diane Andrews-Clarke to some legal remedy on behalf of herself and her children. Consider just one of her claims—breach of contract," he said.

> This cause of action—that contractual promises can be enforced in the courts—pre-dates Magna Carta. It is the very bedrock of our notion of individual autonomy and property rights. It is among the first precepts of the common law. . . . Our entire capitalist structure depends on it.
>
> Nevertheless, this Court had no choice but to pluck Diane Andrews-Clarke's case out of the state court in which she sought redress . . . and then, at the behest of Travelers and [the Travelers-hired utilization review companies] slam the courthouse doors in her face. . . .
>
> This case, thus, becomes yet another illustration of the glaring need for Congress to amend ERISA to account for the

changing realities of the modern health care system. Enacted
to safeguard the interests of employees and their beneficiaries,
ERISA has evolved into a shield of immunity that protects
health insurers, utilization review providers and other managed care entities from liability.

In the months after Young's ruling, Andrews-Clarke declared bankruptcy, arranged for her parents to take care of her children, and
checked into a psychiatric institution. She was hospitalized twice
more for depression.

It has taken Diane Andrews-Clarke a dozen years to put her life
back together, to build up the insurance agency that she inherited
from her father so that she can make her payments on the white clapboard house to help her girls cope with the chaos of their early lives,
and—recently—to remarry. She tries to stay away from selling health
insurance or employer benefits, sticking mainly to homeowner and
auto insurance policies. She also spends a lot of time telling clients
about ERISA. Her explanation goes like this: "You've got a good employer, you've got to figure you have good health insurance. Then
you get cancer, and your managed care plan says you should drink
green tea. There's no way you can pay for the regular treatment so
you drink green tea, and that's it."

AS AN ACTIVE PLAYER in the benefit business, Debra Potter remembers reading about Andrews-Clarke's case and about Judge Young's
ruling. She asked colleagues and insurance-industry associates how
such a thing could have happened and remembers being told that
Travelers had fallen behind the times and was having to catch up,
perhaps at the cost of cutting a few corners. She was assured that
nothing like that could happen to her clients. Or, by implication, to
her. With that, Potter put the story out of her mind. By the mid-
1990s, with her own career taking off, it was hard to imagine how
anything could go wrong. A regional bank had purchased the J. V.

Arthur agency, and Potter had been given a promotion. Then, the regional bank had been snapped up by BB&T, and she was offered another promotion. By the end of the decade, she had become so widely recognized as a leader in her field that she had been invited to testify before Congress, had headed a regional coalition on rising health costs, and had been elected president of the Virginia Association of Health Underwriters, an insurance-industry trade group. All the while, the money kept rolling in—$190,128 in 1999, $229,354 in 2000, nearly $255,000 in 2001, according to the family's records.

But Potter was beginning to suspect that she had a medical problem. The first sign came in the summer of 1999, during a Jazzercise class at a local high school. She suddenly felt wobbly and exhausted; she had to sleep for twenty-four hours to shake the feeling. Two years later, in August 2001, while watching her youngest son, Nate, then seventeen, play in a soccer game, she got up to go to the bathroom but her legs refused to budge. As she filled out clients' paperwork that fall, her arms began to ache, then go numb.

Debra Potter was eventually diagnosed as suffering from multiple sclerosis. The progressive neurological disease quickly disabled her. She could not carry the boxes of pamphlets explaining disability coverage to her clients, or stay awake during important business meetings, or sometimes even stand up. It also landed her in a long and costly battle with the company whose policies she had only just been selling, UnumProvident. The insurer questioned whether Potter really was disabled and refused to pay her. Although the company eventually relented, its reversal took three years, and did not come before the Potters had seen their income plunge from almost $300,000 to just $30,000, had run through most of their savings, and had been forced to withdraw Nate from college because they could not pay his tuition. Nor their legal bills.

UnumProvident executives deny that the $10.5 billion-a-year insurer mishandled Potter's case, and some independent experts agree that the company may have had at least some grounds for its initial refusal to pay because MS can be a tricky disease to diagnose in its early stages. But the number of roadblocks that the company threw in Potter's path and the fact that, even with all of her expertise, it took her so long to overcome them suggest what awaits less well-equipped Americans who think they're protected from a financial free fall in case of illness.

Potter's search for an answer to what was happening to her medically began in December 2001, when she went to Winchester Neurological Associates to see Dr. Patrick M. Capone. Capone's notes over the following year show a physician in search of a diagnosis. He suspected multiple sclerosis from the outset, but an MRI turned up only one wedge-shaped lesion in Potter's brain, instead of the two lesions required by newly adopted diagnostic criteria for MS. So he wrote in his notes that he couldn't prove she had the disease until further symptoms appeared. He tried out other diagnoses as well, but at least initially couldn't nail down any of them to his satisfaction. He noted in passing that his patient showed signs of depression and prescribed an antidepressant, but otherwise made little mention of her state of mind.

Finally in May 2002, he wrote that Potter was suffering from "chronic fatigue syndrome" and "possible" MS. He warned that "her fatigue is such that she is now in danger of losing gainful employment in spite of heroic efforts on her part."

While Capone wrestled with a diagnosis, Potter's supervisor at BB&T, Edwin E. White Jr., noticed that she looked increasingly tired, had trouble carrying the twenty or thirty pounds of paper she'd typically take to a client meeting, and was beginning to miss work, according to subsequent documents in the case. As Potter's troubles deepened, White took over more and more of her responsibilities.

Potter says that she discussed with her bosses the possibility of having to go out on disability. She says that White and other BB&T executives, in turn, discussed the issue with UnumProvident and were assured that—whether her diagnosis was MS or chronic fatigue syndrome—she would be covered under BB&T's group disability policy with the insurer's Provident Life and Accident arm. Potter set herself one final goal: visiting her top one hundred clients to explain what was happening with their accounts. She only made it to six before she had to leave work on May 30, 2002. A few weeks later, she filed for disability.

Although UnumProvident describes the problems in the handling of Potter's claim as isolated, the parallels with problems uncovered during the 2004 investigation by the fifty state insurance regulators and the 2005 investigation by the California insurance department are striking. For example, investigators in the 2004 probe concluded that there was a "bias" in the way UnumProvident's in-house medical staff interpreted the records that claimants submitted to prove their disabilities. "The bias," the regulators wrote, "was reflected in attempts to focus upon any apparent inconsistencies in the medical records or other information supplied by claimants, rather than attempt to derive a thorough understanding of the claimants' medical condition."

Although Capone in his medical records made comparatively little of Potter's psychological state, documents show that UnumProvident officials seized on his note that she showed signs of being depressed. Within two weeks of receiving her claim in early July 2002, an in-house nurse was e-mailing Potter's claim handler to alert her that Capone "has noted that there is an anxiety/depressive factor present which could be significant."

Disability insurers have a considerable financial interest in concluding that a disability has psychological, rather than physical, roots. Most policies—including the one that covered Potter—place a two-year limit on the benefits a company must pay for persons disabled by "mental and nervous disorders." By contrast, most disability claims with physical causes must be paid until the claimant turns sixty-five. In Potter's case, that meant the difference between UnumProvident's owing about $295,000 and owing more than $2.5 million.

In September, a second nurse, reviewing the records in the case but not consulting Potter herself, prepared a report that quoted Capone's notes from his first meeting with Potter that there was "clear evidence" of anxiety or depression. What the UnumProvident report failed to mention was that in the very sentence before the one saying there was "clear evidence" of anxiety, Capone wrote that his first guess about what was causing her problems was a "demyelinating disease" such as MS.

During their 2004 and 2005 investigations, state regulators said they found many instances where UnumProvident denied benefits "on the grounds that the claimant had failed to provide 'objective evidence' of a disabling condition" even where the company's claim forms did not require such evidence. In Potter's case, company documents show that within three weeks of receiving her disability claim, UnumProvident officials were on the phone to Potter complaining that her condition was "self-reported" and saying they needed objective evidence that something was wrong with her. "We must have medical records from the doctor where he finds out what is the problem and diagnoses the problem," company official Mark Hicks wrote that he told Potter in an early August call.

After their probe, the state regulators accused UnumProvident of placing an "inappropriate burden on claimants to justify eligibility for benefits." Among other things, the regulators said they found evidence that UnumProvident was engaged in a company-wide effort "to shift the burden of responsibility to the claimant to provide . . . records in support of a claim," rather than investigate a claim's legitimacy on its own. On August 15, 2002, five weeks after receiving Potter's disability claim, UnumProvident denied it, writing that "we find no medical evidence to support your inability to perform the duties of your occupation. The medical evidence we have received does not indicate the severity of symptoms you claim to have."

In internal documents both before and after the denial, company officials complained about not having received a particular blood test that they said could have helped confirm Capone's secondary diagnosis of chronic fatigue syndrome. Although Potter had signed releases giving the company the right to order up almost any test it wanted, there is no record that anyone at the insurer did so. It did not notify Potter it wanted the test before denying the claim.

On September 9, Potter wrote the company, pleading with it to reconsider its decision. "After helping so many people with disability claims personally in the past, I never expected this to take so long or be so difficult," she said. "Please address this appeal as soon as possible. Money is very tight and it is hard enough to deal with my illness with a positive attitude."

Capone followed up with a series of memos, culminating in one on November 1, 2002, that read:

> The patient . . . does have an abnormality on her MRI and could conceivably have multiple sclerosis. This cannot be confirmed as of yet. Nevertheless, she more than meets the diagnostic criteria for chronic fatigue syndrome. This has significantly incapacitated her, making gainful employment impossible at this juncture. There is no basis to support that her complaints are anything other than legitimate. Clearly, not having total knowledge of the pathophysiology of a disorder is no basis of the denial of its existence.

On November 11, UnumProvident denied Potter's appeal. Among the reasons cited in its denial letter was the lack of the blood test the insurer said it wanted in order to check for chronic fatigue.

In the period that followed, the Potters burned through most of their savings, pulled Nate from $19,000-a-year Roanoke College, and canceled their annual family vacations. Documents show that BB&T made several appeals on Potter's behalf, but UnumProvident stood by its decision to deny her claim. On its own, BB&T appears to have given Potter the equivalent of about a year of her previous pay. When

Potter herself tried to get the insurer to reconsider, she was sent her four-inch-thick claim file and told the case was closed.

All doubts about Potter's diagnosis vanished in August 2003, when she was hospitalized for eye pain and an inability to control her right eye. The eye problems, Capone said, clinched it: She had MS. The following July, Social Security declared Potter totally disabled and began paying her benefits. But it took UnumProvident almost another year to budge.

UnumProvident CEO Thomas R. Watjen refused to comment on the particulars of the Potter case, but pointed to recent declines in customer complaints and lawsuits as evidence that the company's claim-handling problems are behind it. James Sabourin, Unum-Provident's communications vice president, said that company officials initially denied Potter's claim because of inadequate evidence of her disability, but subsequently gathered more evidence and changed their minds. "We received new information along the way, and with that new information we reached a different conclusion, one that's based on the bigger picture rather than focused on a specific symptom or disease," he said.

However, the files that the insurer sent to Potter after it closed her case suggest that UnumProvident's decision to reverse itself occurred only after Potter retained Jon Holder, a Bar Harbor, Maine, lawyer. It was Holder who provided the company with new information about Potter's condition and notified the insurer that Social Security had concluded that she was totally disabled.

Although the insurer would eventually send Potter a check for the back benefits that it now agrees she was owed, the check did not include the several hundred thousand dollars in legal fees that it cost her to get the company to change its position. She and Holder are now asking UnumProvident to pay these amounts as well. And the check for back benefits took three years to arrive. Asked recently about the three-year wait, UnumProvident spokesman Sabourin said that Potter, Holder, and, by implication, BB&T were as much to blame as his company for drawing out Potter's case, although he refused to explain why. "Could we have done better? Quite possibly," he said. "But to suggest that we were solely responsible for this claim taking as long as it did is not accurate."

How could an insurer, whose policies Debra Potter had been selling as protection against economic upheaval, put her through a hazing so severe that—even with all of her knowledge of insurance and the help of a lawyer—it took her three years to get the benefits she deserved and left her family's finances in tatters? How could a health plan like Diane Andrews-Clarke's deny a benefit that its own documents said it would provide and, when her husband died untreated, leaving her to raise the couple's children, give her no legal recourse? How could a law that had been labeled the "greatest development in the life of the American worker since Social Security" be so completely turned against those same workers? By the end of the 1990s, such contradictions seemed to be pushing the Supreme Court to alter the way it interpreted ERISA. Many people thought the justices would finally come to grips with the huge change in benefits since the 1970s, especially the shift from group pensions to individual retirement accounts and from fee-for-service to managed health care.

In one case, where executives with farm-equipment maker Massey Ferguson used "deliberate deception" to convince more than 1,000 employees to switch health and other benefits to a money-losing subsidiary that eventually went bust, the court seemed to encourage these hopes for a judicial course correction. It ruled that the federal benefits law was not, after all, solely focused on protecting plans; it could also be used to force employers and insurers to make awards to individuals as well. In other decisions, the court appeared to trim back the sweeping preemption that had prevented states from regulating benefits, especially health benefit plans. The justices suggested that states could prohibit insurers from asserting the special legal status for their decisions on claims that placed an almost insurmountable burden of proof on the plaintiff, as had happened in Potter's case. They also appeared to authorize states to set up review panels that people denied coverage by their health plans could turn to for an independent assessment of their claims. The high court even seemed to signal that people might, under some circumstances, sue their health plans for money damages in state court, which could have put new pressure on providers to treat plan participants fairly. Writing about one of the rulings in mid-2001, health law authority Peter J. Hammer said it showed "the Court's desire to see state tort law [read lawsuits] play a greater role in policing managed care conduct."

But the legal springtime was short-lived. In a recent series of decisions written by conservative justices Antonin Scalia and Clarence Thomas, the court returned to its earlier position on ERISA. In one case, the justices issued a decision that meant even plan participants who suffered substantial costs—physical or financial—because of benefit denials could not be awarded "compensatory damages" under the law. Indeed, in most instances, the court held they were ineligible for *any* money even if they won, including the back benefits they had been denied. And in its June 2004 ruling called *Aetna v. Davila*, the high court decided that almost all disputes between employer-provided health care plans and their participants—even disputes over proper medical care—are covered by ERISA, so people cannot sue their plans for malpractice. "The cases have been greeted with despair in the scholarly and practitioner world. They are imposing a terrible toll of injustice," lamented John H. Langbein, a Yale law professor. Langbein prides himself in being a conservative; among other things, he considers corporate pension plans little better than the illusory financial pyramid schemes named after Charles Ponzi, who duped thousands of New England investors in the 1920s. But Langbein is outraged by the high court's ERISA rulings and has said so, in no uncertain terms, in a series of biting law-review articles with titles like "What ERISA Means by 'Equitable': The Supreme Court's Trail of Error . . . ."

AT SIX FOOT TWO AND 245 POUNDS, J. D. Lind was not accustomed to sitting around. So he tried to make himself useful even with his MS and blindness. He tried to do repairs around the house he shared with his wife, Linda. He sought to mow the lawn. He signed up for a $5,000 online computer course with Villanova University, figuring that maybe he could become a project manager even if he himself could no longer do construction. But he drove a screw through his finger, ran the couple's riding mower into a tree, and realized halfway through the course that no one was going to hire him. "Nobody wants a guy who can't drive on a construction job. Hell, I can't put my hand in front of my face and be sure it's there," he said.

In May 2004, the Linds sued Aetna in state court and sought compensatory and punitive damages on grounds that J. D.'s ability to function had been destroyed by the company's insistence he take drugs other than those prescribed by his doctor. When the Linds acted, the Oklahoma couple found themselves in the same predicament as Potter and Andrews-Clarke. Aetna's lawyers used the Supreme Court's early rulings on ERISA to have the case removed from state to federal court. Lind's lawyer, Jason Aamodt, was confident that they still had a strong case because of the more encouraging thrust of the court's recent "springtime" rulings. Aamodt called particular attention to decisions in a previous Oklahoma case: Under certain circumstances, a federal appeals court had held, persons who believed they'd been injured by their managed-care plans could sue for money. Aamodt thought the Linds' circumstances matched those in the previous case.

But on the very June day when lawyers' briefs were due in the Linds' case, the Supreme Court handed down *Aetna v. Davila*. Aamodt struggled to put some distance between the Linds' situation and that of the patient in *Davila*. But Aetna's lawyers argued that *Davila* threw into doubt the Oklahoma appeals court decision on which Aamodt had pinned so much hope. In addition, the company's lawyers said, Aetna had written language into its plan that gave its claims decisions specially protected status.

In 2005, federal district judge Terence Kern ruled, "Nothing distinguishes the facts at hand from *Davila*. The plan documents permitted [Aetna] to do all of the things it did in changing Mr. Lind's medication. . . . That Mr. Lind suffered damages from [Aetna] exercising its rights . . . is simply not actionable. . . . Under current law, one cannot be made whole where ERISA governs." On Halloween of 2006, Kern's decision was upheld by an appeals court.

"The tough part has been watching a big man like J. D. go down," Linda said. "That, plus I'm going to have to work until they throw dust over my face."

"This isn't me," Lind said of himself in his current condition. "If I could do some kind of work or get [Aetna] to pay for what they've done to me, I could accept it. But not this way, not being helpless like this."

RIPPLES FROM THE SUPREME COURT'S recent decisions reached not just health plans but 401(k)s and savings plans as well. In a move that alarmed even the conservative Bush administration, appeals court panels cited the high court's recent ERISA rulings as protecting 401(k) plan administrators who fail to follow the explicit orders of account holders to make investment changes in their accounts. In doing so, the appeals courts returned the law to its thirty-year-old pot-of-money roots, and in the process left retirement-account holders effectively unprotected.

As a result, when the manager of James LaRue's 401(k)-like savings-plan retirement account ignored his orders to change his investments and thereby cost him an estimated $150,000, LaRue was told—as Potter, Andrews-Clarke, and Lind were told—that there was nothing he could do about it. ERISA protected the investment-firm manager who fouled up the account, not LaRue.

In LaRue's case, a three-judge federal circuit court panel cited a Scalia-authored Supreme Court opinion that plaintiffs' appeals to "vague notions of a statute's 'basic purpose' are inadequate" to secure the kind of damage claim being made. If Scalia's rejection of arguments based on the law's "basic purpose" sounded like a rejection of his cherished notion of "original intent," there was not any higher legal authority to say so. The appellate panel went on to declare that, since LaRue's loss was solely his, rather than being suffered by all members of DeWolff, Boberg's savings plan, ERISA barred him from collecting anything. LaRue had other options, the panel added: "He could, for example, seek an injunction compelling compliance with his investment instructions," the judges suggested, apparently choosing not to notice that this advice came a little late to be useful; even court injunctions can't roll back time in the stock market.

The appellate court's ruling against LaRue took the Bush administration by storm. Administration lawyers quickly filed a brief asking the panel to rehear the case. The brief warned that the judges' decision "could undermine if not eliminate the ability of participants of [401(k)] plans, which nationally hold approximately $2.9 trillion in assets . . . to recover monetary losses. . . . [T]he decision leaves LaRue and individual plaintiffs like him without any means whatsoever to recover losses caused even by the most egregious fiduciary breaches."

The panel promptly reheard the case and came to the very same decision. The case appealed to the Supreme Court. On February 20, 2008, the high court effectively reversed its earlier rulings that ERISA could only tend to the overall soundness of employee retirement plans, but not provide substantial relief to individual beneficiaries who have been wronged. In a nine-to-zero decision, it recognized that big pensions and their pots of money are largely gone. "[T]hat landscape has changed," wrote Justice John Paul Stevens. In their place are individual accounts such as 401(k)s and savings plans like James LaRue's. So it only makes sense, the court reasoned, that the law should apply differently to these new types of retirement arrangements, and that individuals such as LaRue should, after all, be able to sue for losses when their accounts are mishandled. LaRue, investor advocates and the Bush Labor department all heaved great sighs of relief.

But there was a little-noticed—and deeply discouraging—aspect to the new ruling. Although the justices specifically asked lawyers on both sides to brief them on whether they should expand their decision in the LaRue case beyond retirement to cover the entire universe of employee benefits that comes under ERISA, they ultimately decided the case just on retirement. That means that James LaRue and 401(k) account holders are helped. But for Debra Potter, Diane Andrews-Clarke, J. D. Lind, and anyone else who receives their health care or disability insurance—or almost any other benefit besides retirement—through their employers, there is still no relief in sight.

"ERISA has basically become a plague upon the people it was designed to protect because the Supreme Court has interpreted ERISA remedy in an extremely crabbed and narrow way," said Yale law professor Langbein. "The court, in *LaRue*, had the chance to revisit its earlier mistakes in ERISA remedy law. But they didn't go there."

3

THE NUMBERS

FOLLOWING THE EXPERIENCES of Richard Coss Jr. and his father, of Debra and Ron Potter, of Diane Andrews-Clarke, of J. D. and Linda Lind, or of James LaRue can give you a feel for how the lives of individual Americans have grown simultaneously more prosperous and more precarious. What individual stories alone cannot do, however, is tell you whether the setbacks suffered by these people are the sorts of misfortune that have always befallen an unlucky few, or instead represent something new and different in America. Are they simply part of life's bargain? Or do they indicate that the U.S. economy has developed a disquieting tendency to dish out troubles of increasing severity? And even if the economy has developed such a tendency, the individual stories cannot answer whether the kinds of losses that people experience are usually offset by compensating gains. Is the payoff for losing your job the possibility of a better job at higher pay? Does struggling over coverage under your employer-sponsored health plan ultimately result in more care and greater payouts? To answer these questions—and to begin figuring out what the economy's changes mean for you—requires looking at a lot of Americans to see whether their circumstances are changing in broadly similar ways, both for better and for worse. In other words, it requires moving from case studies to statistics.

Making this move is not quite as simple as it might seem. Although the United States probably collects more numbers about itself than any other nation on earth, almost none of these figures are the kind that let you follow actual individuals as they move through their lives, doing such things as providing for their families, paying for their homes, and saving for school and retirement. Most government statistics—whether about unemployment or the number of car owners—involve taking snapshots of random samples of people, then comparing those snapshots with previous pictures to see if one can spot a trend. The problem is that human beings live not from snapshot to snapshot but continuously, and they don't care half as much about what's happening to a random sample as they do about their families and themselves.

With the help of experts, I set out to assemble a set of numbers that comes closer than the conventional statistics to measuring the economic circumstances of people and their families in ways that are both important and more familiar to them. I have not been the only one to try my hand at this. But I think I have looked broadly at the trends in the economy and have come up with a set of statistics that usefully portrays economic America as it looks from the doorstep of working households up and down most of the income spectrum.

Most of the numbers in this chapter come from a set of data called the Panel Study of Income Dynamics (PSID), which is one of the few surveys that follows the same nationally representative group of families and their offshoots, and has been doing so since the late 1960s. That means we can keep tabs on particular men and women as they have moved through their lives. We can watch as their incomes have risen with raises, promotions, and new jobs, or fallen with pay cuts, layoffs, and illnesses. We can see couples as they have married or divorced; parents as they have raised their children, put them through college, and sent them into the world; and kids as they've grown up and started families of their own. By looking carefully, we can see individual triumphs and tragedies. Most important for our purposes, we can see whether there have been any changes in the way that people go through all of these very human activities and the way that the activities are rewarded, punished, or ignored economically. And we can examine whether, if something goes wrong, a family is more likely than before to take a big financial fall.

This is not the conventional way of looking at the economy. At least it's not the approach that shows up in most news stories about the unemployment rate, housing starts, or changes in the cost of living. The commonly reported economic snapshots have produced a lot of positive headlines over the past few decades, if not the past few months. So if, as I am doing, I'm coming up with a different way of looking at the economy that shows a very different picture than those in the snapshots, it is important that you understand what I am doing and see both its strengths and weaknesses. To begin with, the panel study has been going on so long that some of its data go back to the age of computer punch cards. That's important because having a lot of data over a long time period reduces the likelihood of temporary blips skewing the analysis. But it also means that the data can be tricky to work with. Over the years, many of the original people have dropped out or died, but they have been replaced largely by their descendants. In recent years, database officials have been forced by government funding cuts to survey families only every other year, instead of annually. All of this can affect data quality and force you to change the way you handle the numbers. You should ask questions about the techniques that I and the experts who helped me used. There are different ways to perform these calculations, and some give somewhat different results. For those who are interested in the technical details, more information can be found in the endnotes and in the Methods section on page 325. But it would be unfortunate if, amid questions about method and data quality, the central substantive question of this book got lost: namely, how to account for an America that is growing securely more prosperous even as many, perhaps most, Americans are growing less so. And it would be a shame if certain facts ended up obscured—among them, that the nation's economy has changed substantially over the past thirty-five years and especially the past twenty-five years; that those changes have helped many lead materially better lives; that this improvement has come at the largely hidden cost of significantly boosting the odds that when something goes wrong, individuals and their families can take steep financial falls from which they have a harder time recovering.

Ultimately, the aim of laying out the numbers in this chapter is to give you a sense of the dimensions of the problem and how many people are being affected. But the numbers have a second, more immediate, purpose. Journalism involves talking with people and reporting what they have to say. There is plenty to recommend this as a way of learning about the world. But there's always a question about whether a reporter has tilted the outcome of his findings by talking mostly with people who support the point he wants to make. The numbers are intended to assure readers that I have *not* tilted my findings. The numbers show that what is happening to the individuals whose stories I tell is happening to America as a whole, or at least to that vast middle of America where most of us live— the huge and heavily populated region between the superrich and the destitute.

The Panel Study of Income Dynamics has followed a representative nationwide sample of families and their offshoots for nearly forty years. It started with 5,000 families and has now grown to about 8,000 families. Over the years, it has collected information on more than 65,000 people, in many cases spanning most of their lives. Although much of the information is financial, survey takers have also asked panel study members about housing and health, child care and charitable giving, automobiles and education. Recently, government statisticians began experimenting with methods to replace surveys like the PSID by using powerful new computer techniques that can scarf up all the records on, say, people who pay into Social Security and match them up with income tax records. But these techniques are still experimental and, because of confidentiality concerns, are off-limits to most researchers. That means that the PSID remains the most comprehensive publicly available record of family earnings and income in the United States and, in fact, in the world. It is run by the University of Michigan and is principally underwritten by the National Science Foundation.

Since the panel study data are broadly reliable and also follow families from a wide range of backgrounds over many years, it is well suited for an examination of whether the experiences of the families in this book reflect a significant nationwide pattern. Richard Coss has had years when he made a very good living, as much as $140,000 in 2007 dollars. The problem is that, unlike his father, he couldn't maintain a string of good years. Periodically, he has found himself out of work and out of money. Debra Potter was making an even better living—more than twice as good—until she was blindsided by disease and her insurance failed her. What Coss and Potter have in common is that both suffered sharp economic reverses. They both saw their incomes take big dives. To see whether the odds of experiencing similarly big income swings have gone up, I began by using the panel study's data to look at the households of working-age adults. I limited my analysis to workers between the ages of 25 and 64. Using this age bracket excluded the potentially distorting income swings that could have occurred if I had included younger people who were just finishing school and getting started in the workforce. At the same time, confining myself to the 25-to-64 age group limited the effect of downward swings that can come at the other end of a work life, when people are retiring. In defining what constituted a steep dive, I was flying a bit by the seat of my pants. I wanted to pick a sum big enough that most people would agree that it was a painful amount—something none of us would wish upon ourselves. I settled on one-half of a family's annual income. By this measure, families that had been making $30,000 a year and saw their income fall to $15,000 would be counted. So would families that had been making $250,000 and experienced a drop of $125,000. And I compared what the data showed for the early and mid-1970s, the early and mid-1980s, and the early and mid-1990s. Because of the nature of the PSID, I had to put off for a bit bringing the figures up to date, although I would do so before I was finished.

During the early and mid-1970s, 2.8 percent of panel study families lost half or more of their annual income between any one year and the next. By the early to mid-1990s, that fraction had more than doubled to 6.1 percent. In themselves, these numbers may not seem like terrible odds. And they were accompanied by some modest-sized increases in the fraction of families that saw their incomes jump by 50 percent or more. However, the odds of a big loss add up. Facing a 2.8 percent probability each year, your chances of seeing a 50 percent income drop in at least one of five years is about 13 percent. Facing a 6.1 percent probability, your chances increase to about 27 percent—

Big Gains Rise, Then Fall
The percentage of American families whose annual income jumped 50% or more increased through the 1990s, then declined.

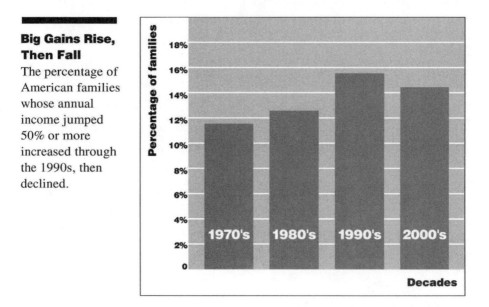

or more than one in four. And the figures that bring the comparisons up-to-date suggest that the odds of big income plunges have climbed substantially, and they have not been accompanied by anything like a comparable-sized increase in the likelihood of income jumps. The figures show that the odds of families seeing their income drop by half or more during any two-year interval have gone from roughly 1 in 20 in the 1970s to 1 in 11 by this decade. That last number is roughly equivalent to your chances of catching the flu in the next few years. And while the 1-in-20 chance of experiencing a big income dive during the 1970s was accompanied by nearly 1-in-9 odds of having one's income jump by half, today's sharply higher chances of a big loss have not been accompanied by anything like a comparably large increase in the chances of a big gain.

The figures alone offer no clue about why the chances that a family's income swings up and down are so much greater than they used to be. We can at least imagine completely benign explanations. Perhaps more Americans are taking more sabbaticals or changing careers more often in ways that leave them leading more satisfying lives even if the changes disrupt the steadiness of their income. Or perhaps

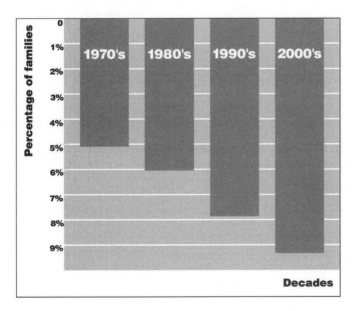

Big Losses Rise
The percentage of American families whose annual income took a dive of 50% or more has steadily increased since the 1970s.

more are working as consultants or class-action lawyers who can hit it rich, but can go for long dry spells between the fat years. Or maybe the economy has simply grown more competitive—so that while it takes away bigger chunks of income, it also adds back still bigger ones in what many people consider fair trades.

Whatever the explanation, the figures show that the stories of Richard Coss, Debra Potter, and the others you've met so far are not the experiences of a statistically unfortunate few. The numbers from the PSID study reveal for the first time that something about the economy has changed in ways that make the experiences of Coss, Potter, and the others more common than they were in preceding decades. Although not apparent in the standard statistics and not noted by most economists, something about the economy is growing more turbulent, and its effects are reaching down into the heart of America's individual households.

To GET AT WHAT THAT SOMETHING is and the potential trouble it spells for you and your family, we can look to the people whom we've been following for hints about what to watch for. We know that Coss's problems began with job loss. With Potter and Lind, it was disease. With Andrews-Clarke, it was the death of a spouse. LaRue incurred a serious financial loss. And we know that in the case of most of these people, the initial blow was greatly magnified when business and government programs in place for much of the past century to buffer Americans against setbacks proved of little help. What was the experience of the panel study families?

In looking at these families, I applied the test of the two economists I mentioned in the introduction, Richard Burkhauser and Greg Duncan, who, in turn, were building on the work of earlier academics who had tried to figure out exactly how the hardships of the Great Depression fell on the shoulders of most American families. The evidence showed that it wasn't just stock losses or unemployment, but any of a number of common destabilizing life events that let trouble seep in during the Great Depression. When considering today's families, I selected seven such common life events: divorce or separation; a big decrease in a spouse's work hours; a substantial decrease in the head of the household's work hours due to unemployment; a big decrease in the head's work hours due to disability or retirement; a big decrease in the head's work hours due to illness; the death of a spouse; or the birth of a child. Then, I calculated how often panel study families experienced any one of these seven events during the 1970s, the 1980s, the 1990s, and the first half of this decade. Finally, I analyzed the data to find out who of those who did experience one of these life events saw their income take a hit of 50 percent or more.

The frequency rates for these events occurring were just about what you'd expect given the history of the past thirty-odd years. Between the 1970s and 2000s, the odds of a household head suffering a major spell of unemployment decreased as the national unemployment rate went down. By contrast, the odds of a couple getting divorced went up along with the national divorce rate. Overall, the chances of being struck by any one of the seven events during the course of a decade fell slightly.

But when you turned from the frequency or incidence of these events to the economic impact or consequence, the story was the exact opposite. The fraction of families who saw their income slashed by half or more when hit by unemployment climbed from about 17 percent to almost 26 percent; the fraction suffering similar-size declines when hit by a divorce or separation jumped from about 30 percent to about 36 percent. Even seemingly positive events such as childbirth were more likely to be income-rattlers—in large measure because families have become more dependent on the incomes of working wives who have to take time out to have their children. During the 1970s and early 1980s, only about 7 percent of panel study families in which a child was born saw their annual income fall by at least half. By now, that fraction has climbed to 10 percent, an increase of one-third. Overall, the fraction of families whose incomes were

cut in half after being hit by any one of the events rose from 14 percent to 20 percent, an increase of more than one-third.

IF YOU READ THESE NUMBERS and think there is no cause for concern, consider this: Births and deaths, divorces, unemployment, illnesses, and injuries are among the bedrock events of life, examples of
the "what ifs" that come with being human. During earlier eras, these
sorts of setbacks were usually made manageable with the help of extended families, employers, and government. In fact, in some instances, families, employers, and government have continued to play
their traditional roles during the past three decades. For example, the
combination of medical research (much of it government funded),
employer-sponsored health insurance, and healthier habits on your
part and your family's has helped reduce the chances that you will die
during your work life or that you will lose your spouse. So far, so
good. But then comes that last set of numbers. Chillingly, they reveal
that the economic danger posed by these events has been quietly
climbing so that, by today, if you're struck by one of them, you and
your family face a more than 1-in-5 chance of seeing half your family
income vanish.

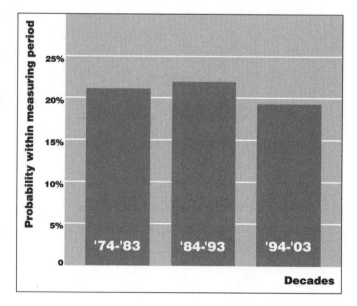

Declining Incidence
The probability of any of a panel of income-threatening events happening to your family has declined since the 1970s.

Of course, all of this talk of taking such economic blows is premised on the notion that one of these bad events will actually happen to you. Most of the time, most people manage to dodge the bullets. Most families are not like the Cosses, Potters, or Linds. In fact, the figures from the panel study suggest that, right now, the chances of getting nailed over the course of a decade by any one of the seven events that we've been looking at stands at about 20

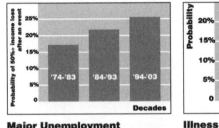

Major Unemployment

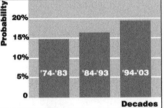

Illness

Rising Consequence

However, when a threatening event does occur, the probability of your family's income falling 50% or more has jumped.

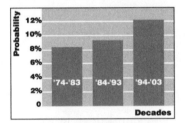

Work Loss of Spouse

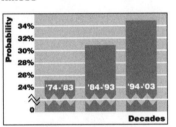

Retirement or Disability

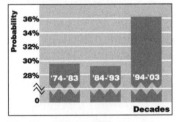

Divorce or Separation

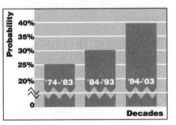

Death of a Spouse

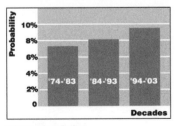

Birth of a Child

percent. So there is a temptation to say that the other 80 percent of Americans can breathe easy. But can they really? Or has the economy come to operate in ways that leave even families that have not yet sustained bad blows more vulnerable to them, and to their economic fallout? To answer these questions, we need to find some way to measure the risks, or odds, of bad economic events befalling people *before* those events actually strike. We need to see whether those risks are on the rise.

This is a harder assignment than you might think, even though the past generation has been a golden age in the development of techniques for measuring and managing risk. The difficulty is that most of the new mathematical methods for predicting the odds of bad outcomes and most of the financial inventions for shaping, sharing, and shifting risk have remained the exclusive preserve of financiers, corporate executives, and technical experts who serve them. New risk-management tools help health insurers tailor policies to avoid people who are apt to file many claims—or to charge them prohibitively high premiums. Similar tools enable credit card issuers to pick out the most profitable people—those who run huge balances and pay hefty interest charges but do not default. Others assist consultants in coming up with variable pay schemes and flexible work schedules that let companies boost output while minimizing the cost of keeping unneeded employees on the clock. What all these new statistical tools and techniques do not do is provide much aid to American families.

"Managing risk is really what finance—not just insurance, but banking, venture capital, hedge funds, the stock and bond markets—is all about," said Yale economist and finance theorist Robert J. Shiller. "And finance should concentrate on our ordinary riches—our means to ensure that families are provided for if something goes wrong, that there will be money for a house, an education, a business idea or retirement," he said. "Risk management tools should be widely available in a democratic and innovative society, but they are

not. . . . With the exception of some experiments in home equity insurance and some financial products like 401(k)s and home equity
loans, most households have pretty much the set of risk management
tools that they had a generation ago—traditional insurance, the basic
rules about diversifying your financial investments, the cautions
about debt and savings."

Lacking tools to assess the risks families face, we must borrow
methods from elsewhere in the economy. And the most obvious
place to borrow is from the stock market. Although the ardor for
stocks has cooled somewhat since the tech bust of 2000, the corporate scandals of 2002, and the options debacle of the past few years,
the stock market remains, in most people's eyes, the very model of
what a free-market economy is supposed to be—as well as the embodiment of our wildest hopes for a new, democratized, and fabu-
lously wealthy future. The most widely used risk measure in the stock
market is something called a "beta."

Betas work by following a single stock's price as it bounces up and
down and comparing those bounces to changes of an overall market
measure such as the Standard and Poor's 500 Index. The movement
of the overall measure captures what the market and the economy as
a whole are doing. Any bounce in the individual stock price above
and beyond the ups and downs of the market is considered to be the
risk specific to that stock. The general idea behind using bounce, or
volatility, as a risk measure is that the more and larger the bounces,
the more likely it is that a shareholder could get caught short, want-
ing or needing to sell shares when the price is down. Although stock
betas measure both the upswings and the downswings of a stock's
price, professional investors pay almost no attention to the upswings.
Plenty of other ways exist to gauge the rewards of a stock investment,
like the profits you can reap when you sell for a gain. What investors
want to know from a beta is the stock's risk.

The groundwork for using betas to look at families' economic
circumstances was laid more than a decade ago by two prominent

researchers, Peter Gottschalk, an economist at Boston College, and
Robert A. Moffitt, the Johns Hopkins University economist and editor of the *American Economic Review*. The core of their thinking
was simple enough, although it involved some complicated math.
Much of the economics profession, the two reasoned, had devoted
itself to taking snapshots of people's earnings and incomes, figuring
out how the levels of earnings and incomes stacked up, and deciding whether the gap between the top and the bottom—economic
inequality—had widened. But economists had not spent much
time looking at how earnings and incomes behaved between the
snapshots—what journeys those earnings or incomes had taken between one time and another, and between one level and another.
For example, how did a family whose income began at $50,000 and
five years later stood at $55,000 make it from the lower number to
the higher number? Did its income rise in neat $1,000 annual in-
crements? Or did it take big leaps in some of the years and steep
plunges in others? The answer might not matter to economists
looking at the whole population, but it could matter mightily to individuals. A big downward plunge could cost families their homes
or deprive children of higher education, for instance, and the losses
might not be recoverable even if the family's income eventually
climbed back to where it had been before the bad times hit.

Gottschalk and Moffitt's original interest was not in coming up
with ways to measure the risks of these sorts of things happening to
families. It was in examining how much of the recent growth in economic inequality was—as almost all economists assumed before the
two wrote—the result of a permanent widening between those at the
top and bottom of the economy and how much was the result of
transitory swings in people's earnings and income. In trying to answer this inequality question, however, they developed measuring
techniques that look remarkably like a beta. Like the overall market
measure in a stock beta, the trend in a family's income over, say, five
years—and more especially the trend in the incomes of a whole

group of families, such as all of those in the panel study sample—captures where the economy generally is pushing people. Any income swings over and above that trend represent the specific risks that a family bears. As with a stock beta, the idea behind using swing or volatility as a risk measure is that the greater the income swing, the greater the chance that a family will be caught in a downdraft when a crisis strikes, and the harder it will be for that family to work its way back to firm financial ground.

By adapting the idea of the stock beta to family income, we now have a way to see whether the economic circumstances of *all* families—not just those like the Cosses, Potters, or Linds—have been changing in ways that leave them more prone to trouble. We have a way, in other words, to look at the other 80 percent of panel study families who thus far have not experienced a big income drop. And since the panel sample is broadly representative of the U.S. population as a whole, we have a way to look at the other 80 percent of all American families and determine whether they are on secure or shaky ground.

So what does our new measure show? It shows that the income swings of individual families have grown substantially over the past twenty-five to thirty years. It shows that the increase has affected families who've suffered setbacks such as illness and layoff and also those who've skated by seemingly unscathed. And it shows that the swings have shaken almost everyone—from working poor families earning $20,000 and $30,000 a year to working rich families making $200,000 a year or more; from younger families to older ones; from high school dropouts to college graduates—and by now have reached into the majority of working American households.

"The long-run trend in the volatility of earnings and incomes in the United States has been upward," said Moffitt. "The earnings and incomes of families have grown increasingly unstable over the last generation. All other things equal, rising income instability suggests that families from the working poor to those fairly far up the income distribution are bearing more economic risk."

In the past three decades, the typical income for middle-of-the-pack families has risen by about 23 percent. Panel study families in the middle saw their average incomes—measured in 2007 dollars—rise from $56,375 in the early and mid-1970s to $69,406 in the early and mid-2000s. The Census figures for the same median families are slightly lower, but increase by a similar percentage amount.

But the path that most of these households have followed in getting from their 1970s incomes to their 2000s incomes has hardly traced the neat upward sloping line that was once the norm. Instead, a growing number of families have found themselves on a financial roller coaster, with their incomes taking increasingly wild leaps and plunges over time. In the early 1970s, the inflation-adjusted incomes of families in the middle of the income distribution typically swung within a range whose outer borders were plus $9,546 or minus $9,546. By now, those typical swings have reached plus or minus $17,692. In percentage terms, the swings have risen from about 17 percent up or down to almost 26 percent—or by half.

The volatility increase has been even greater among low-income families, those who, on average, make less than all but one in ten American households. Since 1970, the average annual income of

**Rising
Volatility**
The incomes of
American families
are swinging up
and down more
dramatically now
than they did in
the 1970s.

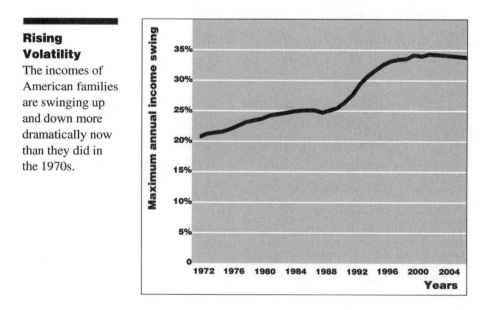

these low earners has barely risen from a little less than $22,066 to $23,008. But the income swings that have accompanied this increase have been dizzying. In the early 1970s, the inflation-adjusted incomes of most low-income families bounced around in a range of about $6,591 up or down. But that's now jumped to more than $12,000. In percentage terms, the income volatility of low-earner families has climbed from 30 percent to almost 50 percent, or by two-thirds.

Perhaps most surprising, rising volatility has not been confined to families at the bottom or in the middle of the economy. Since the early 1970s, the typical incomes of families at the 90th percentile—that spot in the economic pecking order where only one in ten families makes more—have risen 54 percent. Panel study families at the 90th percentile saw their incomes climb from $103,241 in the early and mid-1970s to $158,528 by the early and mid-2000s. Yet even these highly favored families saw the volatility of their income, the amount that it swung around on its way from one level to another, increase as much as their end-to-end gains. Most families began the era exposed to potential swings of no more than 16 percent up or down, but ended it facing the possibility of yo-yoing swings of 28 percent. That's

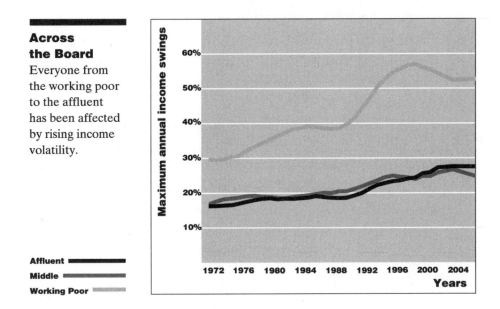

Across the Board
Everyone from the working poor to the affluent has been affected by rising income volatility.

Affluent

Middle

Working Poor

a 69 percent increase in the level of volatility. In dollar terms, the increase was from about $16,860 up or down to more than $43,600. Stop for a moment and imagine what would happen to your life right now if your annual income plunged by $43,000. Even if it eventually rebounded—and not all do—could you keep up your car and mortgage payments, continue your kids' music lessons, and keep children on the hockey team? And the numbers don't look much better when you go up one more notch to the 95th percentile— where families are making so much money that only one in twenty earns more.

IN RECENT YEARS, economic trouble has fallen particularly hard on those who are poorly educated. In addition to lowering the wages you can earn, lack of education raises the chances that you will experience big and destabilizing income swings. But it turns out that having an education—even a college or graduate school education— doesn't provide the same kind of surefire protection against volatility that we've come to expect it to provide against so many other kinds of economic danger. To be sure, families headed by high school dropouts have substantially more unstable incomes than those headed by high school graduates and just about everybody else. But once you get beyond dropouts, most of the conventional wisdoms about education and economic stability go out the window. High school graduate families, families headed by those with some college but no degree, and those headed by college graduates have all seen their chances for big fluctuations in their income rise. Indeed, all three have risen roughly in tandem, suggesting that the level of education needed to achieve some kind of insurance against economic upheaval has ratcheted upward, and that a graduate or professional degree is the new bachelor's degree. And even that may be too optimistic; the volatility of those not just with college degrees but with advanced degrees (MBAs, JDs, MDs, and PhDs) has recently caught up with that of people with lesser degrees and, at least in the most recent figures, is at about the same levels as that of high school graduate–headed families—not likely what parents and students had in mind when they plopped down still more money and dove in for yet another round of education.

At least part of the reason that education has provided less protection against income volatility is that even many college-educated young people are having a hard time getting launched in their adult careers. In their early years, many young people are forced to piece together part-time jobs, temporary assignments, and internships, and await yet another round of education—this time at graduate school—before making it to full economic adulthood. The slow arrival at adulthood may be part of a still-larger trend: an economy that, as it has grown increasingly competitive, has encouraged employers to squeeze labor costs by, among other things, hiring fewer young workers into permanent full-time jobs in order to save on training costs. The trend may have a matched-set bookend at the other side of the age spectrum: an effort by employers to get older workers out the door faster in order to cut the number of high earners and those most likely to raise a company's health care costs. Instead, they have focused much more intently on workers between ages thirty-five (largely trained) and fifty-four (little danger yet of a heart attack, cancer, or other expensive medical event). Of course, some companies have taken the effort to squeeze labor costs one step further and focused on hiring cheap young workers, but not into regular jobs. In the spring of 2007, Circuit City, the consumer electronics chain, announced they would lay off 3,400 prime working-age workers, not because of any problem with their performance but simply because they'd accrued too many raises and become too expensive.

The pattern shows up in the volatility of the numbers. The amount that the incomes of households in all age ranges—those headed by people between 25 and 34, by those between 35 and 54, and by those between 55 and 64—swung up and down within a tight band of only a few percentage points of each other during the 1970s and much of the 1980s. But from the late 1980s until very recently, the swings of younger households, and especially of older 55- to 64-year-olders' households, have been sharply higher than the swings experienced by those in the 35- to 54-year-old group. The implication is that economic risk has been shifted onto families at the two ends of the age spectrum.

The income, education, and age numbers all suggest that the volatility increase of the past generation has been widespread and deep-running. But many people are still likely to have doubts about it, or question the notion that it means families are bearing greater risks. If such a big change had actually occurred, some will ask, why hasn't anybody spotted it before now? Others will argue that we've just lived through an atypical era of extremes during which a relative few Americans walked away with a huge chunk of the nation's income and wealth while another very small segment of the population plunged to new depths of degradation. Isn't it possible, these skeptics will say, that the numbers showing a big jump in income volatility have been caused by a handful of outliers—the Oprah Winfreys

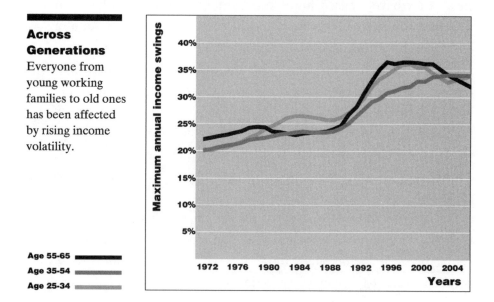

Across Generations
Everyone from young working families to old ones has been affected by rising income volatility.

Age 55-65
Age 35-54
Age 25-34

who've gone from rags to riches and the Ken Lays or Dennis Koz-lowskis who've gone from corporate riches to rags—while the rest of us are really in no more danger than we ever were? The answer is that it's possible. But the numbers strongly suggest it isn't so.

To see this, let's not divide families by income or educational lev-els, where it's at least conceivable that a few households' wild swings are throwing off the volatility numbers for everybody else. Instead, let's divide families by their volatility levels. That would mean we'd take all of the families in each measuring period who ranked in the 99th percentile of volatility, where only 1 percent of panel study fam-ilies had bigger income swings, and put them together. And we'd take all of the families, for example, in the 85th percentile, where only 15 percent had greater swings, and put them together, and so on down the line. What we'd know by sorting people in this fashion is that the person in the 99th percentile was there because his or her own fam-ily's income took a huge leap or plunge, not because somebody else's family who happened to be in the same age or educational or income category took a leap or plunge and threw the numbers off for every-body else. Similarly, what we'd know about a person in the 50th per-centile is that he or she was there because his or her family's income took a middle-of-the-road swing. Then, by watching how the size of the swings of each of the volatility categories changed over time, we'll be able to see how deeply into the panel study families—and there-fore how deeply into America as a whole—the growing instability of income is cutting.

There's zero surprise in many of the results that you get by look-ing at the data in this fashion. Those with the most volatile incomes have absorbed the biggest increases in volatility during the past three decades. The volatility of those in the 99th percentile has nearly dou-bled. The volatility of those in the 85th percentile has gone up by half. What is striking, however, is that substantial increases continue right on down through the ranks of panel study families and, by corollary, right on down the ranks of almost all American families.

Those at the 50th percentile, for example, have seen the volatility of their income rise by one-quarter. The picture that emerges is that of a nation where 40 to 50 percent of working families have seen few changes in their lives, while the remaining 50 to 60 percent have experienced significantly rising income volatility. And with it have come substantially increased odds of seeing the economic pins knocked out from under you and your family, even in cases of comparatively minor setbacks like a spell of unemployment or the birth of a child. Hardly the standard picture of the American Dream.

Many experts and commentators simply cannot believe that, amid the prosperity that has been evident for most of the last 25 to 30 years, most American families face previously unrecognized risks.

Deep into America
Volatility has increased for the majority of Americans, both those with relatively stable incomes and those with extremely unstable ones.

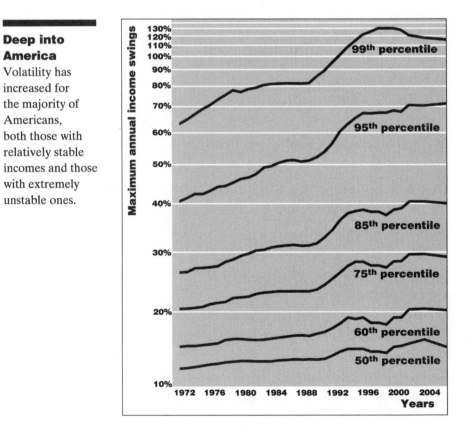

If the numbers show income volatility to be widespread, that its growth has been deep-running and its reach now extends up the income and educational pecking orders and across age groups, then there must be some benign explanation. Conservative *New York Times* columnist David Brooks has advanced one such explanation. "The main reason incomes have grown more volatile over the past decades," Brooks wrote recently, "is motherhood. . . . As women play a more significant role in the economy, their movements in and out of the labor force to care for children increase volatility."

On its face, this explanation has much to recommend it. The entry of women of childbearing age into the full-time labor force, in fact, has been one of the biggest social and economic events of the past generation, and the source of one of the biggest changes in the structure of families and families' finances. Even so, women tend to play a different role in the workforce than men. Disproportionately, they step out of the job market not just to have children but to care for them when they are ill or devote more time to them when they're having problems. They are also statistically more likely than men to interrupt careers to care for sick or elderly parents.

On closer examination, however, there are three flaws with Brooks's argument. Teasing out these flaws helps to explain why the economic consequences of something going wrong for a family can be more severe than in the past. It also illustrates why spotting the increased danger to families has proved so difficult.

The first is that volatility numbers for women simply don't do what Brooks says they do. For most of the past three decades, women's earnings volatility has gone down, not up. And a lucky thing, too, since the volatility of men's earnings has done exactly the opposite. For almost two decades, from the 1970s through most of the 1980s, the two trends offset each other and helped dampen the increase in the volatility of overall family income. Only in the late 1980s and early 1990s did women's earnings volatility start to rise. By that time, most mothers had gotten into the labor market, and the majority were moving toward working full-time or nearly full-time. Even then, it does not appear that it was motherhood that caused the volatility increase, but rather that women's economic roles had become more and more like their working-husband counterparts. As a result, over the past fifteen years, the volatility trends of women and men have begun to operate in lockstep, wiping out the offsetting effect and apparently helping to send overall family income volatility upward.

Brooks's argument has another much more important problem, which he implies though never says outright. That is that in most cases, women's wages represent discretionary or extra income for their families—money, in other words, that makes things easier but for which there are no terrible consequences if it disappears. As a result, when working women take off time to have kids or care for them or other relatives and their families' incomes go down, it's no big deal. If Brooks had assumed otherwise—namely, that women's wages are crucial to their families' standards of living—then there would be nothing benign about volatility that comes with women going in and out of the workforce. It would mean that the economy is now operat-

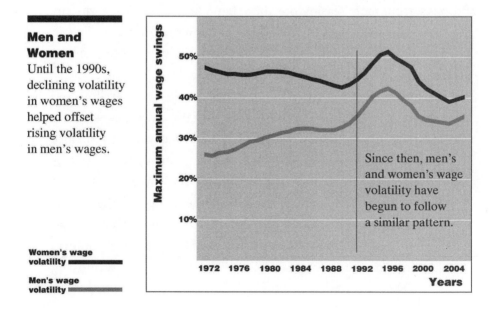

Men and Women
Until the 1990s, declining volatility in women's wages helped offset rising volatility in men's wages.

Since then, men's and women's wage volatility have begun to follow a similar pattern.

Maximum annual wage swings

50%
40%
30%
20%
10%

1972 1976 1980 1984 1988 1992 1996 2000 2004
Years

Women's wage volatility

Men's wage volatility

ing in ways that put families in terrible double binds. They need the money from women's wages, but they also need the women's work at home or elsewhere inside the family. In such a world, whichever decision women make, the results are bad for them and their families. That doesn't sound much like the American Dream, either.

The volatility numbers drawn from the panel study show just how important women's wages, and in fact the wages of both partners, have become to families hanging on to their economic stability. What the figures show is that, as long as both adults work and never step off the treadmill of two earnings, they can maintain a stability that single-earner American families enjoyed a generation ago but have since lost. What they also show is that the minute that one earner stops producing, or that a family begins to switch back and forth between fielding one earner and two, the family income is launched on a financial roller-coaster ride that has grown increasingly wild over the past three-plus decades and especially the past twenty-five years. It's hardly the picture of a household economy in which women's wages are superfluous.

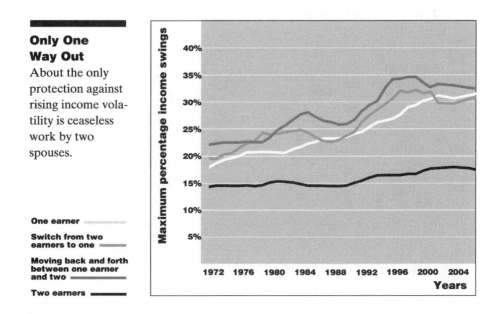

**Only One
Way Out**
About the only protection against rising income volatility is ceaseless work by two spouses.

One earner

Switch from two earners to one

Moving back and forth between one earner and two

Two earners

BEYOND BROOKS, there is another explanation that has been offered as a means of taking the sting out of rising income volatility, and it has gained ground recently among economists. It's that you shouldn't measure how well Americans are doing by their incomes. You should measure it by what's happening to their consumption. This idea might come as a surprise to people who work for a living and have always assumed there was a close tie between wages and well-being. But as with motherhood, the idea has a certain surface plausibility. After all, people don't generally decide whether they're going to buy a house or send a child to college based on dips or pops in their paychecks. They look to the long run and to how well they think they can reasonably expect to do in the future. And in fact, there are statistics that show that the consumption of Americans up and down the economic ladder changes much less than either the levels or the swings of their incomes.

Two problems crop up when we look not at income but at how much people buy. The first is a numbers problem. If we have difficulty measuring families' incomes even with surveys like the PSID, we have vastly bigger problems measuring their consumption. What people buy keeps changing, and what counts as the same thing keeps changing. Is buying a flat-screen TV today the same as buying one of those big, bulky television sets of ten years ago? Such changes cause the survey on which those who make this argument depend, the government's Consumer Expenditure Survey, suffers from a variety of difficulties. The second, and more important, problem has to do with how Americans are managing to continue consuming at the same or even higher levels despite their increasingly unstable and often stagnating incomes. The basic answer is borrowing; Americans are more able to borrow money than ever before via credit cards and home equity loans. And they are doing so at unprecedented levels. Theoretically, such borrowing is a good thing. It enables people to tide themselves across bad times without having to rely on business or government safety nets and to pay off their debts during flush periods. Unfortunately, as recent events such as the subprime mort-gage mess illustrate, a substantial fraction of people are doing no such thing. They're simply borrowing and consuming, and then bor-rowing and consuming more. Rising debt, like rising income volatil-ity, has much the same effect on families: The more of either, the greater the chance that a family will end up financially toppled.

THE PROPOSITION THAT people face a greater danger of taking steeper financial falls today than they did a quarter century ago may not be familiar, but it should not come as a great shock. After all, the economic policies that the nation adopted beginning in the late 1970s and continues to live with today—those of deregulation, scal-ing back safety nets, and promoting free markets—are all premised on the notion that working Americans will accept more risk in return for the opportunity of greater reward. Free-market advocates ac-knowledged that the old policies had buffered people against the worst economic blows, stabilized families' incomes, and let them build on what they had. But the old policies had also purportedly caused the economy to ossify and workers to lose their incentive to excel. The whole point of free-market reforms was to make the econ-omy more competitive by putting a higher premium on winning. This, of course, also increased the chances of losing. Family incomes might swing around more—down as well as up. But it was hoped that the end result would land most workers on top.

In fact, that's pretty much what many prominent economists think has occurred. They find nothing surprising about the idea of family income volatility rising. On balance, they see the quarter-century experiment in promoting prosperity as a grand success. "On the whole, we have moved toward a freer market, a more competitive economy and a richer one," said University of Chicago economist and Nobel laureate Gary S. Becker. "There has been a shift toward people taking more risk on themselves . . . and the economy has gained for it."

The big question for individuals and their families, however, is not whether the economy as a whole has gained but whether they themselves have done so. Have those who've shouldered the greater risk—whether knowingly or not—enjoyed the benefits of greater rewards? There is no single answer to this question. Clearly, the wealth of many families—and not just those at the very top—is up. The stock of their houses, cars, and home electronic centers; the extent of their travel; and the elaborateness of their medical care have all expanded. But as a straight-up trade-off—more income risk for more income reward—the story of the past three decades or so has been a much more mixed one than most Americans realize. Working families have faced ever-changing—and, to a substantial extent, more perilous—risk-reward bargains. And these mixed results have included not just families at the bottom or in the middle of the economic pile but also those with substantial six-figure incomes.

These kinds of risk-reward trade-offs are what the free-market revolution of the past twenty-five years was meant to be about. They are the sort of calculations and comparisons in which professional investors regularly engage. And, although it may not be clear to most people, they are the kind of assessments that working Americans are now supposed to be making in their own economic lives every day.

To assess what taking on the new risk-reward trade-off means, it may be most illuminating to look at families in the economic middle—those making around $70,000 today. Such families are presumably better able to withstand modest economic hits than lower-income families that are living closer to the edge financially. During the 1970s, such families enjoyed a comparatively good run. Although most saw their incomes swing up or down as much as 19 percent, on average they ended each year 0.6 percent ahead of where they began. By the end of the decade, the volatility of their income—and therefore the extra increment of risk they'd taken on—had increased 10 percent, or about $1,600, and the level of their income was up from where it had been at the beginning of the decade by 6 percent, or

$3,235. Essentially, they'd been rewarded with a reasonable increase in annual income for a moderate addition to risk.

However, the trade-off during the 1980s and the early 1990s was not nearly as balanced. During the 1980s, the incomes of families in the middle fluctuated as much as 20 percent up and down. But families were not compensated with increased income growth; in fact, the growth rate declined slightly from the 1970s. By decade's end, volatility was up almost 13 percent, while income was up less than 4 percent. During the early 1990s, volatility rose 13 percent to peak at 25 percent. But income increased a mere 3 percent. The bottom line was more risk for precious little reward.

Only since the late 1990s have families in the middle seen anything like good times return, although on substantially different terms than during the 1970s. Between 1995 and 1999, such families saw their incomes climb $5,270, or about 8.1 percent. The increase was accompanied by a 1 percent increase in volatility. This was a case of more reward for somewhat more risk—an acceptable trade. Similarly, between 2000 and 2004, incomes reversed course and fell, but so did volatility—not a bad deal, but not a very good one, either. The trade-off between risk and reward for families in the economic middle seems to have settled at a new equilibrium, with risk about 51 percent higher than it was in the early 1970s, as compared to only a 23 percent increase in reward.

Even among families at the 90th percentile, those now making about $160,000, the risk-reward trade-offs have grown increasingly unfavorable. During the 1970s and the 1980s, most 90th percentile families saw their incomes swing as much as 19 percent up or down. But even as they swung, they kept climbing. The result was that while the income volatility these families experienced was up, so were their incomes, which rose by more than 29 percent—that is, more reward for comparatively little additional risk. Matters took quite a different turn during the 1990s and the first half of the 2000s. Although these families continued to see income gains, they also encountered substantially higher volatility. The income of most 90th-percentile families rose more than 18 percent, much of it in the late 1990s. But the growth has been accompanied by an increase in income swing of nearly 40 percent. By the first half of the 2000s, the growth in volatility was outpacing that of income. The bottom line had now become somewhat more reward, but substantially far more risk.

THESE NUMBERS SHOW THAT we lead economically more dramatic lives than most of us realized. And they show that, for a large number of us, that is not only true but increasingly true. The percentage of people experiencing truly huge annual income swings—50 percent up or down—is on the rise. Moreover, the numbers show that the kinds of events that have always bedeviled working families but once caused only moderate damage—those layoffs, illnesses, injuries, and divorces—are now much more apt to wreak economic havoc. Over the past three-plus decades and especially the past twenty-five years, almost twice as many of the families hit by any of the seven income-threatening events that I examined closely have gone on to see their incomes plunge by half. Even families who have *not* been hit by economic misfortune—and that's the large majority at any given moment—are at greater risk of being toppled *if* trouble makes its way to their doors. That's what the increase in income volatility tells us. And it goes a long way toward explaining why, even in the midst of a sustained economic expansion, so many Americans felt so uncertain about their economic circumstances.

Perhaps what's most important to members of the middle class is that these numbers show that it's not just the poor, the uneducated, or those unfortunate enough to live in America's economic trouble spots who now face greater odds of being toppled if something goes wrong. The game has turned on families across the spectrum—from the working poor to the reasonably affluent, from the Rust Belt to the Silicon Valley. For better or worse, the rising risks of a big economic setback are proving to be extremely democratic.

4

JOBS

On a typical morning in America, 90 million people wake up, hurry through their personal rituals—dress, fix a bite to eat, get the kids off to school, check the news, walk the dog—and go to work. Another 30 million follow at some point during the day. What these jobs pay is important. With the exception of a tiny sliver of millionaires and billionaires, wages are the single greatest source of income for working Americans. Nothing else comes even close—not stock investments, cashed-in home values, government checks, or dumb luck at the lottery.

But there's more to work than wages. Meet someone new, and one of the first things you're likely to ask is what they do for a living. Tell someone what you do, and you'll have gone a long way toward pegging yourself in their eyes. Where we live, what we wear, how we talk, and who we talk to all heavily depend on where we work. What we can plan for—what we can realistically dream of—for ourselves and our families turn largely on our jobs. The simple act of going to work and coming home frames our days and gives them structure.

For most Americans, the opposite of work is not kicking back, but chaos. As a result, any change in the nature of work—in the basic stuff of what a job is, how long it lasts, what it provides, and what happens next—will ping-pong through our politics and our personal lives.

And something about the basic stuff of jobs has changed, although economists can't agree on precisely how to describe the change or how pervasive it is. As signs that something new was happening began to emerge in the late 1970s and early 1980s, some analysts declared that we were witnessing the "deindustrialization of America." The core of the nation's workforce—its high-paid manufacturing jobs—was being hollowed out, and more and more people were being left to get by on menial work. When the economy confounded these prophets of trouble by manufacturing more goods with fewer workers and creating tens of millions of new jobs—many of them high-paying—a new generation of economists dashed to the opposite extreme and declared that a high-speed, high-tech economy would lift almost everyone to greater, more secure prosperity. But this view, too, has stumbled. Something important about jobs in the United States is, in fact, being hollowed out, and in ways that leave millions of Americans more vulnerable to taking steep financial falls. Part of it is the manufacturing middle of the workforce, just as the original critics had said. But the trend has crept into other areas of the employment world as well, affecting both white-collar professionals and blue-collar union members—people like both E. Paul Fredo and Ron Burtless.

By most conventional measures, Fredo is an American success story. The fifty-nine-year-old son of a coal miner, he made almost $200,000 in his peak year, enough to place him in the top 2 percent of American wage-earners. As a financial manager for the Hornell, New York, unit of Alstom, the French bullet-train manufacturer, he lived the expense-account life, spending most nights in hotels and jetting to meetings in Washington and Paris. But look carefully at Fredo's circumstances and a less appealing picture begins to appear—one that says a lot about making a living in America today. By the time Fredo joined Alstom in mid-2003, he'd become an itinerant executive, a contract worker brought in for a particular job, then sent packing. "They tell me every Friday whether to come back or not," he said during his stint at Alstom. Between his last regular job as the chief financial officer for a Pittsburgh steel-plant equipment maker and his hiring at Alstom, Fredo was unemployed for nearly two years and watched his income drop by two-thirds. After being cut loose by Alstom, he ran through two more jobs before landing in his current position as an accountant for a pump manufacturer. The pay is half of his peak earnings, but comes with employer-provided health insurance, something he'd spent the past few years scrambling to hang on to so that he could make sure that his high blood pressure and his wife Donna's diabetes would continue to be treated. "We come from the old school that you work hard and give it your all, and the job will be there for you," said Donna. "It's different today."

FROM HIS PERCH several rungs down the economic ladder, Burtless, fifty-two, has seen similar economic changes in his own life—with similarly damaging results. Unlike Fredo, Burtless never aspired to the executive suite. Instead, more than three decades ago, he went to work as a union electrician at what was then Bethlehem Steel Corporation's giant Burns Harbor, Indiana, mill on the southern shores of Lake Michigan. Until recently, he seemed the very embodiment of middle-American stability, with a $60,000 annual wage, two grown daughters, a red Ford pickup, and a five-bedroom suburban home. Yet Burtless has had the economic struts kicked out from under him repeatedly: in the early 1980s when the steel industry nose-dived; in the early 1990s when the added security of his two-income household broke down after he and his working wife divorced. And it happened yet again a few years ago when, in rapid succession, Bethlehem collapsed, he was badly injured on the job, and the workers' compensation system that was supposed to protect him failed. At that point, Burtless found himself on the verge of bankruptcy. He was forced to wait three years for the workers' compensation payments he was owed to cover more than $90,000 in medical bills. In the time since the accident, Burns Harbor has been sold twice, and Burtless has managed to hang on to his job, but only by accepting more than a decade's delay in his pension. "I'm just thankful to have the work," he said.

If we wanted to be hard-nosed about it, we could dismiss Fredo's and Burtless's troubles as old news. After all, both live in the Rust Belt, work in manufacturing, and were tied in one way or another to Big Steel, which has gotten hammered during the past twenty-five years. We might even wonder whether the two veterans of the old economy showed the requisite energy, resilience, and adaptability by switching jobs, jumping to other industries, or moving into other sectors of the economy as trouble headed their way. The problem with this reaction is that the very same kind of upheavals are occurring without fanfare or much public attention elsewhere in the economy—in vanguard industries, not just fading ones, in boomtowns, not just backwaters.

The reason these blows to the security of jobs have attracted so little attention is that they do not register in the headline statistics commonly used to take the pulse of the American economy. Indeed, until very recently, the headline statistics barely registered blows of any kind. National output marched more or less steadily upward. The country's employment total rose from 100 million twenty-five years ago to more than 145 million by 2007. The unemployment rate has dropped from an annual average of nearly 8 percent from the mid-1970s through the mid-1980s to about 4.5 percent during the past few years. Median real wages—the earnings of those at dead-center of the economy—have increased 15 percent. Looking at this economic box score, one might fairly ask, "What's the problem?"

The problem is that each of these top-down economic statistics could have improved in precisely the fashion it did, and a growing number of Americans could—and did—still find themselves with increasingly turbulent work lives and unstable personal finances. To see how, consider employment. Over the past quarter century, the U.S. economy recorded a net gain of 45 million jobs. But how that gain was achieved makes all the difference in the world to the kinds of lives that working Americans were able to live during these years. If the gain, including 2007's addition of 1.3 million positions, had come about in steadily rising annual increments, then a comparatively small proportion of workers would have gotten new positions each year while everyone else would have kept doing pretty much what they had been doing, and the overall effect would have been quite stable. By contrast, if the gain was the result of wild swings of hiring, firing, and quitting, then millions of workers would have had a very different experience—racing in and out of jobs, uprooting their lives, and struggling to adjust to new work assignments and often drastic changes in pay and security. The evidence is that the country's job growth occurred in the latter, not the former, fashion: Neither the twenty-five-year increase nor the 2007 gain was the result of anything close to an orderly process. In both instances, the increases were the products of gigantic swirls and churns. The path to 2007's job gain alone involved about 55 million people—the equivalent of more than one-third of all working Americans—leaving their jobs and 57 million hiring on in new positions. The same instability can be found inside virtually every one of the nation's standard economic statistics. Whether it's employment, unemployment, the gross domestic product, or national income, each is a net number that has risen neatly until recently atop an almost inconceivable amount of job creation and destruction, worker arrivals and departures, company births and deaths, pay raises and cuts, output growth and shrinkage. And it is inside the churn, rather than atop it, that people live and work.

Of course, economic churn or turbulence may not be entirely bad. Many economists believe it confers special powers on the economy: Because Americans are more accustomed to changing jobs and even careers than workers in most other major economies, the United States has an easier time adopting new efficiency-improving technology and adjusting to setbacks such as jumps in energy prices. And so long as job creation outstrips job elimination and new opportunities open up faster than old ones disappear, people ought to be able to find new work, perhaps even at better pay and under more favorable conditions. But even as sunny an observer of the U.S. economy as President George W. Bush acknowledges that there can be such a thing as too much turbulence. In a television interview in October 2007, he conceded that "a couple of factors . . . trouble Americans. One is that there's a lot of churning in the job market. In other words, if you're under thirty, you're likely to have had seven jobs by the time you're thirty. And older people like me take a look at that kind of volatility or some would call it excitement in the job market, and they wonder whether or not this job turnover is going to affect them."

And the turbulence means that the standard statistics are not very reliable guides to how people actually lead their economic lives, how the economy actually treats them, especially during those key moments of transition between jobs. The commonly watched statistics are also not good at telling us whether the treatment that individuals and families receive from the overall economy is changing for the better or the worse. It is when one begins to look for indicators that do provide such guides that the cracks begin to appear.

One gauge of what people actually experience in the economy is job tenure—the length of time employees are typically with the same employer or in the same job. Ceaseless change may be fine for the economy as a whole, but it can be a bear for anybody trying to lead a life, plan a future, or raise children. These activities, which—along with work—make up the core of most people's lives, require some degree of stability. Job tenure is one way to measure stability. In the late 1970s and early 1980s when the nature of work was beginning to change, economists didn't focus much on tenure. They spent their time arguing about the quality of jobs, and whether "good" jobs were losing out to "bad" ones. By the time they got around to the simpler question of how long a job lasts, they couldn't find much of a trend— in part because the booming economy of the late 1990s was making almost everything about jobs look great. Now, however, more than a half decade away from the '90s boom with few signs of a repeat performance in the wings, there's a slowly growing consensus that yes, job tenure is declining; yes, the fraction of Americans with the same employer for ten or twenty years or more is going down; and yes, these changes have increased the chances that what once would have been a modest setback can now send a working person's fortunes plunging. Many economists see the new reality as, on balance, a plus: some added risk, but an increased likelihood of much greater rewards. In other words, they see it as a new form of "stability"—less static than the old kind and perhaps a bit more emotionally stressful, but, in the end, better for almost everyone.

Unfortunately, as the numbers in Chapter 3 demonstrated, this rosy hypothesis doesn't seem to jibe with what has been happening in most people's lives in recent years. Except for workers who find themselves in hot sectors of the job market—a piece of good fortune that itself may be short-lived—those who must change jobs frequently often have trouble maintaining their income levels. Benefits such as health insurance are interrupted or even lost, especially in an economy that now relies on smaller companies to create many of its new jobs; small companies, especially start-ups, rarely offer the full range of benefits that remain common—if more expensive—among large, established employers. Moreover, the rush of new technology represented by such things as globe-girdling fiber-optic cable along—with the doubling of the workforce with the sudden integration of China, India, and the former Soviet bloc into the world economy—means that there's no turning back. Indeed, the decline in job stability has only just begun.

WASHINGTON HAS BEEN SURVEYING how long people stay with their current employers since the early 1980s. The numbers for men are easiest to grasp because men have played the same role in the U.S. economy for the entire period, which makes possible apples-to-apples comparisons. Working-age women, the majority of whom are now in the full-time workforce, were still in transition during the 1980s, making similar apples-to-apples comparisons difficult. In 1983, male wage and salary employees in the prime of their work lives, aged 45 to 54, could expect to be with the same employer nearly 13 years on average, according to the federal Bureau of Labor Statistics. By 2006, the latest year for which figures are available, BLS statistics show that number had dropped by more than one-third—to 8.1 years. Slightly older men, those 55 to 64, who were once typically with their employers more than 15 years, are now with them less than 10 years.

In a recent study using Census data on more than 800,000 people, labor economist Henry Farber compared the job tenure of younger and older men at the same point in their working lives. He found that the average amount of time those who started their work lives in the 1990s have spent with the same employer was only half that of those who started in the 1940s and 1950s. Even when Farber adjusted for such factors as the increasing numbers of immigrant workers—who haven't been in the United States long enough to amass long work histories and therefore tend to push down the averages—he still found a 25 percent difference. Farber also found that women's tenure, after rising for some years, has fallen into line with men's. "Analysis of the best data on job tenure through 2006 shows clearly that there has been a substantial decline in the average length of time workers have been with their employers, as well as a substantial decline in the likelihood of long-term jobs," said Farber, a Princeton economist.

DECLINING JOB TENURE does not signal the end of all long-term jobs in America. Figures show that from the mid-1970s until the mid-2000s, nearly half of middle-aged men, and well over one-third of middle-aged women, hung on to what most would consider long-term positions, sticking with their employers for at least a decade. And shorter job tenure doesn't necessarily mean that a new job will be worse than the one you leave. In their book, *Economic Turbulence: Is a Volatile Economy Good for America?*, economists Clair Brown, John Haltiwanger, and Julia Lane recently argued that more frequent job changes and reduced tenure actually helped people into better jobs and careers. "Over time [workers'] job changes result in improved jobs," the authors wrote, adding that "most workers eventually find successful career paths." The evidence for the trio's optimistic conclusions is, however, much, much thinner than the authors suggest.

The authors slide past the key question of whether people improve their jobs and careers because of turbulence or despite it. And they disregard several measures that, like tenure, are aspects of the overall economy that people experience for themselves and loom

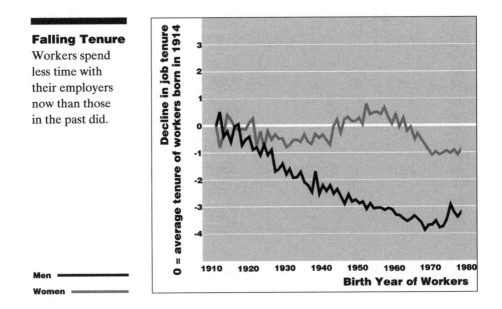

Falling Tenure
Workers spend less time with their employers now than those in the past did.

Men

Women

large in how they judge their own well-being: First, the chances of getting laid off from your job—fired—have not fallen during most of the economy's recent run of growth, but have risen. Second, the typical amount of time workers are out of work if they do get laid off has gone up. Finally, the personal cost of being unemployed has gone way up, even for the economy's most favored and protected workers—college-educated professionals like Paul Fredo.

FREDO WAS BORN in a Pennsylvania coal town called Spangler. His father, according to his son, lost his mining job to automation, his pension to union corruption, and his life to black lung disease. The son was determined to have a better go of it. He hauled himself up the way many poor kids do: He joined the military, spent four years in the U.S. Air Force, including time in Vietnam. Then he enrolled in night school at the University of Pittsburgh, studying accounting. During his early career, he worked for a dairy, a nuclear waste processor, and a company that sold tire-making equipment. For a period of thirty years, he rose steadily, working long stints with one employer after the next and switching only when a better job presented itself. Since the start of this decade, however, Fredo has been hit with every one of the forces that are now rattling American workers' lives— shrinking job tenure, layoffs, long spells of unemployment, benefits that come nowhere close to matching those he had before his time out of work, and big wage declines. That he nevertheless managed to keep himself in the upper ranks of wage-earners, at least until recently, is less a tribute to the economy than to Fredo's scrappy refusal to be beaten. His story shows that, while the overall economy may prosper, individuals—even individuals who have carefully plotted out their work lives—can be sent tumbling with little help from business or government to break their falls.

Records show that for most of Fredo's adult life, his earnings moved progressively higher. He earned $8,000 in 1970, $25,000 in 1980, and $64,000 in 1990. By 1985, at the age of thirty-seven, he had snared a vice president's title. "I'm going up the ladder," he remembers thinking. "It's time to settle down." He and Donna picked out a design from a Ryan Homes catalog and had a house built along the Ohio River north of Pittsburgh—a blue aluminum-siding and brick colonial with four bedrooms, two and a half baths, and a fifteen-year mortgage. Throughout most of the succeeding decade, their confidence in the future seemed fully justified.

Fredo's income began to dance around during the 1990s. More and more of it came in the form of bonuses rather than straight pay—up $25,000 one year, down $5,000 or $10,000 the next. Still, by 2000 he was pulling in more than $160,000 annually as chief financial officer for Pittsburgh-based Voest-Alpine Industries, Inc., which at that time was a $200 million-a-year American subsidiary of a much larger Austrian firm that made equipment for steel plants. He was convinced that he was in line for the top spot at Voest-Alpine; during his eight years as CFO, he had helped lead the company from just 14 employees to 450. But in October 2001, Fredo got caught in one of the U.S. steel industry's periodic downdrafts. As the industry swung from boom to bust, Voest-Alpine began winnowing its executive ranks. Instead of a promotion, Fredo was handed a pink slip.

The layoff stunned his family and friends even more than it did Fredo. "I called my fiancée and said, 'Dad's been downsized,'" his younger son, Stephen, recalled. "She said, 'Did the company go under?'" Don Battaglia, a Pittsburgh computer consultant who'd worked for Fredo, was equally incredulous. Fredo had seemed the most secure executive at the company. "I was convinced he'd be the guy who turned out the lights," Battaglia said.

Fredo began his search for another job with a leg up on most Americans. He'd been granted six months of pay—roughly twice the severance employers typically give laid-off workers. Fredo and his wife, Donna, had hundreds of thousands of dollars in savings—most of it squirreled away for retirement, but available in case of emergencies. They had almost finished financing their sons' college educations. And they had recently paid off their mortgage. In addition, the couple knew how to scrimp. They quickly canceled plans to trade in their 1998 Chrysler sedan for a new vehicle. They drew up a bare-bones budget for groceries, utilities, Christmas gifts, and the occasional trip to the hair salon for Donna. They started collecting buy-one-get-one-free coupon books at the local Walgreens.

With his family finances ready for a lean time ahead, Fredo pulled down his copy of the Iron and Steel Institute directory. Before, whenever he went looking for a new job, he'd landed one by writing to a few of the companies in the book and calling a couple of Pittsburgh employment agencies. This time, however, he came up dry. He eventually pitched 900 companies. For his trouble, he said, "I got two callbacks and an interview that didn't go anywhere."

By the spring of 2002, with his six months of severance gone, Fredo had changed tactics and begun attending Priority Two, a job networking group at nearby Northway Community Church. There, the group's director, Charlie Beck, offered some advice: "You've got to have a hook so they remember you." Fredo considered the technique demeaning, but he began telling potential employers to remember him as "PAC Man," for "planner, analyst, and cost saver." He had business cards printed up with an image of the little yellow video-game figure chomping its way across the surface. The effort produced a few temporary consulting assignments that paid better than the alternatives— a $10-an-hour customer service position at a local Verizon Wireless call center or a job as a checkout clerk at the neighborhood supermarket. But he soon discovered that landing a decent temp job was almost as difficult as nailing down a good permanent one.

As his severance pay ran out, Fredo had to rely increasingly on government-provided unemployment insurance. In Pennsylvania, the maximum benefit in 2002 was $442 a week. Since he had been making so much money before he lost his job, the state program replaced only a small fraction of his previous income and thus provided him with little financial protection. In addition, his employer-provided health insurance expired, a big blow because of his high blood pressure and Donna's diabetes. For a while, Fredo managed to maintain his old medical policy under COBRA, the federal law that requires companies to permit laid-off employees to continue coverage for eighteen months—provided that they, not the former employer, pay the premiums. Eventually, he switched to a less generous policy, which still cost $800 a month, no small sum when there's almost no money coming in.

As 2002 turned into 2003, the Fredos hunkered down further. They cut their weekly offerings at church. Donna gave up one of her favorite activities, sending packages of toys and party favors to the children in the North Carolina special-needs class taught by her son Joseph's wife, Maureen. The effects of the family's altered circumstances produced subtler changes as well. As a boy, the Fredos' younger son, Stephen, had waited up to put his father's dinner in the microwave when he got home late. Now a new ritual was developing: Fredo would get up at seven in the morning to have coffee with his son before Stephen headed off to work as a systems analyst at Children's Hospital in Pittsburgh. Then the elder Fredo would trudge upstairs to spend the rest of the day—and often much of the night—in a guest bedroom, glued to his computer screen, searching for work. As Stephen's July 2003 wedding approached, Fredo acknowledged that he was getting desperate. His annual income was down to about $48,000. That's when the call came from the U.S. unit of Alstom, the French bullet-train maker.

The contrast between his position at Voest-Alpine and what Alstom offered embodied everything that had changed about the nature of jobs. Here he was being asked to be the Alstom unit's chief financial officer, by one measure its number-three or number-four person and able to sign legal papers on its behalf. He'd eventually be paid close to $200,000 a year, along with a travel budget that would keep him on the road almost continuously and provided most of the other trappings of a senior business executive in the new global economy. The only problem was that he was a "temp," without benefits and security or even the knowledge of whether he'd be called back the next week. But Fredo jumped at the position. This was a chance to make up lost ground from nearly two years of joblessness and, perhaps as important, the opportunity for an executive comeback. And for a while, it worked.

After replenishing family savings and paying for health insurance, Fredo traded in the 1998 sedan for a royal-blue 2004 Chrysler Concorde. And nearly one year into his Alstom stint, he and Donna prepared to celebrate their thirty-fifth wedding anniversary in grand style. Each of the one hundred family and friends whom they put up at the Airport Sheraton in Pittsburgh would receive a party box containing Teaberry gum, a tiny Etch A Sketch, and a refrigerator magnet showing the average income ($8,547), price of a loaf of bread (23 cents), and cost of a gallon of gas (35 cents) in 1969—all reminders of the year they married. "I wanted something retro," Donna explained, "but I didn't want the whole anniversary to be retro."

A few weeks before the July 3 soiree, Alstom notified Fredo that his services would no longer be needed. A French executive would take over his job, working on the same week-to-week basis. The couple went ahead with the anniversary celebration, then Fredo spent the next four months looking for a new job. He landed one that came with a $120,000 salary and seemed to promise a return to regular employment, but it lasted only four months. A second evaporated in similar fashion. Finally, in 2005, he found a job as an accountant for a pump manufacturer. Although it pays less than half his previous peak earnings, it includes good health insurance. He says that he's given up any hope of making it back to the top of the executive heap. He figures he can slide through to retirement without doing too much damage to his finances. "Do I think I've got something more to offer? You bet. If this is the best I can find, I'll take it," he said of this current job. "But the way they've got this country organized right now, there's no way they're getting the best out of people."

ECONOMISTS TEND TO DISMISS stories like Fredo's either as special cases (the Rust Belt adjusting to the new economic reality) or as otherwise unrepresentative. They argue that the nation's overall unemployment statistics show that the chances of losing your job are slim and falling, not rising, as Fredo's experience might suggest. With the national unemployment rate below 5 percent until recently, for example, the odds of being jobless are less than 1 in 20. That's not nothing, but it's considerably more favorable than the odds of having at least a minor accident that we accept when we get into our cars. The problem with this approach, however, is that the overall unemployment rate understates the risk of joblessness faced by a typical worker. Among the reasons, the employment totals that the government uses to calculate the jobless rate include 25 million part-timers, many of whom are not seeking full-time work. And the unemployment numbers include millions of mostly young people who are starting out and simply haven't found a job yet, or others who stepped out of the workforce to get more schooling or start a family or some similar reason and are just coming back into the labor market. The numbers also include those who are briefly out of work because they quit old jobs on their way to taking new ones.

The odds that the overall unemployment rate captures are simply not those that most concern the bulk of Americans who work full-time to support themselves and their families. What concerns these people are, first, the odds that they could be going along, doing their jobs, not quitting or being fired for breaking the rules, and suddenly find themselves thrown out of work. What also concerns them—perhaps even more—is the possibility that, once out of work, they could find themselves unemployed for a very long time.

Economists have a name for the former—displacement—and the government has been tracking it since the early 1980s. They call the latter long-term unemployment, and Washington has been tracking that since the late 1940s. The combination is a breadwinner's nightmare. That's not simply because it means losing the pay and employer-provided health insurance that most of us depend on, or because government-supplied unemployment insurance benefits may make up only a tiny fraction of the losses if one ends up out of work, but because it's a classic case of suffering an economic blow through no fault of your own.

In tracking displacement, the government tries to zero in on just this group of people who are unemployed through no fault of their own. To do this, survey-takers focus on workers who had held their positions for three years or more at the time they were laid off and so presumably were doing good jobs and were loyal, conscientious employees. What survey-takers have found is that during most of the 1980s, the number of these workers who lost their jobs to displacement closely followed the fluctuations in the overall economy. When the economy sank into recession, the number of displaced workers went up, and when the economy recovered, the number went back down again. But in the years since then, the pattern appears to have changed. Now, the number of longtime jobholders who lose their positions begins to rise more sharply even before the economy goes

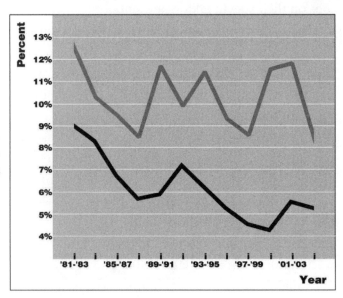

Greater Chance of Displacement Unemployment and the risk of displacement—or job loss through no fault of your own—used to move in tandem. Now you can be displaced almost anytime.

Unemployment Rate

Job Loss Rate

into recession and falls more slowly after the economy recovers. One way to illustrate the change is to match up the job-loss rate owing to displacement with the overall unemployment rate. Farber, the Princeton economist, has produced such a match and finds that the gap has widened over the past twenty-five years even with the recent fall in the displacement rate. What that means is that the odds of losing your job to displacement have increased since the 1980s, that displacement can occur not just in bad economic times but also in good ones, and that you have to wait for a much longer run of good economic performance before the displacement rate finally comes back down. The bottom line: Even in a time of low unemployment, the chance of losing your job through displacement—and therefore no fault of your own—has gone up.

AND NOT ONLY HAVE those chances gone up, but so have the chances that once out the door, you remain out for a long time—with all the risk of severe financial damage that long-term unemployment entails. The government defines long-term unemployment as being out of

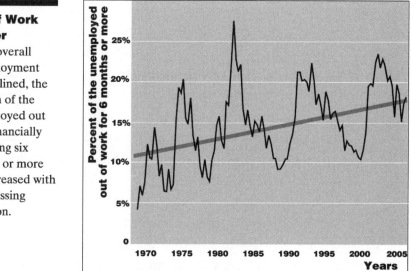

Out of Work Longer
While overall unemployment has declined, the fraction of the unemployed out for a financially damaging six months or more has increased with each passing recession.

work six months or more, largely because unemployment benefits typically run out after six months. As with displacement, the number of people who are out for six months or more goes up and down with the ups and downs of the economy. So does the fraction of the total population of the unemployed that long-termers account for. But with each passing business cycle, the number and fraction have ratcheted upward so that long-termers, who accounted for about one in ten jobless workers in economic good times during the 1970s, account for about one in five workers in what until recently were comparably good economic times.

JOB TENURE, DISPLACEMENT, and long-term unemployment would not be such big deals were it not for the fact that their growth has been accompanied by yet another negative development. After all, the number of people suffering no-fault-of-their-own job losses in the three-year period ending in 2005, the latest for which numbers exist, totaled 3.8 million. The number of long-term unemployed in recent years has hovered at around 1.3 million. This, at a time when employment totals about 145 million, is not a huge fraction. The problem is that the cost of being among these few million job-losers and long-term unemployed has climbed substantially in terms of lost wages and benefits. What once were only moderate threats to working families' finances have become potential calamities. One study looked at people who lost full-time jobs between 2001 and 2003 but were fortunate enough to find full-time replacement positions, and so were comparative winners in the job-loss process. What it found was that these reemployed people made, on average, 17 percent less than they would have made had they managed to hang on to their original positions. That was double the wage loss of the late 1990s. And, since annual raises are fairly modest in most job categories these days, it is difficult to impossible for those who lose jobs to catch up after they go back to work. The losses were particularly pronounced among the very people who are generally considered best prepared to cope with the new economy—college graduates. Some workers fresh out of college in the 1990s were lucky enough to ride the high-tech boom to big-money jobs, but they were hardly the majority. Nevertheless, the 1990s was a good time to be in the job market. Neither the high-tech winners nor recent graduates who landed more conventional positions would have believed that the golden job market of that era could have changed so dramatically that by the beginning of the current decade, the penalty for losing one's job would have rocketed. On average, college graduates who lost their jobs in the early 2000s ended up with wages in their subsequent jobs that were more than 20 percent lower than what they would have made had they held onto their original positions.

When people try to assess dangers of almost any sort, they tend to break the problem into two parts: How likely is it that a bad thing will befall me? And how bad could it be if it does? It's on this last count that the economic changes of the past twenty-five years have had their most disruptive effect. As with so much else about the present economy, the dangers are like rifle shots: The risk that you'll be laid off has risen only modestly—or perhaps not at all, as some argue. But the danger is substantially greater than it used to be that, if you *do* lose your job, you could find yourself out of work for a long time and be forced to take a steep pay cut in order to land a new position.

Of course, the dangers are not evenly distributed. You're more likely to lose a job if you're a high school dropout than if you have graduated from college. But the protective padding provided by such things as college degrees is wearing away. As a result, the hazards and the potential for more damaging consequences are creeping up the economic ladder. Today, if you have a college degree and lose your job, you're apt to be out longer and take a proportionately bigger hit to your earnings than workers with less education. It is developments such as these that help explain the paradox of an American economy that seems ever more prosperous while millions of working Americans feel increasingly less secure.

AT ABOUT THE TIME that Paul Fredo was landing his first civilian job in the early 1970s, the Nixon administration created a task force to examine the country's readiness for competition in what even then was an increasingly global economy. The subsequent study and report became a wide-ranging examination of the condition of jobs and work. And, looked at through contemporary eyes, it offers startling evidence of how drastically policies and attitudes have changed over the past three decades. The Nixon White House was nobody's idea of liberal; no one would ever accuse the president of being soft-hearted. But the task force that his administration commissioned would be laughed out of court by modern advocates of the no-promise society. To begin with, the group devoted considerable time to a sympathetic exploration of how unfulfilling many workers found their jobs to be. Its report, issued in 1973, was called *Work in America* and, unexpectedly, became a best seller. Reading it today, you can experience a sort of mental vertigo.

The panel, chaired by James O'Toole, then a young aide to Nixon's Department of Health, Education, and Welfare secretary, Elliot Richardson, worried that working Americans were growing dangerously alienated from their jobs and hence from society. What can make a present-day reader feel a little dizzy is where the report puts the blame for job dissatisfaction—not on workers but on corporate managers. These managers were causing problems in their organizations, the report suggested, because they failed to understand the deeper psychological meaning that jobs held for their workers. "Work," the report's authors wrote, offers "status, family stability and an opportunity to interact with others in one of the most basic activities of society." And, the authors warned, "if the opportunity for work is absent or if the nature of work is dissatisfying, severe repercussions are likely."

The report barely mentioned the backstory behind the concern over the emotional well-being of ordinary workers: a bitter strike that had occurred in 1972 in Lordstown, Ohio, site of what was then General Motors' newest auto assembly plant. The plant had been hailed as the U.S. auto industry's belated answer to foreign competition, a sleek, highly automated facility that would meet the quality and productivity challenges of Toyota and other overseas carmakers. Despite these grand goals, the plant was plagued by problems and discontent from the beginning. The actual roots of the trouble lay deep in the unique culture of General Motors; its relationship with its biggest union, the United Auto Workers; and, to some extent, the radical changes under way in manufacturing technology. But beyond the specifics, "Lordstown" became synonymous with the idea that something was deeply wrong with the way big U.S. corporations related to workers and their jobs. Some management specialists pointed approvingly at Swedish carmaker Volvo, where teams of assembly-line workers took part in decisions about everything from new products to new manufacturing techniques. Lordstown turned into something much bigger than an argument about manufacturing jobs, however. It became the workplace equivalent of the Vietnam War protests and spawned the notion of "blue-collar blues," a sort of roiling discontent with the unfulfilling content and strict regimentation of factory work. If workers in general did not begin to find their jobs more meaningful, it was argued, then the discontent at GM's new plant in Ohio would burst out in factories and offices everywhere.

Citing a contemporary poll by the Labor Department, the Nixon administration report ticked off some of the top twenty-five things people wanted from their jobs. Among them: "interesting work," "good pay," "opportunity to develop special abilities," "job security," and "seeing the results of one's work." Subsequent polls in later years show the wish list hasn't changed much down to the present. But the authors concluded that a substantial majority of working Americans were not getting anything like what they wanted. The panel called on American business to help fill the gap by replacing strict notions of mechanical efficiency with the idea of "social efficiency," or improving job quality while still boosting profits.

Viewed from the perspective of the early twenty-first century, the vision represented by such ideas seems little short of romantic. Richard Nixon has gone into the history books as one of the most hard-nosed politicians of his age, yet the ideas embraced by the assessment of American workers that his administration put forth could be mistaken for a liberal daydream. And nothing more graphically illustrates how much has changed about the economy and how we view it than what the report had to say about two subjects of concern: the role of women and the alienation of American workers generally. On the first, the report barely caught the change in women's roles that was just getting under way and by now has utterly changed both the economics and the personal dynamics of American families. It said, "Housekeeping may still be the main occupation of American women, but it is no longer the only occupation. . . . In the past, a woman's sense of self-identity and main source of satisfaction centered on the husband's job, the home and the family. Today, there are alternatives."

From the perspective of today, there was a similarly dreamlike quality to the report's assessment of its second subject, the roiling dissatisfaction among the nation's industrial workers. The cure that Nixon's commission proposed was self-employment. "This element of the American Dream," it said of self-employment, "is rapidly becoming a myth, and disappearing with it is the possibility of realizing the character traits of independence and autonomy by going into business for oneself."

In the years that followed publication of *Work in America*, the United States would pursue both self-employment and a larger role for women in the workforce with a vengeance. The result, however, would not always—or even usually—be the greater sense of self-fulfillment and job satisfaction that the Nixon-era officials had envisioned. Meanwhile, the problems that have actually developed in recent decades have turned out to be vastly different from the concerns that agitated Nixon's analysts and their peers.

To begin with, the flood of women into the full-time workforce during the past generation was driven only partly by hunger for self-realization and such society-wide factors as the opening of wider opportunities for women that began during World War II. The determination of younger women to nail down dependable careers was spurred in no small part by the rise in postwar divorce rates. More generally, the evidence suggests that by far the biggest factor in drawing women into the labor market has been the simple desire for more money to live better lives in a more expensive society. More recently, the trend was reinforced by a recognition that the stability of men's jobs was declining, along with both employer-provided benefits and government safety nets. So the arrival of women in the workforce provided families with important financial ballast just when they needed it most—ensuring that households would have a second income-earner in case anything happened to the first.

THE ROLE THAT WORKING WOMEN now play in the financial security of their families, however, is not quite the unmixed blessing it is sometimes portrayed as being. For starters, whereas a working wife reduces the risk that a family will see its income dive to zero if the husband becomes unemployed, having two jobs *raises* the risk that a family could see a substantial—perhaps 50 percent—income drop. Two workers are exposed to the possibility of job loss or interruption, not just one. The extra downside exposure might not be that important if two-earner families operated as though the woman's income were mad money—something extra that the family didn't really have to have. But almost none operates that way. Wives' earnings are now integral to their families' basic living standards. An analysis of two decades of the government's Consumer Expenditure Survey, Washington's tally of what Americans buy, shows that the fraction of consumption and income going to big-ticket items like houses, cars, and schools has, if anything, risen slightly to more than 50 percent, even as the number of families' earners and the size of families' income have climbed. This suggests that most two-earner families are, in effect, living up to their incomes, operating on the assumption that they have both spouses' earnings to spend. It also suggests that many families face a much tougher adjustment if something goes wrong. Second incomes are not being spent primarily on luxury items that can be readily sacrificed if a job disappears. Instead, the money is going into the kinds of basic spending that are not easy to shrink, and, if shrunk, entail big, painful changes.

The size of these so-called consumption commitments "puts families in a bind," said Raj Chetty, a University of California-Berkeley economist who specializes in the study of risk. "It means that if they are hit with an economic shock such as an illness or layoff, they have to adjust to it by making bigger changes in the part of their budget that is still not locked in."

There is one last point that needs to be understood about women and work: Notwithstanding the fact that a large majority of wives and mothers now work full-time and make a crucial contribution to their family income and quality of life, there are still important differences between the work patterns of men and women. Women still tend to go in and out of the labor force more often, to take more leaves, and to work part-time or on nonstandard schedules more often than men. That's because women, much more so than men, are the ones who serve as the buffers between the work world and their families. They take off work to have children. They take off work if a child is having trouble at school or a parent is sick. These adjustments are necessary if two-earner families are to accommodate the increasingly insistent demands of the economy and still function as families. However, the adjustments have a downside. They mean that women's wages are more volatile than men's—more likely to be interrupted or curtailed. And they mean that if women make big adjustments like taking time off, the much-vaunted benefits of the two-earner families suddenly vanish—for both members of the partnership.

Both the benefits and the potential risks of having women and men become something close to coequal breadwinners have—along with many other changes—made the contemporary world of work a much more hard-edged place than it was three or more decades ago. As a result, the Nixon-era idea that employers must focus on their workers' sense of self-fulfillment now seems wildly idealistic. In any case, it was soon overtaken by harsher realities.

Ron Burtless, now in his early fifties, was among the first to discover the change. He never intended to be an economic guinea pig. And after three decades of work, he's just grateful to have survived.

Since Burtless has spent his work life in Big Steel, it is easy to see his story as a Rust Belt relic, but don't be too quick to dismiss it as an artifact of history with no contemporary relevance. The upheavals that battered steel are not so different from those that have subsequently plagued companies far removed from heavy industry—those in telecommunications, insurance, and banking, among others. Moreover, the way that Burtless's steel company employer treated him when hard times arrived matches the way firms in these other industries have been treating their workers. His experience with the government safety net is not unique to manufacturing, either. A steelworker may not be the anachronism he seems in present-day America; in fact, his work experiences are becoming increasingly commonplace.

A COLD WIND blew off Lake Michigan and across the dunes that surround Bethlehem Steel's Burns Harbor plant on the day in March 1975 when Ron Burtless went to work as an electrician. But Big Steel was at its zenith, and there was nothing to discourage him from taking a job that seemed as durable as the heavy sheets of steel that rolled out of the plant. So confident were industry executives about steel's permanence on the American landscape that they had recently signed a landmark labor pact with the United Steelworkers union. Called the Experimental Negotiating Agreement, it gave Bethlehem what amounted to a no-strike pledge from the union. What the union got in return was perhaps the richest package of wages and benefits in the history of the industrialized world.

The accord, which covered Burtless, promised an indefinite string of 3 percent raises. In an era when oil embargoes and Soviet grain deals had sent prices flying, it provided complete protection against inflation above and beyond the 3 percent. It set the stage for improvements in health-, dental-, and eye-care coverage; extra unemployment and workers' compensation in case of layoff or injury; and even employer-paid "sabbaticals" for plant veterans, an idea broached a few years earlier by Nixon's *Work in America* task force. In short order, the agreement helped Burtless more than double his income—from $13,500 in the mid-1970s to more than $32,000-plus in the early 1980s. The money gave him the wherewithal to buy a three-bedroom ranch house near the plant and an American Motors Javelin with a V-8 engine and dual exhausts. Burtless got married, and set himself a long-term goal—to stay with the company until March 2005, when he would hit the thirty-year service mark and be entitled to an ample pension and health insurance for life. At that point, Burtless would be only fifty years old, and he could do almost anything that struck his fancy at almost no risk to his economic security. "It was going to be my freedom," he said.

But in 1982, Big Steel buckled. In short order, steel producers ditched the groundbreaking labor accord, and Bethlehem cut its workforce from nearly 80,000 to 34,000. Sabbaticals were out, but that was the least of it: Wide-ranging cutbacks hit Burtless and other steelworkers like a tornado. To this day, Burtless is foggy about exactly what happened. All he remembers is that neighbors in his suburban subdivision, all steelworkers, began to go bankrupt and lose their homes to foreclosure. The value of his own house plunged, to be followed quickly by his income, which dropped in inflation-adjusted terms from $35,000 in 1982 to $30,000 five years later. His marriage fell apart and with it his family, which now included two little girls,

Mary and Patty. Before steel's collapse, Burtless said, "I figured my income would keep right on rising, that it was like a sure thing that I could plan around." Instead, "here we were giving givebacks"—the term for unions agreeing to forgo wage gains and other benefits they had previously won. "It made a mess of everything."

Over time, Burtless managed to rebuild a semblance of his former life—first by signing up for all the Sunday and holiday shifts he could get, then by winning legal custody of Mary and Patty, and finally, in 1992, by remarrying. His new wife, Toni Brown, was a fellow electrician at Burns Harbor. By that time, Burtless was earning more than $50,000 a year. His new wife brought an extra $50,000 a year to the household, almost doubling the family's annual income. In 1993, the couple built a $150,000 five-bedroom, three-bath house to shelter their new clan, which was made up of Toni and her four children from a previous marriage as well as Ron, Mary, Patty, and eventually Patty's young son, Nicky. They outfitted the place with cherry furniture and a thirty-five-inch Magnavox TV. They also took out several loans and a $30,000 second mortgage to finance a parade of motor vehicles that included, at various times, a van, a sedan, a Jeep, a truck, a motorcycle, and a Dodge Caravan. In 1996, they bought into a vacation time-share in the Caribbean.

At about $1,500 a month, their mortgage payments weren't exorbitant. And as the family settled in, and as Mary and then Patty got their own places, Burtless and Brown were able to handle their day-to-day costs easily and even to stash away $72,000 in a 401(k)— about twice what Federal Reserve statistics show a typical family saved at the time. Unfortunately, the good times did not last. In 2000, the couple split up in a bitter divorce. Among other things, Ron had to give up half of the 401(k) money.

Once more, Burtless got himself back on his feet, and Bethlehem Steel was doing the same. After a succession of losses through the 1980s, the company posted a profit in four of five years after 1993. It spent close to $1 billion modernizing Burns Harbor and other plants and began winning back market share from foreign rivals. Among the many advantages of Bethlehem's return to profitability was that it was allowed to run its own workers' compensation program instead of being required to buy expensive outside insurance against industrial accidents, as most companies must do by law. At Burns Harbor, the program was backed only by a sort of standby policy from another corporate giant, Illinois-based Kemper Insurance Companies. It was an arrangement that Burtless had no reason to pay any attention to—until Easter Sunday, 2003.

From his first day at Burns Harbor, Burtless had worked at the front end of the steelmaking process, where coal is turned into coke by heating it to 2,300 degrees. The coke is combined with limestone and iron ore to form molten cast iron. The molten iron then goes to a blast furnace, where it is transformed into steel. At close to midnight on Easter, a locomotive delivering thirty-six tons of fire-red coke to be quenched with thousands of gallons of water suddenly stalled. Burtless, the electrician on duty, was dispatched to find out why. As he reached for the ladder to scramble up into the engine cab, he fell—his legs plunging into a nearby runoff trench of boiling water. Train operator Ron Lewis still recalls the scream: "It was like in the movies when somebody's getting electrocuted."

By the time Lewis located Burtless, he had clambered out of the ditch and was talking rapidly, joking about having been "lobstered." He insisted he wasn't badly hurt, but the plant ambulance raced him to a local hospital, where the doctor took one look at his legs and sent him on to Loyola University Medical Center's burn unit in Chicago. In the weeks that followed, Burtless remembers Patty getting on the phone and describing Nicky's day at nursery school to distract him from the pain. The nurses came in every day at three in the morning to debride the wounds, scraping away the damaged layers of skin in search of what was still alive. Burtless suffered chills and underwent a lengthy operation in which skin was stripped from his upper thighs and grafted onto his lower legs. Although he didn't know it at the time, the operation was doing more than stripping skin; it was stripping his finances.

After Bethlehem's comeback, the company stumbled again in the late 1990s because of industry consolidations, failed investments, and the unrelenting challenge of foreign competition. On May 1, 2003, when Burtless was still at Loyola recovering from surgery, the company sold all of its assets—but almost none of its liabilities—to International Steel Group, a two-year-old firm set up by investor and "vulture" fund operator Wilbur Ross Jr. At virtually the same moment, Kemper Insurance found itself sinking under a mountain of claims, many of them connected with Enron Corporation's implosion and the priest abuse scandal in the Roman Catholic Archdiocese of Boston. The combination ripped apart the workers' compensation safety net that, at least financially, was supposed to catch Burtless.

The question of who was responsible for Burtless's medical bills remains murky. Lawyers for Bethlehem and the Indiana Workers' Compensation Board said Kemper should be covering the costs of injured workers such as Burtless. Lawyers for Kemper said that the firm was not responsible because Bethlehem stopped paying premiums on its Kemper policy more than a year before Burtless was hurt. Indiana has a law that bans health providers from trying to collect from injured workers, but because Burtless was rushed across state lines to Illinois for treatment, it was not clear whether that protection applied. The upshot is that Loyola, Superior Air Ground Ambulance of Elmhurst, Illinois, and even local St. Anthony's Hospital all dunned Burtless to pay for his care. The bills amounted to $92,075.10—an amount he said he could not possibly hope to raise.

LAST YEAR, more than three decades after the appearance of *Work in America,* its principal author, James O'Toole, now a sixty-something professor at the University of Southern California, returned with a colleague to examine how the themes of the Nixon-era study had played out in subsequent decades. What he found was a substantial increase in the number of women in the workplace, as well as improvement in the kinds of jobs open to them. There had also been a substantial jump in self-employment. But to his mind the biggest change from the 1970s was this: What "most American workers have in common today is that they are bearing increased risk compared to workers of previous generations. Increasingly, employers have transferred onto their workers the . . . risks related to employment security, healthcare, training, career . . . choices, forms of compensation and benefits and retirement," he said.

Unlike many of today's economists, who are still looking to top-down statistics for evidence of a fundamental change in the relationship between employers and employees, O'Toole and coauthor Edward Lawler are categorical in their conclusions. Citing a new survey of Fortune 1000 executives, the two said that employers no longer value long-term ties with employees as they still did in the 1970s. Asked if "loyalty to the company is rewarded," only 16 percent of the executives said yes. Asked if "rewards [and continued employment] are tied to individual performance," more than 60 percent did not agree. "What has emerged," O'Toole and Lawler wrote, "is a social contract in which employees understand they have jobs for as long as they have the right skills and . . . the organization has the resources to pay them. Moreover, corporate executives have become the sole decision makers with regard to determinations about both [the relevance of workers' skills and the companies' ability to pay them]. . . . Employment at will is now a fact of . . . life for almost every worker in the private sector," referring to the legal doctrine that employers can fire employees for any reason or none at all.

The authors' conclusions document what has happened to the first and crucial strut on which families' economic security has long depended: stable jobs, reliable paychecks, and certain benefits. They suggest that a work world that existed as recently as the 1970s, in which the government worried aloud about job quality, employee satisfaction, and a sense of self-fulfillment, is the stuff of a distant and never-to-repeat-itself past. They show that Americans now operate in a harsher environment where the margin for economic error is narrower and chances of steep financial falls are greater. They begin to answer the question of how people up and down much of the income spectrum can feel imperiled even amid economic plenty.

WITH THE ISSUE of his medical bills unresolved, Ron Burtless once more struggled toward self-sufficiency. To save money in the months after his discharge from Loyola, he decided to forgo the $200-a-day medical dressings the doctors had ordered for his legs. Instead, he bought disposable diapers and boiled them into a sort of papier-mâché that he used to swathe his burns. After weeks spent wrangling with St. Anthony's to continue sending a home health aide, Patty and Nicky moved back home, and Patty began taking care of her father.

The sale of Bethlehem Steel did not eliminate the $1,670-a-month pension that Burtless expects to collect someday. But that's only because the Pension Benefit Guaranty Corporation, a federal agency, picked up the obligation. The company's sale did erase the thirty-year finish line that Burtless had been pushing toward for so long. Instead of starting to collect his pension in March 2005 at age fifty, Burtless was told by the PBGC that he now must wait until he is sixty-two. Bethlehem Steel also defaulted on its promise of retirement health coverage for more than 90,000 former and current Bethlehem Steel employees, including Burtless. With no federal agency to guarantee those benefits, they are gone for good.

Without any payments coming in from workers' compensation, and with his pension delayed by more than a decade, Burtless decided two months after his accident to hide his wounds under heavy stockings, apply with the plant's new owners, and go back to work at Burns Harbor. Only three years after the accident did the workers' compensation board finally cough up the $90,000 for medical bills, plus $6,585.60 for the wages he lost while he was hospitalized. He seems reconciled to toiling at the plant until 2016, when he finally will be eligible for his pension. "I'm just thankful to have the job," he said recently. "But forty-one years in a mill seems like a high price to pay to get to retirement."

5

UNJOBS

O N A WARM SPRING NIGHT a couple of years ago, sunset bathed
Atlanta's midtown skyline and brought a gentle glow to the
pink and white blossoms of the flowering trees in Piedmont Park.
Waiting for the start of an open-air concert featuring Grammy
Award–winning country star Jamie O'Neal and an Atlanta girl band
called the Swear, a crowd of some 20,000 people strolled beside Lake
Clara Meer. Onstage, a middle-aged business executive named Bruce
Meyer was receiving a plaque in recognition of his service as chair-
man of the annual Atlanta Dogwood Festival, of which the concert
was a part.

Meyer had taken over the seventy-year-old Atlanta Dogwood Festival, which traditionally opened Atlanta's spring social season, under
less than auspicious circumstances. The preceding chairman had had
a heart attack after his business went bad and had died only weeks
before the 2004 festival. During Meyer's own tenure, he had faced a
racially charged lawsuit involving one of the event's 200-plus ven-
dors. He had struggled with the organization's ragged finances. And

he had moved forward despite a prickly Piedmont Park Conservancy, which never much liked the festival, and a city administration that considered Dogwood a white event in a majority-black city. On this night in 2006, Meyer's swan song as chairman, however, he basked in praise. He was proclaimed a "friend of Dogwood."

Meyer had reason to treasure this public recognition as a civic leader. The time he had lavished on the festival was what members of his temple call *tzedakah* (charity). Equally important, such efforts were, at least until recently, highly valued in the corporate world, whose views Meyer took—and still takes—very seriously. Community service is one of the things expected of a top-flight executive, a business leader such as Meyer, who had held upper-level positions with such corporate giants as WorldCom and Arthur Andersen. Beyond the obligation to give back to the community, Meyer, in candid moments, acknowledged that the contacts he'd made during his time with the festival could pay dividends in new business opportunities. And such opportunities, should they develop, would be a godsend for Bruce Meyer. Because by the time he received his Dogwood award, he had not worked steadily in four years. By the fall of 2007, the string had stretched to more than five years.

In the American economy as it has developed in recent decades, Meyer represents something unique—and uniquely new. He is one of a growing number of highly trained and experienced professionals who are living neither inside nor outside the world of work, but along its margins. You could get pretty close to Meyer and never guess that he's no longer quite the high-level, high-income businessman he used to be—and outwardly still seems to be. Meyer inhabits a new netherworld, the vocational purgatory of the "unjob." Residents of this world display many of the outward trappings of success. They dress well, do lunch, take meetings, network, and keep in touch with contacts. They often live in fancy houses and drive expensive cars. On any given day, they may have important, well-paid assignments from major corporations. The one thing they will not have are real full-time jobs. It's not just that they don't have lifetime employment; fewer and fewer people have that anymore. What Meyer and others like him don't have are the kinds of jobs you can count on to be there next week or next month—that is, the kinds of jobs most of us consider the first prerequisite for a sustainable life. If you can't be sure from one day to the next whether you will have a paycheck coming in, how can you be sure of anything? The answer, at least so far as the material aspects of life are concerned, is that you can't. And the effort to stay afloat, cope with stress, and keep alive the hope that you will soon regain solid ground may be as demanding as any task in the modern workforce. You could almost say that holding down an "unjob" is a full-time job all by itself.

At first glance, an unjob seems like an impossibility. How could someone live in a fancy house, drive a fancy car, and otherwise display the attributes of affluence while lacking a steady job? What do people with unjobs do for money? The detailed answer, as well as the consequences of living this way, is the subject of this chapter. But the short answer is juggle part-time work of a relatively lucrative but unreliable sort: consulting gigs, short-term contracts, and temporary jobs that pay well while they last but evaporate with little or no warning. That, and carefully parcel out your savings, the use of your charge cards, lines of credit, home equity, and whatever else you can find to stretch resources. All the while and at all costs, people caught in this situation must maintain the appearance that nothing has changed about their circumstances. Otherwise, a once-successful worker risks falling into the fatal category of damaged goods.

THE UNJOB may be the least-understood way in which changes in the workplace have remade the nature of employment. Besides boosting the average length of time that people stay unemployed, besides increasing the proportion of the unemployed who are out of work for potentially damaging lengths of times, the changes have given rise to a world with its own rules, traditions, institutions, and imperatives. Moreover, contrary to what you might expect, the unjob phenomenon is growing not solely in the Rust Belt or other economic backwaters but in such economically expanding regions as metropolitan Atlanta. This suggests that economic growth alone—or at least anything short of boom-time growth—will not make the problem go away.

It is easy to dismiss members of this group as undeserving of sympathy. Meyer made enough money during his time in the upper reaches of corporate America and in subsequent consulting assignments to hang on to his house in the expensive Buckhead suburb of Atlanta. He still maintains not one but two cars, a BMW and a Jeep Cherokee. Many people would kill for such a life, or at least think they would. The appearance is deceiving, however. It is a way of life in which anxiety is more common than satisfaction, self-doubt a near-constant companion. Almost every waking moment is devoted to seeking a way out. Meyer and others who have been pushed to the margins of the job market after years of success may sound like members of the new class of entrepreneurial workers that some economists and many conservative politicians like to portray as an emergent blessing. But behind the shell of appearances, these workers are not congratulating themselves or enjoying the experience. To the contrary, they are deeply troubled about what has happened to them. They think it's their fault. And they feel a consuming responsibility to make their way back to solid jobs. They are scrambling to find almost any way to do that. In the meantime, they are terribly exposed to the possibility of even more severe hits. Having no steady income, often no health insurance or other benefits, and no durable financial underpinnings, they live in near-constant danger of losing even the outward trappings of good fortune.

Beyond the pain and insecurity this phenomenon inflicts on its victims, the unjob trend is an especially disturbing aspect of the way the risks of something as basic and indispensable as work are being shifted onto individual workers and their families. For most of

Meyer's career, he and others in similar situations represented the strong core of the U.S. workforce. They were exceedingly well trained. They had kept their skills current. They were positioned in fields that had, and still have, bright futures. Decade after decade, they performed at the top of their games, winning steady advancement as they carried out demanding assignments. And when they fell, the reasons for falling had little to do with unsatisfactory performance or obsolescence: They were pulled down by forces unrelated to their own work and entirely beyond their control.

The reason we need to look at the world of unjobs is not that its denizens suffer more than others; their lives are not as nice as they look, but many people have it much worse. No, the reason to care about the Bruce Meyers of today's economy is that if they can fall after so much success, what's in store for the rest of us?

We may be able to accept the idea that young workers starting out in a changing economy face greater uncertainty than young workers in more settled periods of the past. We may also accept the suggestion that midcareer course corrections could become necessary for veteran workers—getting more training, for instance, or shifting to a new line of work. But it is far more difficult to see how people like Meyer can live their lives in anything like the way they do now—even well past the midpoint of their careers, and even after they have achieved and sustained high levels of success in vibrant segments of the economy for many years—if even then, they can suddenly be chopped down in midstride. The implications of such a brave new world are disconcerting. How could individuals and families plan and conduct themselves over a working lifetime if they had to assume that each week of successful, secure employment might be their last? Who would ever buy a better house, a new car, or nicer clothes and thus fuel the consumer-driven economy? Who could make a commitment to a marriage or long-term relationship or to children with no reason for faith in the future?

No sensible person would argue that society could or should be organized so that there was no risk; none of us expects every job to be guaranteed permanent. That is not the issue. The issue is how far can or should a society go in the opposite direction—toward a world of unlimited personal risk, a world in which even the most seemingly trustworthy promises may hold for years and then suddenly be broken?

ESTABLISHING A CLEAR PICTURE of how many workers are in the world of unjobs is not easy. In compiling its statistics on employment and unemployment, the federal government relies chiefly on information from employers and the unemployment insurance system. That means it operates on the premise that a job is an all-or-nothing affair. The result is that many workers like Meyer can go uncounted, especially after they have been in limbo long enough for their unemployment insurance benefits to run out.

The government also keeps track of something called the labor participation rate, which surveys those of working age who report that they are working or looking for work. The labor participation rate for men has dropped substantially, but most likely for reasons other than unjobs. The rate for women climbed substantially during most of the past twenty-five years. Data on part-time workers, temps, and workers classified as independent contractors are also ambiguous. The percentage of workers who tell government survey-takers they fall into one of these categories has remained fairly stable over the decade Washington has been asking. When the question is put to employers, however, the fraction labeled "temps" increases. The government has not resolved this apparent conflict.

It is possible that the number of part-timers, temps, and independent contractors hasn't changed all that much, but that the number of workers in these categories on a more or less permanent basis—so-called perma-temps—could have risen. Here the data are clearer. The fraction of temp-agency employees who used to do temp work for short periods but now report working at it for a year or more climbed from 25 percent in 1995 to 34 percent in 2005. The fraction of company employees classified as contract employees who report operating for similarly longer periods in their in-between roles has gone from 50 percent to almost 66 percent over the same period.

ONE WAY THAT PEOPLE ARE COPING with the advent of unjobs is by doing what Americans have always done in times of trouble—joining a group and starting a movement. Where previous generations of blue-collar workers turned to unions for help with job trouble, the current generation of white-collar workers is turning to voluntary groups. Some are membership organizations, like the Forty Plus Clubs or the Financial Executives Networking Group, that seek to professionalize the job search of white-collar workers. Others, like LinkedIn, are employment versions of virtual social networks like MySpace. But the vast majority of the groups devoted to helping those wandering the new netherworld of the not-really-employed are church-based. From Priority Two and Joseph's People in slow-growing Pittsburgh and Philadelphia to Crossroads Career Network in booming Roswell, Georgia, these groups attack underemployment as well as unemployment using the precepts of Dale Carnegie, the fervor of Christian evangelicalism, and the techniques of everything from Alcoholics Anonymous to dating services.

Like most movements, this one has developed a language and lore all its own. People are not unemployed; they're "in transition." No one lands a position through such old-fashioned means as help-wanted ads, but by "networking." What counts in getting hired is not your experience or your résumé so much as your "elevator speech," a carefully honed, endlessly practiced, unflinchingly sunny pitch for yourself.

The rise of this self-help movement for people like Meyer has attracted a sharp critic in author Barbara Ehrenreich, who argues that, whatever the groups' motivations, "the *effect* of their efforts is to divert people from the hard questions" about how the economy treats those who depend on it. But most who join the new organizations say that, if nothing else, they help combat the feeling of being alone. And the movement has already netted a big name. Long before George W. Bush became president, back when he was a failing oilman, he joined the Midland, Texas, chapter of a group called Community Bible Study. Though not formally an unemployment support group, it emerged in the mid-1980s to meet the needs of businessmen and others who were suffering through an oil bust that produced bankruptcies, upset once-secure lives, and drove some of its victims to divorce and—in a few cases—suicide. "Hard times have a way of making people draw closer to God," group member Skip Hedgpeth told PBS's *Frontline* show in 2004.

THE FACT THAT the energy and talent of so many people could be so tenuously connected to the economy would seem to be a big story. But with the exception of Ehrenreich, almost no one seems to have taken notice. Clearly, part of the reason almost no one has focused on this corner of the job market is the tireless efforts that most of those stuck in it make to conceal the underlying reality. Meyer has kept his Buckhead house. Allan Hess, an associate of Meyer's who had at least a couple of "c-level," or chief, positions to his name before he was knocked off the corporate ladder, has held on to his 4,500-square-foot home in fashionable Marietta. At one point when Hess briefly let himself believe that a new executive position with a computer data-mining firm called Proficient was going to last, he celebrated by ordering an in-house movie system with surround sound and a 108-inch screen. But his grip on such luxuries soon proved as tenuous as his hold on the kinds of jobs that make big luxury purchases possible.

Beyond their own effort to conceal it, the reason the situations of people like Meyer and Hess go unnoticed may be that they do not fit the view of reality that prevails among most economists and even more national political leaders. Although the conventional accounts take a bow to the idea that today's working people must be ready to switch jobs and even occupations, the switching is almost always described as fitting the safe, familiar pattern: old job to new job, or old job to brief period of joblessness to new and better job. In the upbeat outlook that characterizes today's conventional wisdom, there is no room for the idea that there are other, less reassuring patterns, including ones that carry workers from solid jobs to the economic sidelines and leave them stuck there.

If today's job market includes a significant risk that well-trained and successful workers may be sidelined without warning and through no discernible fault of their own, then getting more training in the form of college education and advanced training does not sound like a convincing antidote for high job turnover. Getting more education and being more adaptable make sense only in a world of smooth job transitions and near-certain employment. In a world of abrupt job breaks and long jobless spells, they look more like an expensive and time-consuming crapshoot.

IN MANY WAYS, Bruce Meyer looks like a role model for young people headed into the corporate world today—in his training, his career choices, and his work ethic. He grew up in Richmond, Virginia, during the civil rights movement. For Jewish families like his, the time and the place combined to put a premium on fitting in. The Meyer family's temple was so intent on not seeming different that for years it conducted its weekly services not on the Jewish Sabbath of Saturday but on Sunday. He went to high school at Trinity Episcopal, and played on the baseball team.

He was raised on stories of how his grandparents had lost everything in the Depression. He saw his father, Milton Meyer Jr., after years on the road selling men's trousers, open his own clothing store in the 1970s, only to have it fail, sending him back out on the road.

The takeaway for the son was that he could not do the same. "There was an expectation of success. They always thought I could do better," the younger Meyer said.

Partly due to his mother's urging, Meyer came home after college and business school at the University of Georgia and took a job in what was then the kind of high-tech field that today's leaders would recommend. He began selling word processors for Lanier Business Products. But he was soon following a girlfriend back to the Atlanta area. When the relationship soured, he threw himself into work, and within a few years had little time for anything else. In 1989, he started working for a small Florida fiber-optic company called Microtel, which was acquired by a larger Atlanta-based discount long-distance carrier called ATC. ATC merged with a still-larger Jackson, Mississippi, telecommunications company called LDDS, which eventually changed its name to WorldCom.

Meyer stuck with the firm and won a series of promotions, ending up in a senior marketing position with WorldCom's operator services division. But along the way, he was put through an executive mixmaster of fifty-seven mergers and dozens of reorganizations that, he said, included reporting to nine different vice presidents in a single year. "The company's view was if you weren't willing to remake yourself perpetually, you couldn't make it," he said. Meyer was willing, but it left him time for almost nothing else.

WorldCom was briefly one of the nation's largest telecom companies before collapsing in 2002 under the weight of an $11 billion accounting fraud. Former CEO Bernie Ebbers was sentenced to twenty-five years in federal prison for his role.

By the time WorldCom imploded, however, Meyer was gone. In 1996, he landed a job with what seemed at the time a corporate Rock of Gibraltar—accounting and consulting giant Arthur Andersen. It was a position that Meyer was convinced would lead to his making partner and locking in all the financial success and personal security that he'd been seeking since childhood. He was hired to market what was initially known as the company's "benefits and compensation" practice. It had been a sleepy backwater at Andersen, where consultants advised corporate clients on how to organize their payment of employees to get the most out of them. But it was an area that was about to be renamed and to take off. The new name was "human capital."

The idea of human capital—that people are a company's principal asset, to be valued and developed like an investment and not used up like office supplies—had been around since at least the early 1970s, when the government's *Work in America* report concluded that a substantial fraction of the nation's labor force was being mismanaged. But the notion took off in the 1990s when a consensus developed that America was entering a new "postindustrial" era in which all or nearly all of us were "knowledge" workers whose brains, rather than our brawn, were what could make or break an organization. In short order, top executives were letting people organize themselves into autonomous work groups, agreeing to share gains from quality improvements with workers, and helping to pay for employees' education and training. What Andersen offered—and what Meyer set about marketing—was something that only an accountant could dream up, a means of measuring and managing the realm of employee ideas. The company's effort culminated in a 1998 book written by three Andersen partners and partially orchestrated by Meyer, according to the book's acknowledgments. It was titled *Delivering on the Promise: How to Attract, Manage, and Retain Human Capital.*

In the book, the authors described their efforts "to develop a comprehensive metric that could be used to rate the effectiveness of human capital." Although they conceded in the book that the "Arthur Andersen Human Capital Index" was still a work in progress, they promised a sequel to update readers on the new measuring device. But there never was a sequel. In the years that followed *Delivering on the Promise,* corporate leaders began to change their minds about human capital. Although they maintained some small-scale changes

like autonomous work groups, they decided that the business world
had become too uncertain and prone to reverses to make the long-
term commitment to employees that a human-capital approach required. No matter what the Andersen matrix might show about the
returns on investment in human capital, it was an idea whose hour
had passed.

IT WAS A REVERSAL that Meyer refused to believe was under way until the very end. When his time came, he was thunderstruck. Even
when Arthur Andersen found itself drawn into the Enron and later
the WorldCom scandals—accused of shredding documents and ob-
struction of justice—Meyer was convinced that both he and the firm
would survive. His faith endured almost to the moment when federal
prosecutors obtained criminal indictments against the firm in early
2002. As Andersen tottered and retrenched, Meyer was among the
first to be let go. Within three months, the entire firm was gone.

Looking back, Meyer said, he should have better prepared himself
for the job loss by snapping up all the company-paid training that he
could get. He should have thrown himself into trade organizations
like the American Marketing Association and begun "networking as
if that was my second job." But he had done none of these things. "I
didn't go on the golf trips. I didn't go to the conventions. I didn't take
a day off."

FALLS FROM CORPORATE GRACE have been increasing since the early
1990s. They seem likely to go right on increasing as the economy
casts about for the right shape for the twenty-first century. And there
has been no shortage of warnings about the trend from economists,
policymakers, and politicians. Yet you would be hard-pressed to find
much evidence of a national response—certainly not in what's publicly available to those who fall out of regular employment, whether
high in the financial pecking order like Meyer and Hess or lower
down like steelworker Ron Burtless.

It's not that the country doesn't have programs to help people move from one job to another, learn new jobs when old ones vanish, or adjust to being steamrollered by global competition. There's a nation-wide "Employment Service" that's supposed to deliver "one-stop" shopping to match employees with jobs and employers with employ-ees. There's something called "America's Workforce Network," which Washington describes as a "federally sponsored nationwide employ-ment and training system . . . committed to helping workers get the skills they need to succeed in our high-tech world and committed to helping employers find the skilled workers they so desperately need." There are also two programs to help people who've lost jobs to trade and global competition by matching them with new jobs, paying for their retraining, and even making up a portion of their lost wages if they are forced to take lower-paying replacement jobs.

But if you've never heard of any of these efforts, you are not alone. Neither have most of the un- and underemployed who'd use the services. The reason is that the programs are tiny, splintered, and underfunded. Money for job networking, placement, and training has been evaporating for three decades. Back in the mid-1970s, the government spent more than $30 billion a year in 2007 dollars on these kinds of efforts through the Comprehensive Employment and Training Act, or CETA. Even if one subtracted the money spent on CETA's "public service" jobs, which were widely considered make-work boondoggles that seldom led to permanent employment, it was still spending more than $20 billion to help ordinary Americans cope with changes in the labor market. Today, it spends about $4 billion— mostly through CETA's successor, the Workforce Investment Act, and the program that underwrites America's Workforce Network. "At this point, our spending on training and re-employment efforts are largely placeholders," said Anthony Carnevale, an authority on the subject who was appointed to major commissions by both presidents Ronald Reagan and Bill Clinton. "It gives politicians something to point to, but doesn't do much good."

The argument that's generally given for cutbacks such as these is that—to date—most public and private attempts to intervene in the job market and make it run more smoothly or fairly have failed. But considering how much America prides itself on its ingenuity and its ability to innovate, it's striking that so little effort is being expended in the search for something that does work—especially since so many national leaders warn that more upheaval is on the way.

THERE IS ONE MORE FEDERAL PROGRAM that was supposed to help people like Meyer and Hess. A federal law passed in 1986 as part of the Consolidated Omnibus Budget Reconciliation Act, or COBRA, gave the newly unemployed the right to hang on to the group health insurance they had while employed. They could keep their employer-based health care for eighteen months, which was seen as time enough to make the transition to new jobs and new job-related medical insurance. The catch was that the unemployed worker had to pick up the full tab for the coverage, plus 2 percent to cover administrative costs. That made COBRA so expensive that only one in four of those who are eligible for it sign up. Hess chose to sign up; the $450 monthly charge ate up two of every four weeks of his unemployment benefits. Meyer decided to take a chance and go without insurance. It was probably just as well. Within two months of laying him off, Arthur Andersen LLP was convicted of obstruction of justice and other crimes in the Enron case and essentially collapsed, making it unclear whether the group health insurance program Meyer could have bought into still existed at all.

IN THE ABSENCE OF GOVERNMENT ASSISTANCE, the burden of navigating from job to job, from unemployment to employment, from unjob back to regular work falls largely on individuals operating on their own.

From all outward appearances, Allan Hess's life is another example of the kind of success that has made upward mobility an American hallmark. Hess was raised in the South Bronx. His ticket out was math. Unlike those hapless English majors or the kids attracted to psychology, he had the kind of aptitude the new economy needed. He went to New York University on a coveted Regents Scholarship. Even before he graduated, IBM had signed him up for a position that paid $16,900 a year, a princely sum for a twenty-year-old in 1979. The job came with a promise of company support for graduate school in the technical field of his choice. But once he completed college, Hess found himself moving up the corporate ladder so quickly there was no time—and no real need—for advanced study. By age twenty-five, he was one of Big Blue's top technical experts handling the Citibank account. By age thirty, he was one of three sales managers in charge of the Chemical Bank account. Eight years later, he was business manager of the company's Internet division and, a year after that, chief evangelist for the Java programming language that became a pillar of IBM's Internet operations.

For almost two decades, until the late 1990s, Hess prospered with the company that, perhaps more than any other in America, embraced the doctrine of "human capital." Embraced it, that is, until it changed its mind and slashed its workforce. It was not until about halfway through Hess's time with IBM that the company ordered the first layoffs in its history and began to dismantle its cushioned human-capital culture. By 1993—with Louis V. Gerstner Jr. as the new chairman and $16 billion in losses during the preceding three years—the firm was in no mood to keep promises to employees about expensive things like grad school tuition. IBM focused on getting rid of people, not enriching their talents. The joke that December was that Gerstner sent out end-of-year greetings to employees that read, "Happy Holidays to Each and Every Other One of You." The holiday joke had barely died before Gerstner made good on the implied threat by cutting the computer giant's 400,000-person workforce in half.

In the years that followed, Gerstner and his successor moved the company two more giant steps away from its old human-capital culture. First, they cut IBM's pension costs by weakening pension promises to older employees. Then they announced that starting in January 2008 they would freeze most of the defined benefit pensions altogether and shift workers into less expensive 401(k)s.

Hess rode out the cutbacks and managed to stay with IBM another five wild years. In his last position as the chief Java spokesman, he was in the air forty-seven weeks out of fifty-two, appearing at conferences on four continents, parachuting in to help major clients. He traveled so much that he "went gold" with three airlines and three hotel chains. Newspaper clips at the time suggest that, as a speaker, he was in almost as much demand as Gerstner himself.

But as Hess's career, IBM's fortunes, and the Internet were all heating up in the late 1990s, he was realizing that the company would never go back to its old ways, reducing the likelihood that anyone, himself included, could count on spending an entire career at Big Blue. He began looking for a safe place to land, and he thought he had found it in an Atlanta-based division of Fortis Insurance. In a display of what he thought was foresight and adaptability, Hess resigned from IBM and became Fortis's chief of e-commerce with a staff of some one hundred people, an $8 million operating budget, and a salary of close to $250,000 a year. At a time when tech friends and colleagues were joyfully diving into dot-coms with zero revenues and nothing but stock options for pay, Hess's job move looked to be as prudent a step as you could ask for in the technology field. He bought a twelve-room, five-bedroom, plantation-style house in upscale Marietta and treated himself to a Porsche 911 Turbo Cabriolet. The safe haven remained safe for exactly sixteen months. Then Fortis merged with a competitor, purged its new e-commerce division, and dumped Hess.

The layoff was a blow, but not as debilitating as it might have been. That's because Hess had learned a few tricks living through IBM's transformation from employee-friendly to lean and mean. While the big salaries were rolling in, he had set aside enough savings to cover two years of living expenses. And he'd bulked up the amount as both his income and expenses rose. He reacted to the Fortis layoff by taking in a boarder at his Marietta house, letting go of the Porsche, and setting about making business contacts in his new and unfamiliar hometown.

WHEN MEYER AND HESS lost their corporate jobs, their soon-to-be ex-employers granted each of them several months of severance pay. That was unusually generous, and it slowed their economic descent. As the day drew near when there would be no more paychecks, each turned to the unemployment insurance system funded by the state and federal governments. In their case, it was run by the Georgia Department of Labor. Hess applied for his jobless benefits at the unemployment office on Big Shanty Road in Marietta. He brought his severance agreement with him to prove that his payments from Fortis were running out. The document showed he'd been pulling down what he estimated to be about ten times what everybody else in line with him that day had made. What Meyer remembers about the process was having to prove that he'd been looking for a job each week by filling out the department's online "Record of Work Search" form. In the box for "Name and Address of Company and Person Contacted" he'd list some of Atlanta's biggest companies and top executives. But when it came to the "Results" box, he had to check "Pending."

In Washington, policymakers have consistently touted unemployment insurance as a safety net that has remained rock-solid through two and a half decades of economic change. They are particularly proud of the system's replacement rate, the fraction of a person's pre-unemployment wages that benefits typically make up. Officials say the rate has stayed steady at about 50 percent.

This stability is more apparent than real, however. Unemployment insurance is a classic case of how changes in the economy, public policy, and individuals' personal circumstances have conspired to fray a public safety net that purports to protect people. For starters, the system compensates only for lost wages. Unemployment insurance does nothing about benefits such as health insurance, which have become almost as important as pay for many workers. Similarly, the system was designed for short stints of joblessness—ones lasting less than six months—even though in today's economy, a substantial percentage of jobless workers are out longer than that. And the program was intended to serve a labor force made up largely of men who'd been working full-time; today, the labor force is increasingly made up of women, part-timers, and unjob-holders. Then there's the matter of the replacement rate.

While the government says that unemployment insurance replaces 50 percent of an individual's pre-job-loss wages, in fact, the replacement claim refers not to anyone in particular but to a mythical worker in the middle of the economic spectrum. In other words, the benefit is capped, and capped in such a way that the fraction of wages that benefits actually replace for a great many workers is much less than the advertised 50 percent. The difference between what the replacement rate seems to mean and what it actually delivers masks two crucial changes in the level of protection the program provides.

The first change was that starting in 1979, the federal government and most state governments began taxing benefits. Even for middle-income workers, that effectively cut the replacement rate to about 40 percent. The second change came about not through government action but through a shift in the labor market—a trend toward greater polarization in wages. Rather than being bunched close together in the middle as they had been for many years, more and more Americans have been earning either a lot more or a lot less than the "average." That's great for the higher-income workers as long as they hang on to their jobs. But it means that if they lose their jobs, they have much farther to fall to reach the unemployment insurance safety net. When they get there, they discover that their benefits don't come close to making up what they've lost. The $250 a week or so that

Meyer and Hess each collected from the Georgia unemployment program amounted to 5 percent of the pre-job-loss wages, not 50 percent. That won't arouse much sympathy from jobless workers struggling just to put food on the table and keep a roof over their heads, but it's devastating for those who experience it—both financially and emotionally—all the more so if the fall involves a family and children. "The employment security system is obsolete for a large percentage of the American workforce," said Georgia labor commissioner Michael L. Thurmond. "Here we have a global economy that's undergoing major changes and workers who are increasingly insecure, and the main federal program we have for dealing with these problems is a New Deal program that hasn't undergone a major revision or reengineering in seventy years."

When Meyer and Hess lost their jobs, they did two things that many upper-level white-collar workers do. First, they began to look around for contacts, people they had personal connections with who could help hook them up with new jobs like the ones they'd lost. Second, they began to look for ways to insulate themselves from future shocks by using their business expertise to launch businesses of their own.

The search for contacts who could help them return to normal employment turned out to be less fruitful than they initially hoped. People who can deliver jobs for others are actually few and far between in our society. Whom do you know who could put you into a good new job? The news was especially bad for Meyer because his employer had just blown up, and for Hess because he'd only just arrived in Atlanta. In short order, each turned to a local job-networking organization called the Kettering Group.

The name conjures up images of oak paneling and thick carpets, and the group's organizers worked hard to give Kettering the trappings of an exclusive club. It accepted only those who made $150,000 or more, operated at the senior executive ranks of a major company for at least seven years, and managed at least twenty-five people and a budget of $5 million or so before being laid off. In addition, a new member had to be sponsored by a current member and approved by the full group. The patina of exclusivity covered a more prosaic reality. The Kettering name did not come from some august and well-wired founder. It was borrowed from a suburban street on which some of the group's first members lived. And even if its members were once powerful and affluent, everyone attending Kettering's Friday-morning meetings in suburban Roswell is either unemployed or so recently reemployed that they stay involved in the group just in case. "We decided to add a certain exclusivity so everybody speaks a common language and can talk to each other peer-to-peer," said Kettering founder Chip Schuneman.

There is something a little disorienting about the idea of an exclusive organization of the unemployed. But such groups are a nationwide phenomenon. And talking to their members makes it clear that these are people who have fallen so far so fast that they need *something* that suggests at least some semblance of their previous lives—if only a meeting to put down on their calendars. Schuneman, forty, had been the vice president of an IBM subsidiary and the chief operating officer of a second company when he was laid off from a $280,000-a-year job around 9/11. He was out of work seven months. After founding Kettering, he landed a new job, eventually rising to become president of a Kaplan, Inc., subsidiary at $340,000 a year. But he was laid off again in June 2006 and has been out ever since, surviving on consulting contracts. Other Kettering members have similar pedigrees. In a May 2000 issue of *Fortune* magazine, Barry Trout was among the thirtysomething consultants featured in a cover story on how dot-coms and other hot firms were going to almost any length to snap up business talent. "I got a call a couple days ago where somebody offered me a Porsche if I took a job," Trout mused to the magazine. "I said, 'I'm not leaving.' He said 'We'd still like you to help us with our business plan.'" Trout hasn't had steady work since 2001.

If the way Kettering was put together sounds familiar, that's be-cause it's part of a long tradition of Americans inventing social groups when society's official and long-standing ones don't suffice. What's flourishing in groups like Kettering flourished in an earlier era in the Shriners, the Elks, and the Loyal Order of Moose.

The problem with Kettering and groups like it across the country is that they appear to be outgunned by the economic forces they are contending against. Although Meyer and Hess say that their Ketter-ing contacts have proved invaluable to them, neither can remember a single job they landed through the group, and Schuneman acknowl-edges that the organization "is not meant to be the whole answer or the safety net" for members. Part of the trouble is simply that job networking and jobless support groups largely involve the needy leading the needy: unemployed people trying to help other unem-ployed people get reemployed.

That's not the only contradiction to be found in these groups and their members, well-meaning though they may be. Here, after all, are people who are staring at the possibility of ruin from the comfort of suburban McMansions, who are using the latest business school techniques to analyze why they are no longer in business, who are furious at Corporate America for throwing them out while trying desperately to get back in. A couple of years ago, Kettering invited members—corporate veterans all—to a presentation sponsored by the business schools of Emory University and the University of Michigan, both of which are training grounds for future executives. The title of the program summed up the whole dizzying situation: "I Can't Stand the Corporate World." Before we yield to the temptation to smile, however, we should pause to consider what better ideas we could come up with to tackle the problems facing these people.

As part of their effort to help themselves, Meyer and Hess took another step that is common among successful businessmen whose careers nosedive. They started a business venture of their own. In this case, together. Along with a third ex-executive, former Kimberly-Clark global marketing director Robert Vonderhorst, they formed a company called Triad of North Atlanta LLC. The tiny partnership sought to track down businesses that the group could buy or invest in. In the founders' buzz phrase, Triad's goal was to generate "multiple streams of revenue." Translation: "We never want to depend on a single corporation for our livelihoods again," said Hess. Or as Vonderhorst put it, "You always hear on the financial side how you've got to diversify. But nobody ever tells you that about your career. That's what we're doing."

Each brought something different to the group. When Vonderhorst lost his job, he already had a company on the side that imported window and door hardware from China. He didn't want to kick in investment money for Triad, but he had his Chinese contacts for anything that the three might want to manufacture. Meyer had his business and social connections. Hess knew tech. On a sunny fall day in 2002, the partners sat in Hess's basement office with an easel, a large flip pad, and a marker. They made lists, which sit there on the easel to this day. The headings were:

"What we know or are familiar with?"

"2003+ Trends"

"What Do We Want?"

"How Much Do We Need?"

Under "Trends," they listed security, work-life balance, military spending, and health care. Under Hess's portion of "What Do We Want?" is his lost Porsche. The three have been looking for deals to do ever since they made the lists. They ran into a machinist who'd come up with something called a "tree frog," a device that attaches to the top of a ladder and helps keep it stable on uneven surfaces. The partners looked into various versions of the thing before discovering they couldn't get hold of the patent. They met with the inventor of a patented home fire escape called "Chains of Life" and went through the same due diligence only to discover the inventor wanted such high lifetime royalties that they couldn't make any money for themselves. They talked to a small Austin, Texas, company about producing a GPS device that kids could wear as a bracelet so parents could keep tabs on them, but couldn't afford the research needed to bring it down to wearable size. Billionaire Paul Allen subsequently underwrote the development of a similar product.

In fact, of all the products the partners have looked into thus far, they've brought only one to market, and it has the feel of a business-school case study more than an actual moneymaking product. They've begun producing disposable slippers for people who have to take off their shoes while going through airport security checks. The trio has taken all the right business steps. They've registered the slippers, called "Airport Booties," and the category of disposable footwear as trademarks. They've convinced the Department of Homeland Security to rewrite its regulations so people can leave the slippers on all the way through security. They've gotten Park 'N Fly, the airport parking company, to feature the slippers on the buses they run from lots to terminals in thirteen cities. They've even attracted some television news attention. The only problem is that they're not making enough money on the slippers even to cover their mortgages.

THESE DAYS, Hess still lives in the spacious minimansion nestled in the curve of a cul-de-sac and surrounded by Georgia pine, live oak, and magnolia trees. The flower beds remain neatly edged, and the front lawn is as velvety as a golf course. Step through his big front door, though, and you pass through the suburban equivalent of a Potemkin village. The house is almost totally devoid of furnishings. Hess has a dining room table and chairs, two beds, a couple of couches, and a huge home entertainment center. Otherwise, there's nothing. Footfalls echo on the bare hardwood floors from room to empty room.

Meyer meets almost every day with one business contact or another. He regularly bids for new consulting work. He's also started looking for a job with a nonprofit agency like the Arthritis Foundation or the American Cancer Society. And he has agreed to chair an advisory board of the Dogwood Festival. But sitting in his kitchen one recent morning, he admitted that he is at a loss to explain why things have turned out the way they have. "Why don't I have a job?" he asked. "I don't know. Just like why am I not married? I don't know.

"A lot of jobs disappear," he said after another moment of thought. "A lot were never there to begin with."

6

THE POOR

"T HE POOR ARE NOT LIKE EVERYONE ELSE," social critic Michael
Harrington wrote in *The Other America*, his 1962 best seller that
played a major role in awakening Americans to the reality of poverty
and helped shape President Lyndon B. Johnson's War on Poverty. The
poor, Harrington wrote, "are a different kind of people. They think
and feel differently; they look upon a different America than the
middle class." How then to account for Elvira Rojas? Or her husband,
José Maldonado? Or a man named Albert Grimes?

In purely financial terms, all three have spent much of their working lives below the official poverty line. Even on their best days, they
make barely one-tenth of what ex–Fortune 500 executives like Bruce
Meyer and Allan Hess, corporate temp Paul Fredo, super–insurance
agent Debra Potter, or ex-banker Richard Coss used to make. Look a
little more closely at their lives, however, and two points emerge:
First, in terms of their goals and core values, they are virtually indis-
tinguishable from members of the vast American middle class. Second, their experience carries a valuable lesson for the rest of us.

Looking at their lives is like watching a Discovery Channel time-lapse film of a gathering storm. The financial cataclysms that strike most of us only infrequently or creep up so slowly we barely notice them suddenly jump into bold relief when we look at the working poor. So, too, does the cause—the quarter-century-long shift of economic risk from business and government to working families across most of the income spectrum.

When Rojas and Maldonado escaped the Salvadoran civil war and arrived in Los Angeles in 1989 as twentysomethings, they barely had a place to lay their heads. And they were stuck well below the U.S. poverty line—currently about $20,400 for a family of four. But by working three, sometimes four, jobs between them and taking whatever they could get—not unlike what Meyer, Hess, and Fredo have had to do in recent years—the couple has managed to assemble much of the stuff of middle-class dreams.

Rojas and Maldonado are crammed in a two-room apartment in the poor Hawthorne section of Los Angeles, but they have a china cabinet with enough matching plates, cups, and saucers to serve sixteen, reflecting their desire for at least the appearance of prosperity that has its parallels in the lives of Meyer, Hess, the Fredos, the Potters, and the Cosses. The Rojas-Maldonados' two young daughters get their health coverage through Medi-Cal, California's public health insurance program for the poor, but they get many of their clothes from Macy's, the iconic retailer to the middle class. The family relies on credit cards to pay for everything from large-screen TVs to emergency-room visits. "That's why I'm really poor even though I work so hard," Rojas said ruefully of her credit card bills. But in this, she is right in the mainstream of American life, where plastic has become both an admission ticket to the good life and a private safety net that encourages people to try to borrow their way across bad times.

As for Albert Grimes, whom we will discuss a bit later, he has displayed the steadfast determination to improve himself and a desire to care for his loved ones that are at the core of middle-class values. He even embraced a conservative faith in becoming an independent entrepreneur as the key to financial security.

Some economists and social policy analysts see Rojas, Maldonado, and Grimes as testaments to the economic strides that America has made over the years. After all, whatever shortcomings the rest of us might see in their lives, the Rojas-Maldonados enjoy a standard of living better than anything they could have achieved in their homeland, and Rojas herself will testify that she believes the American Dream is within her grasp. And even Grimes has made some progress. "We've won the War on Poverty," Robert Rector, an influential analyst with the Heritage Foundation, a conservative Washington think tank, asserts. "We've basically eliminated widespread material deprivation."

But if deprivation is no longer the problem it once was, that hardly means all is well. In many ways, Rojas and the others are the new faces of the working poor, suffering not so much from a dearth of possessions as from a cavalcade of chaos—pay cuts and eviction notices, car troubles and medical crises, hirings and firings—that keeps reversing their families' advances, rattling their finances, nudging them toward the economic brink.

And for our purposes, this is the crucial point: Rojas and millions like her are *not* fundamentally different from most Americans—as Harrington said they were—but remarkably similar. Whatever the gap in current living standards between Rojas and, for example, Debra Potter, there is a broad parallel between the churn and upheaval in each of their lives. In essence, Rojas and today's working poor are living out extreme versions of the economic chaos that now threatens families up and down much of America's income ladder.

There is one more reason we should look in on Rojas, Maldonado, and Grimes and why their stories are important to families that are much better off financially: All of them believe they should strive to improve their lives and have faith that, regardless of obstacles and setbacks, they can make progress. Such a faith is an important and enduring part of what it means to be an American. We may not think about it very often, but the possibility of a better future has always been one of the defining qualities of American life. No matter how or where we start out, we believe we can—if only we try hard enough— end up in a better place.

The belief has been especially strong when it comes to the poor. Poverty has always existed in the United States, and most of us understand it is a painful and unwelcome condition. What we historically have not accepted is the possibility that poverty might be permanent. On the contrary, it has been a tenet of our national creed that the disadvantaged, whether immigrant or native-born, might have to struggle. The struggle might extend over a generation or more. But in the end, for all but an unfortunate few, persistent effort would be crowned by some measure of success. Otherwise, how could we have the American Dream? How could a dream exist without the prospect of a happy ending?

If the risk shifts of the past twenty-five years now produce the kind of economic turbulence that can shatter people's material progress, converting it from a broad advance to one-step-forward, two-steps-back, and if these upheavals occur in the extreme among poor families but are also creeping up the economic ladder to touch middle-class and affluent families as well, then much more is at stake than people's immediate stability. The dream is threatened. That's why the story of what's been happening to Rojas, Maldonado, and Grimes is important for the rest of us. Their lives suggest how quickly the personal advances that we consider part of the very fabric of our national story can be erased.

Some of the elements of the shift affecting these and other low-income families are different from those affecting more affluent families, but what is most striking is the similarity of result. Business and government protections that poor Americans especially relied on— affordable housing programs, union protection of stable jobs with big employers, and the backstop of welfare—have been reduced or eliminated. These losses have been only partially offset by an expansion of programs such as publicly provided health care and the earned-income tax credit—a kind of income tax that pays you if what you make is too low. They also have been offset by a substantial expansion of lending, especially credit card and home mortgage lending, to poor people. The destructive consequences of the last have become all too clear since the collapse of the subprime mortgage market, and the defaults and foreclosures that have followed.

Nowhere are the cumulative effects of these changes more apparent than in the widening swings in income of working families across the economic spectrum. And nowhere are the swings proportionately larger than among working-poor families. During the early 1970s, the inflation-adjusted incomes of most families at the 10th percentile of income, where only one in ten workers in the United States makes less, swung up and down by no more than 30 percent a year, accordingly to the volatility numbers I described in Chapter 3. In terms of impact on people and families, a 30 percent drop in income is huge. But by the mid-2000s, those annual fluctuations had jumped to more than 50 percent, an increase of two-thirds. By comparison, the incomes of most families in the middle of the economy, where half make more and half make less, used to swing up or down about 17 percent and now swing about 26 percent—also a substantial increase in volatility, though swings that are only half the size experienced by the poor. Those at the 90th percentile, where only one in ten makes more, used to swing up and down no more than about 16 percent; now those incomes swing 28 percent, again a substantial increase, and again only roughly half what is experienced by the poor. The greater the swings, the greater the chance a family gets caught in an income downdraft from which it has a terrible time recovering. What these numbers show is that families at every level except the very top have seen the stability of their income grow increasingly shaky and, with it, the stability of their economic lives. For the country's 20 million working-poor families—those making less than twice the official poverty level—the findings are particularly sobering. A family in the middle of this group now runs a substantial risk of seeing its income slashed by half in a given year—from about $24,000 to

$12,000. That is the difference between getting by and being left destitute. To actually advance is another matter altogether. "The only way to improve your life if you're poor today is to be very prudent and make very, very few mistakes like getting fired or splurging and ending up with a lot of debt," said Christopher Jencks, a Harvard University authority on poverty. "Most people aren't that prudent."

WHEN ELVIRA ROJAS headed for the United States, she was twenty-one years old and in search of two things that were hard to come by in her native El Salvador: peace and prosperity. Combatants in that country's bloody civil war engaged in firefights outside her family's home in Acajutla. Her husband had received death threats because of his role as a former military man. In addition, Rojas discovered that despite her high school degree from the Instituto Nacional, the only job she could get was at the local fish-packing plant. She and Maldonado arrived in Los Angeles in May 1989. She quickly found work cleaning houses with two of Maldonado's aunts. He landed a job at a Hawthorne dry-cleaning plant. Between them, they made about $200 a week. But with the average rent on a one-bedroom apartment in the city then running $650, they could not afford a place of their own to live. With nowhere else to turn, they moved in with one of Maldonado's aunts, sharing a two-bedroom house with her five children and four cousins. Rojas and her family slept on the kitchen floor. "I felt bad in the beginning because I had nothing," Rojas said. "I wanted to go home."

As the couple began to make a little more money, they rented a series of apartments. Each was slightly larger than the last, but still they shared a bedroom with relatives. During their first years, Rojas and Maldonado were effectively excluded from federal rent subsidies or state help because they were illegal immigrants. In 1991, the two gained legal status under a program that allowed people fleeing war in their homelands to be counted as refugees. But their new standing was thrown into question in 1994, when California voters approved Proposition 187. The initiative was designed to cut off state assistance to undocumented immigrants, but many legal immigrants in-

terpreted it as a blanket ban aimed at them, too. That's how Rojas interpreted it. She never applied for housing assistance—or almost any
other kind of aid—although it appears from her Social Security
records and tax returns that she would have qualified. "I didn't want
to be a burden on the government," she explained.

It's probably just as well she didn't come to count on such assistance. By the mid-1990s, the state and federal governments were
winding down a variety of programs aimed at helping the poor. One
was a seventy-year drive to help poor families meet their housing
needs. That effort had begun under President Franklin D. Roosevelt,
who decried the conditions gripping America during the Depression.
"I see one-third of a nation ill-housed, ill-clad, ill-nourished," he said
in 1937. In the years that followed, a booming private sector largely
solved the food and clothing problems. And a combination of financial market innovations and federal power applied through a battery
of agencies—the Veterans Administration, the Federal Housing Administration, Fannie Mae, and Freddie Mac—greatly expanded homeownership, especially among the middle class. But that still left poor
families with a housing problem; most could only afford to rent.

Washington's first answer was to have the government build and
run public housing projects. Some worked. Many turned into vertical
ghettos of economic and social segregation. Badly designed for raising
families, they became pockets of pathology, drugs, and crime. In 1974,
President Richard Nixon and Congress came up with a new approach,
the Section 8 program. Instead of putting up buildings itself, the
government would give subsidies to private developers to construct
housing. Then the government would give vouchers to poor families
to help them pay the rent in the new private housing. But developer
subsidies, though beneficial to many families, produced a rash of political scandals in the 1980s and were largely phased out. That left only
the vouchers, which have been cut back in recent years. All in all, federal spending on housing assistance has plunged by nearly two-thirds
in the past three decades, from an inflation-adjusted $85 billion in
1978 to $30 billion in 2007.

More recently, Washington's answer has been to offer tax breaks for the creation of low-income rental housing, but otherwise leave it to the marketplace to decide what gets built. In hot housing markets such as Southern California's, the result has been too little low-cost rental housing arriving too late to help very many people. "We've produced tens of thousands of units recently, but the well's been dry for so long we should have been producing hundreds of thousands," said Jan Breidenbach, executive director of the Southern California Association of Non-Profit Housing, which represents many of the region's low-income housing developers. In the absence of substantial government help, most of the working poor have been left with few good alternatives, especially in thriving urban areas.

Part of what convinced the government that it could retreat from helping to provide low-cost rental housing in recent years was the advent of subprime mortgages and the conviction—for a time—that the market would take care of the problem of sheltering working-poor families on its own by turning them from renters into home-owners. But the subprime dream has blown up on several million families in the form of huge rate increases and foreclosures. That has left working-poor families back at square one, trying to find places to live in overpriced markets.

By 1997, Rojas and Maldonado thought they had found a way out of their housing dilemma. He was making $4,000 a year at the dry-cleaning plant. She was making more than $6,000 dashing between a part-time job at Airline Linen Service in Hawthorne and a temp position with Kelly Services, putting magazines, perfume, and shampoo into those sample packages that direct-mail marketers send out. In the fall of 1997, the couple, together with another of Maldonado's aunts and her children, rented a white stucco bungalow not far from Los Angeles International Airport (LAX). Although the building sagged in the middle and had drainage problems, it featured two kitchens and two living rooms, plenty of space for each family. The house cost Rojas and Maldonado $550 a month. That was more than 30 percent of their earnings, a level the government considers the outer limit of affordability, but they thought they could manage it. The bungalow "felt good because there were not so many of us," Rojas said. "It was the most room I've ever had." That Christmas the two families celebrated by stringing sparkling lights along the structure's faded blue eaves and inviting neighbors to a party.

Politicians, pundits, and academic experts have devoted considerable time to delineating the cultural values and other characteristics of people like Rojas and Maldonado—qualities that are often said to set them apart from the other large bloc of working poor, African Americans. Although often poorly educated and lacking in job skills, these analysts argued, Latino immigrants are different in crucial ways: The immigrants, the analysts said, embrace many of the values and attitudes toward work, family, and personal responsibility of middle-class whites—ideas and values that are said to be less deeply rooted among poor blacks.

Political scientist Francis Fukuyama, in a 1993 paper titled "Immigrants and Family Values," wrote that "the evidence suggests that most Latin American immigrants may be a source of strength with regard to family values, and not a liability. . . . Many Latinos remain devout Catholics, and the rate of church attendance is higher in the Mexican community than for the U.S. as a whole as well." Moreover, Fukuyama said, although many illegal immigrants "are poor and unskilled, they have a work ethic and devotion to family comparable to those of the South and East European immigrants who came to the U.S. at the turn of the [twentieth] century." He suggested these qualities are less common among low-income, poorly educated blacks.

The idea that the influx of Latino immigrants into the ranks of the working poor brings with it a strengthening of traditional American values may be a comforting thought for some native-born citizens— or at least it was until the current outburst against the latest generation of immigrants. But the corollary notion that working poor African Americans are less dedicated to jobs and family is, at the very least, unproven. And the impact of these ideas on public policy can be pernicious: They suggest that—contrary to the claims of those who see poverty as a serious national problem—we don't have to worry too much about the working poor. At least not about the "deserving poor." Before too long, the argument goes, they will solve their own problems and vault up into the middle class, just as every previous wave of newcomers has.

Many of the people in poor black neighborhoods are working just as hard as those in immigrant areas, striving just as hard for—and treasuring every bit as much—whatever small slice of middle-class dreams they can obtain. Blacks and Latinos alike face problems of drug abuse, crime, gang violence, and insufficient educational achievement. And they are having just as hard a time coping with the increasingly tumultuous work lives that the economy has to offer them. Consider Albert Grimes.

GRIMES ARRIVED IN LOS ANGELES a few years before Elvira Rojas, similarly hungry to start over. He came from Cleveland, where his family was a pillar of the African American community. His father, "Big Joe" Grimes, had returned home from World War II and used the GI Bill to buy a house. He opened a barbershop, founded a youth marching band called B. J.'s Raiders, and became a power broker of sorts in Cleveland politics. Meanwhile, Albert Grimes's uncle, Walter Dicks, ran the Cleveland municipal workers union and helped the younger Grimes find a job right out of high school on a city sanitation truck. It paid about $15,000 a year, equal to almost $55,000 in 2007 dollars, and the most Grimes would make during the coming three decades.

Like the executives of the earlier chapters, Grimes got hit by a piece of history he had no control over. In his case, it was one of the fiscal crises that descended on many cities in the East and Midwest during the 1970s and 1980s. The crises had many causes: decaying industries, eroding tax bases, political gridlock, mismanagement, neglected infrastructure, white flight, and so forth. But whatever contributed to Cleveland's particular financial crisis, Albert Grimes was a consequence, not a cause. As Cleveland slashed its city payroll, he lost his job with the sanitation department. Like businesses knocked down by bad luck or bad decisions, cities can eventually get back on their feet, but workers often end up flattened by the crises. Grimes decided not to wait around to see if his municipal job would ever come back. In 1985, at the age of twenty-nine, he left home and headed west to California. At first, he had no trouble finding work with one of Los Angeles's big employers.

FOR MOST OF THE POSTWAR ERA, working Americans could count on big business, even more than big government, to provide safe-guards against economic risk. Unlike corporate America's current passion for temporary workers and outsourcing and lean workforces, business executives after World War II thought it was good business as well as good corporate citizenship to offer full-time jobs with good wages and solid benefits, even to those like Grimes with no college education. "Steady, year-round employment is so right from the standpoint of the employer, so right from the standpoint of the workers and so right for the country as a whole . . . that it is hard to see why we manufacturers have not made more progress in its appli-cation," Procter & Gamble president Richard R. Deupree told an au-dience in 1948.

As the decades passed, Los Angeles became the hub of the nation's aerospace industry, a second home—after Detroit—for U.S. au-tomakers, and a major financial center. The region's largest employers included Boeing, McDonnell Douglas, General Motors, Goodyear Tire & Rubber, First Interstate Bank, and Security Pacific Bank. By the late 1970s, the typical L.A. County workplace had nearly 30 percent more employees than the U.S. average, according to government sta-tistics. In other words, a large percentage of Southern California workers were employed by large corporations—a situation that trans-lated into good pay, good benefits, and a high level of economic secu-rity. "There is a close correlation between firm size, employment stability, and generous compensation," says UCLA economist Sanford

Jacoby, who has written extensively about the new risks that working people face. "Big firms underwrote the creation of America's—and Southern California's—blue-collar middle class."

The job-generating capacity of smaller businesses is often praised by politicians, who like to point out that more than 60 percent of all new jobs are created by firms employing no more than one hundred workers each. But there are at least two problems for workers in an economy of small-scale employers. First, small businesses tend to offer lower wages and meager benefits. Second, most small businesses don't last very long, creating a churning effect in the labor market. According to Census data, for example, even as some 588,000 small businesses came into existence in 2002 to 2003, 521,000 such businesses expired. Among the smallest enterprises tracked by the Census Bureau, those with twenty or fewer workers, only 37 percent stay in business for four years, and a mere 9 percent make it to the ten-year mark. Whatever such numbers may mean for the economy as a whole, they imply an unsettling level of unpredictability for workers—especially as small companies become a bigger and bigger factor in the nation's employment picture.

ALBERT GRIMES experienced these things firsthand. When he first arrived in Los Angeles, Grimes found his way to Sears, Roebuck and its massive warehouse at Olympic Boulevard and Soto Street, where he was hired as a merchandise handler represented by the Teamsters. He did well for himself there. His income rose steadily—from $12,500 in 1987 to $21,000 by 1990 (or nearly $34,000 in 2007 dollars). On top of that, his health care was covered. But in 1992, Sears stumbled, the result of a failed strategy to sell everything from socks to stocks. Grimes soon found himself out of work.

It was a particularly bad time to be jobless. The combination of recession and steep cuts in defense spending at the end of the Cold War walloped Southern California. Unremitting pressure from low-cost foreign producers and wage competition from new immigrants such as Rojas took a severe toll on unskilled workers like Grimes. And any chance that he would be rehired by Sears soon evaporated when the L.A. riots reduced part of the company's warehouse to rubble. The facility was shuttered.

By the time the region bounced back, the nature of employment had changed. Gone were many of the corporate giants that had delivered a generation of blue-collar security. In their place were tens of thousands of relatively small employers. Government figures show that the average size of a workplace has slipped by 18 percent nationally between its peak in the late 1970s and today. The slide was even steeper in L.A. County; the average size of a workplace plunged by more than 50 percent, to fewer than ten workers. This trend, according to Jacoby, "is one of the most important and least-appreciated reasons why so many people are having a tough time making a go of it today."

Certainly in Albert Grimes's case, the shift toward small-scale employers was not a positive development. For several years after losing his job at Sears, he all but vanished from the regular economy. He and his chronically ill girlfriend and the couple's young son lived off a mix of workers' compensation, disability payments, and her welfare checks. In 1995, he resurfaced as a security guard. And, in line with the U.S. economy's free-market transformation, he was now a self-employed entrepreneur. "I set myself up as a corporation," he said proudly.

With the help of a friend, Grimes persuaded a string of businesses in a run-down neighborhood along Bixel Street near the city's center to hire him. For three years, he watched over a dental office, a parking garage, a liquor store, and a methadone clinic. His earnings climbed from $5,600 when he launched his venture to more than $27,000 two years later. He bought himself a used Pontiac Grand Am, a washer and dryer, and leased a Rent-A-Center living room set. In a small way, he was a model of the new American. Then in 1998, he found out how risky the life of an entrepreneur can be: The city snapped up the properties along Bixel Street to make way for the Staples Center, a massive sports complex and convention facility of the kind that were springing up in urban centers across the country. The project hit Grimes like a meteor. The businesses that he had been employed to protect closed down. Demolition crews flattened the buildings they were in and, along with those buildings, Grimes's income. Tax records show his earnings that year went to zero.

AS GRIMES'S WORLD caved in on him once more, Rojas's prospects were looking up. She was still shuttling between the airline laundry service and her job packing samples when one of Maldonado's cousins told her that the dishwashing department at the Wyndham Hotel on Century Boulevard near LAX was hiring for the four-to-midnight shift. The position was full-time, paid more than $7 an hour, and, because the workers were represented by Hotel Employees and Restaurant Employees Local 814, it came with paid holidays and family health insurance. The latter would prove particularly important when Rojas suffered a miscarriage in 2001; her health plan picked up the tab for more than $5,000. Rojas saw the job as a turning point. Until then, virtually everything she had in her life had belonged to her in-laws. "If we used dishes," she remembered, "they were theirs. If we watched TV, it was theirs." All that would change when she went to the Wyndham. "I knew at that point I would have my own things," she said.

By 1998, Rojas and Maldonado had more than doubled their income, to $26,000 (more than $33,000 in today's dollars). The couple began assembling the pieces of a middle-class life. Rojas bought china by Royal Prestige. She purchased a Levitz Furniture hutch in which to display the dishes. She and Maldonado acquired a couch, a bed, and a dining table. They shelled out for two large-screen TVs and signed up for satellite-dish service. They bought a 1987 Plymouth Sundance to go with their aging blue Toyota Camry. And they traveled. "We would go to Las Vegas and Disneyland," Maldonado recalled. "We had more money to spend."

When the first of the couple's two daughters was born the following year, Rojas was so eager for her to be part of the fabric of America that she resisted entreaties to name her Maria after five of Maldonado's aunts, and instead gave her the name Katherine. She would make a similar choice when their second child was born in 2004, rejecting Maldonado's suggestion of Elvira in favor of Melanie. The new job let Rojas dream about owning a house, where, she said, "my daughters can have their own rooms" and "maybe one day I can take care of my grandchildren if I have some." Any thought of returning to Central America was gone. "Here," said Rojas, "my family will go a lot further than in El Salvador."

In the summer of 2000, the Wyndham's owners announced that they were closing the hotel for renovations. Rojas remembers hearing ominous rumblings that more would change than the color of the lobby, something about the parking attendants' jobs being contracted out. But she was not worried. To tide her over during the shutdown, Local 814 had steered her to a job at a unionized Burger King at LAX. The fast-food outlet offered a wage-and-benefit package almost as good as what she was making at the Wyndham.

About a year after it had closed, the hotel on Century Boulevard reopened. Only now, the sign outside read "Radisson." The Wyndham name wasn't the only thing that was gone. So was the union. That reflected a broader trend sweeping corporate America for more than two decades. Unions represented 17 percent of the nation's private-sector workforce in the early 1980s but counted less than 8 percent as members by 2007. Rojas could have her dishwashing job back, the new management told her. But instead of $8.89 an hour, her top wage at the Wyndham, she would be pulling down only $7.50 at the Radisson, with no family health insurance. She signed on anyway and, to make ends meet, kept her job at Burger King as well. It was hard running between two jobs again, but the family's income finally seemed to be stabilizing. As it turned out, their financial roller-coaster ride had only just begun.

For the poor, the most dramatic of all the safety-net cutbacks that the government has engineered in the past twenty-five years came in 1996. That's when a Republican-controlled Congress passed and a Democratic president, Bill Clinton, signed the Personal Responsibility and Work Opportunity Reconciliation Act, overhauling the nation's welfare system. The law sought to push people off the dole and into work. In doing so, it essentially reversed the poverty-fighting strategy that Washington had pursued since the 1960s, which promised poor Americans a certain minimal standard of living no matter whether they worked or not. By now, the 1996 law has reduced the nation's welfare rolls by more than 3 million families, or almost two-thirds, and has sliced inflation-adjusted cash welfare payments from more than $17 billion to about $5.5 billion. Those numbers are not in dispute—unlike just about everything else related to welfare reform.

Advocates hail the measure as a spectacular success, saying it has increased the incomes of many poor people, which, among other things, has caused a steep drop in poverty among black children. Others have denounced it as a failure, saying that more than a third of all welfare recipients still have trouble feeding their families and half are still poor—in many instances, poorer than they were before.

In Grimes's case, his family has remained largely unaffected by the law's "work first" requirements. That's because California has maintained relatively generous benefits and because Grimes's domestic partner, Jacqueline Harvey, has a chronic intestinal disease and is exempt from work requirements. She has thus continued to collect benefits off and on from the state's cash welfare program, CalWORKs. She now receives more than $600 a month. But Grimes himself has been staggered by another lesser-known element of the 1996 act—a significant toughening of child-support enforcement rules. This part of the law built on other efforts that began in the 1970s to go after absentee parents and compel them to help support their kids. Grimes and Harvey's son, Albert Jr., was born in 1988. Grimes was *not* an absent father, but nine years later, when he applied for custody of a nephew, the Los Angeles County district attorney's office sued him for child support for Albert Jr. The DA took action even though Grimes and Harvey had lived together since before their son's birth and, they and several relatives say, Grimes always helped raise Albert Jr.

Grimes declined to contest the suit. He says he thought he had to go along with the support order as a precondition of obtaining custody of his nephew and as a means of ensuring that Harvey would continue receiving publicly funded health care. There was also concern that establishing Grimes as a parent in the house, as could have happened if he'd fought the child-support case and won, might have jeopardized Harvey's eligibility for welfare. The law on all this is unclear, but there's nothing unclear about what happened when Grimes decided not to fight. The court entered a child-support judgment against him. And the effect on the Grimes household's finances has been devastating. California courts not only have imposed high monthly support payments in cases like this—often with little regard for a parent's ability to comply—but have also added interest charges at a 10 percent annual clip for past-due amounts.

Did the tougher policy help poor single mothers and their children? A 2004 study by the Urban Institute, a Washington think tank, found that past-due child-support payments in California have soared to almost $17 billion from $2.5 billion in the past decade. But most of the money charged against the fathers is earmarked for state coffers—not for the children who need support. "The system was largely about welfare-cost recovery, not helping families," said Curtis L. Child, who stepped down a few years ago as head of the state's Department of Child Support Services. That agency was created in 2000 to remove enforcement power from county district attorneys and restructure the system. "In imposing these huge judgments on fathers, we're confronting these men with an awful choice: go underground, which is just what child-support enforcement was intended to stop, or let themselves be financially ruined," Child said.

In August 1997, Grimes was ordered to start sending the county $173 a month in current payments, plus an additional amount for past-due support totaling $4,900. When he fell behind after his Bixel Street business collapsed in 1998, the past-due total began to swell. It now tops $10,000. And remember, Grimes is not a deadbeat dad.

IN ONE GREAT CLAP, the 9/11 terrorists brought down the Twin Towers in New York and shattered Americans' sense of security. Quietly and largely unnoticed, they also shoved many people such as Elvira

Rojas down the economic ladder. Immediately after the airline attacks on New York and Washington, police and other security agencies in Los Angeles imposed such tight restrictions on LAX that it
took Rojas five days to reach Burger King. When she finally made it
back to work, she found that her manager had cut her shift to just
four hours. Within a couple of weeks, she was laid off. Things were
little better at the nearly deserted Radisson. Rojas's hours there were
reduced to practically nothing.

Over the next fifteen months, Rojas grabbed whatever hours she
could at the hotel, and she began ironing clothes at Hermosa Clean-
ers in Hermosa Beach. It was a tough schedule even before she got
pregnant in 2002. And still it was not enough to keep her family's income from sliding almost 20 percent from its 1998 high to less than
$22,000. So she and Maldonado turned to what has become one of
the few reliable financial resources left for many financially belea-
guered Americans: their credit cards. In May 2002, Rojas was rushed
to the emergency room at Robert F. Kennedy Medical Center in
Hawthorne, where she suffered a second miscarriage. This time, with
only minimal health insurance from the hotel, she put $2,000 of her
$4,000 medical bill on her MasterCard. "I didn't have the money oth-
erwise," she said.

As THE CREDIT CARD INDUSTRY emerged in the late 1950s and '60s,
some expressed concern that even well-provisioned middle-class families would be unable to resist the lure of instant credit. Betty Furness,
President Lyndon Johnson's consumer affairs adviser, warned that
credit cards were "modern traps" that would turn Americans into
"hopeless addicts." But over the past twenty-five years, card issuers
have not let up in pushing their products. And they have reached out
for ever more low-income households. Federal Reserve figures show
that in the early and mid-1990s, families in the bottom fifth of the
economy nearly doubled their use of credit cards, and by 2004 nearly
one-third of families in this group were carrying median balances of
$1,000, about twice what they'd carried a decade earlier. The fraction

who were sixty days or more past due in payments had climbed from 10 percent to more than 15 percent and has risen sharply since. Political leaders and many analysts applaud the greater availability of credit. President George W. Bush has portrayed it as part of a "personal responsibility" crusade, a drive to give people more control over their own lives. Gregory Elliehausen, a finance expert then with the industry-sponsored Credit Research Center at Georgetown University, said that the spread of cards and other lending is part of a sweeping "democratization of finance" that has allowed poor families to operate more efficiently by, for example, buying decent cars to get to work. In the same vein, economists Dirk Krueger of the University of Pennsylvania and Fabrizio Perri, a University of Minnesota economist who has served on the staff of the Federal Reserve Bank of Minneapolis, say that families of all incomes can now increasingly rely on loans, rather than on business and government safety nets, in times of trouble. They borrow their way through the bad patches and pay down their debts in flush periods. The problem comes when there are no flush periods.

Some of the items purchased on Rojas's and Maldonado's credit cards can seem frivolous or extravagant—the TVs, for example, or the $150 set of sepia-toned studio photographs of Katherine and her mom dressed in feather boas and gowns. But most of the charges appear to fit the definition of safety-net spending. Beyond the emergency room charge, there was $130 for a new fuel pump for Rojas's Toyota and $170 to repair the power steering. There was $300 at the start of one month to cover rent and a $1,000 cash advance that Rojas said went to help a brother bring his wife to the United States from El Salvador.

IN THE SPRING OF 2000, two years after Grimes's Bixel Street business failed, he found a job as a security guard five blocks away at Ernst & Young Plaza. And for a while after the September 2001 terrorist attacks, the building's owners and tenants treated Grimes and his coworkers with newfound respect. Managers listened to his suggestions about how to improve safety at the forty-one-story structure. He was promoted to "lobby ambassador," a sort of informal emissary to the building's tenants and visitors, and then to lobby supervisor. His annual earnings climbed back above $20,000, and he began to imagine himself becoming a director of security. "My goal was to have a facility of my own," Grimes said. "I thought I should have a situation where I'm in control."

But for most of the past few years, Grimes has been anything but in control. In February 2004, after a dispute with their landlord, he and his family were evicted from their apartment on Fedora Street, where they had lived for a dozen years. All that he was able to save from the place were three mattresses, two chairs, and a Sony PlayStation. By April of that year, he had run through several thousand dollars paying for a $90-a-night motel room while he looked for a new apartment. He and Harvey eventually rented a two-room Hollywood walk-up for $875 a month, or more than 40 percent of their combined income. Before long, he again fell behind on his court-ordered child-support payments.

In July, things took another turn for the worse. After a series of clashes with his boss, Grimes was ordered out of the Ernst & Young tower and told he would be reassigned. Instead, he quit. In the three years since, he has worked for the Service Employees International Union on a campaign to organize security guards in the city's high-rise offices. What responsibility Grimes himself may have played in his problems on the old job is hard to assess. But even assuming he could have done more to get along with his bosses, it seems evident that the potential penalty for being a less than perfect employee can be extremely high in today's economy. And as Harvard's Christopher Jencks suggested, it's hard for most of us not to make at least some mistakes.

Still, like the model middle-class American he still hopes to be, Grimes is determined to recover from the latest round of reverses. He dreams about what his father had—a house, a secure job—and is convinced he'll fare as well someday. "I'm trying to get back to what he had," Grimes says.

A MONTH AFTER GRIMES was forced out of the Ernst & Young tower, Rojas and her family were evicted from the Burin Avenue bungalow where they had lived for seven years. A developer has razed the place and put in half-million-dollar townhouses. The family might not have been able to stay there much longer anyway. A week before they moved, Maldonado was laid off from the dry-cleaning plant to make way, he said, for new immigrants willing to work for less. He has since gotten a new job, packing items at a warehouse for minimum wage.

The family's new apartment is so small that the bedroom is a single mass of mattresses and cribs. The hutch and couches fill the living room to overflowing. And the cabinets in the kitchenette are so stuffed that Rojas must store her supply of infant formula in her car trunk. But the couple has plans—to turn around the slide in their income, to look for a house, to make sure that the girls continue all the way through school. "I don't want them to be struggling like us," Maldonado said.

Rojas is making other plans as well. Soon after arriving in the United States, she took out a loan to finance her future at the Inglewood Park Cemetery. She now owns two plots at the cemetery's Mausoleum of the Golden West, and recently signed papers to pay $82.79 a month for the next five years to buy two more. By the time Rojas is finished, she will have spent more than $20,000 in total. But she's convinced it's worth it. "Now if I die, I won't have to worry about my funeral," she said. "I won't leave my family with a financial burden." It is a concern that even the sternest advocates of "personal responsibility" may not have had in mind.

BY THE SPRING of 2008, the subprime mortgage discussed earlier in this chapter had caused America's financial markets to crack, threatening widespread trouble. Subprime mortgages are a classic example of an innovation that had the effect, if not the intention, of lifting risks and responsibilities from government, which once bore them, and placing them on individuals and families. They were designed to let mostly poor families buy their own homes. But their invention

relieved Washington of much of a job it had had since the Great Depression, that of helping many of these same families by providing
them with affordable—usually rental—housing.

In fact, subprime mortgages have helped millions of families into
homes they will keep. But the mortgages have also strapped more
than one million others with financial obligations they can not meet.
As these families began to default in growing numbers during the
summer of 2007, their failure to pay caused banks and investors to
take losses and raised doubts about an entire generation of financial
instruments that came of age with the subprime, complex bundles of
mortgages and other assets that somehow won triple-A credit ratings
and were supposed to be safe and sound. Market advocates argue
that the turmoil is simply part of the innovation process and will
eventually subside, leaving behind a new and useful tool. But from
the vantage point of early 2008, the doubts—and the dangers—to
the financial markets and the economy and to our home values, savings and jobs seemed to be growing larger and larger.

7

HOUSING

FOR THE GREAT MAJORITY OF AMERICANS, by far the most valuable single asset they will ever own is the house they live in. A house is also their biggest, most tangible, rock-bottom cushion against economic adversity. On average, 60 percent of the value of American homeowners' material possessions—60 percent of *everything* they own—is accounted for by the value of their primary homes. For the least wealthy half of homeowners, that number is 75 percent. As these figures make clear, Americans may be the world's most insatiable consumers, but the value of all those Infiniti FX SUVs and Sony Bravia flat-screen TVs pales compared with houses when it comes to significant economic assets. In all but a relative handful of families, so do the stock portfolios, certificates of deposit, and 401(k)s that are taken as evidence of our new financial sophistication. Indeed, the sheer size of houses on the landscape of families' finances illustrates a largely unnoticed fact about Americans: that for all the talk about the democratization of the stock market and the emergence of a new investor class, the economics of most American families remain pretty much what they have been for generations. The biggest "piece of the rock" most of us will ever have is the place where we go to sleep at night.

Housing has grown all the more important because of big changes during the past two to three decades in what constitutes an American home and who gets to own one. Today's houses bear little resemblance to the simple boxes of post–World War II Levittown. The average new house is now 1,000 square feet bigger than that of a quarter century ago. Many of these larger houses are the product of a building boom that covered the landscape with suburban villas and made granite countertops as ubiquitous today as Formica was in our parents' time. Especially along the East and West coasts, hot real estate markets have contributed to a gilding of the American home. But even though we may deride some of the structures as "McMansions," they are not the New World equivalent of the stately homes of England or the châteaus of France. All but the most out-sized are the residences of more or less middle-class families, not the landmark domiciles of the truly rich. And to the extent that homes have grown, their role at the center of families' finances has expanded, not contracted.

In tandem with the physical growth of homes has been an expansion in the economic range of homeowners. That's because the financial industry invented new ways to make mortgage loans to millions of lower-income people whom lenders had previously avoided. Some lenders covered the greater risk of default by charging higher interest rates; many enticed borrowers with low initial monthly payments that ballooned over time or with adjustable interest rates that also started low but were subject to market fluctuations. These so-called subprime loans (the term refers to the lower credit-worthiness of the borrowers, not to the interest rates) are the reason that, since the early 1990s, the fraction of Americans who own their own homes has increased to nearly 70 percent—up from 65 percent, where it had remained stuck for the previous thirty-five years. An increase of 5 percentage points may not seem all that large, but it represents a jump of almost 12 million homeowners. For more than a decade, that expansion in homeownership was the poster child of the American Dream, cited by both President George W. Bush and President Bill Clinton as proof that the economy was not simply expanding but spreading its benefits to more and more people. Since the implosion of the subprime mortgage market in 2007 and the tremors that it has sent through the nation's financial system, those benefits seem nowhere near as clear. But the importance of housing—to the economy and to individuals' economic circumstances—could not be more apparent.

What has made homeownership so critical to family security is not just the sheer dollar value involved, important as that is. Our houses have been—and, to a substantial degree, still are—immense forced savings machines that compel us to accumulate assets against a rainy day. Homeowners set aside a substantial part of their income each month to make mortgage payments. For the most part, these "investments" are left untouched for decades while they quietly appreciate in value. A few people might dream about the cars they could buy or the trips they could take if they could lay their hands on the increasing value of their homes. But at least until recently, that was mostly just daydreaming, and for most Americans it still is. Unless they are ready to move or face a serious cost such as a tuition bill or a gargantuan crisis such as death or divorce, only a minority of people actually tap into the value of their houses. Indeed, only a minority draws money out of their houses even after they've grown old, despite the fact that most financial experts think that this is precisely what old people should do.

Given the tremendous importance of homeownership for American families and the amount of attention people lavish on their houses—fixing and improving existing homes is almost as big a business as building new ones—you might think that any significant change in the security of those houses would be big news. But it hasn't been. Instead, quietly over the past twenty-five years and especially over the past fifteen years, much of the protective padding that houses historically offered has worn thin, leaving many people bearing more, not less, financial risk without realizing it.

Paradoxically, one cause of this erosion has been the refinancing revolution. Until recently, refinancing is widely considered a modern marvel and a boon for homeowners. In many ways it was. By enabling homeowners to rewrite their mortgages with comparative ease, it allowed people to chase interest rates down during the long period in which they were falling. That in turn enabled families to safely afford bigger houses or enjoy smaller monthly mortgage payments. And it provided people with the ability to take protective steps by borrowing against their houses to tide themselves over in bad times or to handle truly big expenses. But along with these benefits has come a protection-eroding side effect: The refinancing revolution has given people the ability to act out that old daydream, to break into their nest eggs and use the money to shop—to buy things that may add to the immediate quality of their lives but provide little of long-term value. By being able to refinance for a larger amount than you owed on your house based on the increased market value of the structure, you were able to get ahold of a portion of that increased value right away, rather than saving it or waiting until you sold the house. According to one recent estimate by former Federal Reserve chairman Alan Greenspan and a colleague, somewhere between seven cents and twenty cents of every dollar of ownership value pulled from American homes through refinancing between 1990 and 2005 went to consumption. That meant it was no longer available to serve as protective padding.

But there is another and much bigger reason that houses may not provide their owners with the kind of bulwark against economic misfortune that the houses once did: radical changes in something most homeowners give only passing thought to—their homeowners' insurance. With almost no fanfare, the $600-plus-billion-a-year property casualty insurance industry has launched a series of revolutionary changes that appear to be reducing the risks that insurers bear and increasing the dangers that millions of homeowners must shoulder. Behind a screen of almost indecipherable technical language and fine print, insurance companies have made profound changes in the policies most of us rely on. The companies have also deployed an arsenal of sophisticated new techniques for pinpointing risk and avoiding it, which translates into higher premiums or no insurance at all for many of those the companies decide might make expensive claims. Proponents of the property insurance revolution insist that the changes are making things better, but the weight of the evidence thus far suggests that the opposite is true—at least for policyholders. In many cases, the protection they've bought and paid for is not what it once was, or what many think it still is. As a result, homeownership has become a powerful example of the way families' lives have been growing simultaneously more prosperous and more precarious with barely a trace to let people know what is happening.

THE MODERN REMAKING of homeowners' insurance began on a bone-dry Saturday in October 1991, when a group of construction workers reportedly tried to burn some building debris in the Oakland Hills section of Northern California. In the process, they incinerated several acres before the Oakland Fire Department knocked down the blaze. Just to be on the safe side, the fire crew left its hoses in place overnight. Two hills over, the Scott-Ferguson family—Peter, an architect; his CFO wife, Teresa; the couple's two daughters, then six and thirteen years old; and Peter's invalid mother, Frances Gray Scott—knew nothing about the event. Neither did most of their neighbors.

Sometime around nine o'clock the next morning, firefighters returned to collect their hoses, according to a subsequent grand jury report. When some of them kicked up the "duff"—the thick mantle of ash and charred wood left behind by a wildfire—sparks flew up and ignited a tree. Meantime, Peter and Teresa Scott-Ferguson had embarked on a day trip to watch an auto race in Monterey; one of their daughters had gone with them, while the other stayed with friends. The elderly Mrs. Scott remained at home, where her caregiver helped her dress and eat breakfast. Then, as she did every Sunday, the caregiver drove out of the hills and down to church. She had no idea that, as she was leaving, the new blaze in the Oakland Hills had roared out of control. The first house caught fire at 10:58 AM, according to the grand jury report. Within an hour, nine hundred houses had burned to the ground. The Oakland Hills fire, as it came to be known, would ultimately claim twenty-five lives, among them that of Mrs. Scott.

For the families involved, the fire was a personal tragedy. Both survivors and Oakland's emergency service agencies have analyzed the episode over and over again, trying to figure out how things could have gone so wrong. They have never come to a final conclusion. There is no such ambiguity, however, about another facet of the Oakland Hills fire: the lesson it taught the Scott-Fergusons about how far America has gone toward shifting the risks and burdens of misfortune onto individuals and families—and in the process reducing the degree of economic protection offered by homeownership. The focal point of the lesson was their house insurance.

The cutbacks in homeowners' insurance started simply enough. Insurers became worried about their own costs and began making adjustments in the policies they sold. They sought to control what they paid out in claims by reducing some of the protections they provided homeowners. By now, the effort has gone high-tech in a fashion that some regulators, economists, and consumer advocates say expands the possibilities for adjustment almost limitlessly, a development that could leave many policyholders paying steep new rates, unable to find coverage at any cost, or strapped with policies that leave them uncovered in crucial ways.

The makeover began with the nation's last major run-in with natural disaster prior to Hurricane Katrina—a string of catastrophes that included the Oakland Hills firestorm and a couple of earthquakes, all in California, as well as Hurricane Andrew in Florida in 1992. Taken together, these disasters destroyed tens of thousands of homes, displaced hundreds of thousands of people, and, among other things, drove eleven Florida insurance companies into bankruptcy. The surviving insurers in Florida and other companies nationwide responded by seeking state help and by beginning to change the terms of homeowners' policies to narrow what companies would cover. They successfully lobbied state regulators, for example, to lift the government requirement that they provide individual coverage for the wind and quake dangers that had just cost the firms so dearly. Responsibility for these losses was shifted to a set of state-created agencies that are by now either financially overwhelmed or charge so much for coverage that the number of people buying the protection has plunged. In addition, private insurers began rewriting the terms of their policies to restrict what they covered and to shift onto policyholders the burden of ensuring that the coverage is adequate. Industry executives portray the changes that were made as onetime affairs, intended to rein in overbroad interpretations of the companies' responsibilities. "Insurers think of what they're doing as bringing policies back to what they thought they were selling in the first place," said Rade T. Musulin, a prominent official with the American Academy of Actuaries, an industry professional organization, and a former vice president with Florida Farm Bureau Insurance Companies. Regulators just as adamantly assert that insurers have been substantially shrinking the coverage they offer, and they worry where the process will end. "Insurers are taking on a helluva lot less risk than they used to," said former California insurance commissioner John Garamendi, now the state's lieutenant governor.

In fact, when the country encountered the next run of big disasters that culminated in hurricanes Katrina and Rita in 2005, insurers again demanded that states—and this time, Washington as well—come to their rescue. The companies slapped new restrictions on what their policies covered. And big firms, such as Allstate, the nation's second-largest property casualty company, canceled all or parts of more than 1 million policies from New York to Washington state; the company announced it would sell no new policies in parts or all of every coastal state from Maine to Texas, plus California. Most companies also jacked up the premiums they charged policyholders in areas prone to hurricanes and earthquakes. In some cases, premiums jumped as much as 100 percent, although when 2006 and 2007 brought no major storms, those rates dropped back down, at least for the time being. The combination of policy restrictions in the wake of the disasters in the late 1980s and early 1990s and the post-Katrina coverage cutbacks and cancellations has paid off handsomely for insurers. Despite Katrina and a string of other big storms in 2005, industry profits that year hit a record $45 billion. And with no major storms the following year, profits climbed to more than $64 billion. Experts predict that 2007 will turn out to have been yet another stellar year for industry profits.

The policy cutbacks are now being supplemented by new high-tech methods of assessing prospective customers that could have vastly greater, and in many cases more dire, effects on policyholders and indeed on the basic concept of insurance. The property casualty industry is in the midst of a technological arms race. It is embracing a new generation of powerful computer techniques to learn everything it possibly can about you—or at least people very much like you. The industry is collecting data on individuals' health, houses, cars, and personal habits. Industry leaders assert that the aim is to allow insurers to better understand the risks they bear and thus protect themselves, but also to fine-tune the coverage they can offer customers. "Because of the adoption of these techniques, policyholders can choose from an increasingly wide array of coverage at different price points, and companies can better manage the risks they bear and therefore assure customers that they will be around if people need them to pay claims," said Robert P. Hartwig, president and chief economist of the industry-backed Insurance Information Institute.

Yet the industry's growing use of computer-aided techniques to microanalyze its customers is also beginning to produce side effects that seem to undermine the very nature of insurance itself. New catastrophe-modeling techniques are helping insurers pick precisely where they think disasters such as hurricanes, wildfires, and terror attacks are most likely to occur. New "data-mining" methods are giving companies the power to use a person's income, education, ZIP code, and other personal information to predict the likelihood of that person filing future claims. Armed with such data, companies can raise rates or avoid providing coverage altogether, leaving it to state-created insurers of last resort—or to homeowners themselves—to deal with the dangers. The techniques have had the effect of squeezing those who most need insurance—those, for example, at higher-than-average risk of encountering a problem, those with low and moderate incomes, or those who've suffered job setbacks. In the process, the companies may be cutting at the very heart of how insurance works.

It may seem counterintuitive, but what gives insurance its unique ability to protect people is precisely its imprecision. It begins with pooling together large numbers of policyholders, all of whom pay moderate premiums in exchange for protection. Since the vast majority don't suffer catastrophe in any given period of time, the combined premiums are more than adequate to take care of the small minority who do run into trouble. Only if the risks and costs are spread out in this way does the system work—at least for policyholders. Companies have always distinguished certain types of people—such as smokers or bad drivers, who run particularly high risks—and have charged those customers more or refused coverage. But such distinctions have been few in number and narrow in scope; they did not prevent the assembling of big pools of policyholders. As the industry refines its computerized techniques, however, and expands its ability to "slice and dice" customers and applicants, Texas insurance commissioner Mike Geeslin—among others—worries that "the risk-transfer mechanism at the heart of insurance could break down." If that happens, Geeslin warns, "insurance will stop functioning as insurance."

For the Scott-Fergusons and others struck by the Oakland Hills fire, several months would elapse before they bumped up against seemingly esoteric subjects like this. First came the tragedy.

BY THE TIME the elderly Mrs. Scott's caretaker reached church and looked back to see the conflagration, police had blocked off the roads into the hills. She began pleading with officers to send someone to save Mrs. Scott. The Scott-Fergusons' thirteen-year-old, Ginny, and Peter's sister, Jane, began calling 911, making the same plea. Ginny subsequently tracked down the portion of the 911 tape on which her voice can be heard offering to provide the home address, only to be told that that wouldn't be necessary. Ginny and Jane also called Mrs. Scott and told her to get into the shower in hopes that it might provide her some protection. They were still talking with the elderly woman at 1:30 PM, more than two hours after the blaze roared out of control. Over the course of that time, police and fire officials dispatched four teams to retrieve the woman. The first two got lost. A third reached the house, looked in the windows, and, seeing no sign of Mrs. Scott, who had taken refuge in the shower, left. By the time the fourth team arrived, the house was engulfed in flames. Days later, the family found Mrs. Scott's whitened skeleton in the ruins.

Peter Scott and Teresa Ferguson made two decisions in the wake of the disaster. The first was not to sue the City of Oakland for its bungled performance, but instead to put their energies into demanding changes to protect against a repetition of the catastrophe. The second was to collect on their insurance and rebuild. "I was going to stand on my [new] roof and scream, 'You're not going to drive me out of here,'" Scott remembers thinking at the time.

Together with their neighbors, the couple got some fast action from the city. Within months, they'd helped force out the old fire chief and won passage of a bond issue for a new firehouse and equipment to fight wildfires. Within eighteen months, they'd gotten the city to set up a network of warning sirens. Fire hydrants were made compatible with those of surrounding communities. And the old radio system was modernized; at the time of the fire, it was so inadequate that thirty-five fire companies, several neighboring fire departments, and the police shared just two frequencies.

Matters went quite differently when it came to the Scott-Fergusons' plan to rebuild their house. The problem was with their insurance. At issue was whether the insurer—and the insurers of thousands of others in the fire—had agreed to replace the houses and their contents whatever the cost or whether instead they were obligated to pay only up to a certain dollar limit.

In the early 1990s, when the Oakland Hills fire occurred, the standard policy for the vast majority of homeowners in California and much of the rest of the country was a so-called guaranteed replacement-cost policy. Industry executives said that the phrase "guaranteed replacement cost" was really intended as a marketing gimmick, that these policies also included a dollar limit, and that the firms had never intended to cover more than this amount. Homeowners and government regulators, on the other hand, took "guaranteed replacement" to mean just that—the insurer would replace a destroyed house no matter what the cost to the firm.

Peter Scott and Teresa Ferguson assumed they had a guaranteed replacement-cost policy at least in part because of a series of telephone conversations they happened to have had with their insurance agent in the months immediately prior the fire. When a colleague of Ferguson's complained that she'd had trouble collecting on an unrelated homeowners' claim, Ferguson made her husband dig out the couple's policy and call their agent, Donald Tindell. "Did he say we were covered?" she remembered asking Scott after his conversation with Tindell.

"I guess I didn't ask it quite that way," Scott replied.

"Well, call him back," Ferguson insisted.

The couple said they were told they were fully covered. To make sure there was no confusion about what that meant, they put together a thirteen-page list of everything from their kitchen plates to the grand piano, plus a full description of the structure, which Scott had designed, and sent it off to the agent. But when the Scott-Fergusons called the agent the night of the fire and mentioned what a lucky thing it was that they'd sent him the list, the reply came back, "What list?" And when Scott showed up at the agent's office unannounced and demanded to see his file, it included no list. Efforts to track down Tindell or the now largely defunct Baltimore-based USF&G proved unsuccessful.

Without an assurance of full coverage but nonetheless determined to rebuild, the couple turned their finances upside down. Before the fire, they had paid off almost their entire old mortgage and were debt-free. After the fire, they began borrowing like fiends. They each pulled $50,000 out of their 401(k)s. When they learned they were eligible for a low-cost mortgage through the Federal Emergency Management Agency, they borrowed another $100,000. When Ferguson heard that Wells Fargo was offering fire survivors ninety-day interest-free loans, she snapped up still more cash. Meanwhile, Scott designed the replacement house to be built in stages that stayed tightly within the budget they had. The building was well on its way to completion before USF&G came through with any money.

Saying they'd received no detailed list of items to be covered, the insurer offered the dollar limit of the policy, but not a penny more. However, when Ferguson discovered that she'd deposited a copy of the list with the couple's lawyer and that the package included a cover sheet that showed when it was sent to the insurance agent, the firm quickly settled for about $400,000, or about 25 percent more than the policy limits. By the Scott-Fergusons' reckoning, that still left them $150,000 short of the cost of rebuilding. The combination of the shortfall, their new mortgage, and their children's educations has kept the couple working well beyond the customary retirement age. At seventy-four, Scott would like to slow down. "Maybe in three to five years," he mused a couple of years ago.

Besides the twenty-five dead, the final tally on the Oakland Hills firestorm was 3,354 homes destroyed and $1.7 billion in insurance claims paid. In the years that followed, insurers sought to avoid getting caught in such a costly and contentious mess again. They began phasing out "guaranteed replacement cost" policies and replacing them with a type of policy that shifted responsibility for ensuring adequate coverage from insurers to policyholders. But the way they did so left many homeowners either unaware of the change or baffled by its implications.

The confusion started with the simple choice of a name for the new type of coverage: "extended replacement cost." Those policyholders who noticed the language change were left to guess that the switch from "guaranteed" to "extended" meant they were getting less, not more, coverage. But even noticing the change was a challenge. That's because unlike most business insurers, who change policy terms by canceling the old contracts and requiring the two sides to sign new ones, most residential insurers simply mail out notices that policies are changing. Insurers defend the practice, saying that the notices are explicit and are approved by state regulators. But many notices seem almost purposely designed to leave policyholders confused about what's at stake in the change.

Finally, and perhaps most mysteriously, there was the matter of how it was to be decided what would constitute adequate coverage under the new "extended" policies. Insurers no longer guaranteed to replace a destroyed home no matter what the cost to them. Instead, the firms promised to pay only up to a certain stated dollar amount, plus, typically, an extra 20 to 25 percent. But what should that dollar amount be in order to get replacement-level protection, and who should pick it? Unless they happen to be contractors, almost no one knows what it would cost to replace a home—the cost of building materials, the expense of meeting new building-code requirements, or what local contractors charge. By contrast, insurers know a great deal about these costs and, since the mid-1990s, have had the added advantage of increasingly sophisticated software programs to help them estimate the figure to within a few hundred dollars for almost any house in the country.

After Oakland Hills, insurance companies would only use this wealth of information to suggest dollar amounts to which policy-holders should insure. Fearful of getting locked into the same legal responsibility for full replacement that they'd borne under the old "guaranteed" policies, companies left the final decision up to home-owners. In theory, this shouldn't have caused much of a problem. After all, isn't it in the interest of insurance companies to suggest large dollar amounts so as to collect large premiums? The answer may be yes in theory, but things don't seem to have turned out that way. It appears that many insurers lowball their estimates, perhaps out of concern for losing customers to competitors or because they want to avoid high-dollar claims. Whatever the reason, the net result is that millions of homeowners are running greater risks of loss than they think they are, and greater risks than they used to bear under their old "guaranteed replacement cost" policies. By one reputable estimate, almost 60 percent of Americans do not have enough insur-ance under their "extended" policies to replace their homes, and the shortfall may be as much as one dollar out of every five needed to do the job.

If you think it's implausible that insurers would lowball estimates and forgo premiums that they otherwise could collect, try this exper-iment: Get a contractor to give you a rough estimate of what it would cost to rebuild your house. Or use a computer estimating site like AccuCoverage.com (http://www.accucoverage.com) to get a rough figure. Then call your insurance agent. First, find out what your "Coverage A" is. This is the amount allotted to replace the structure of your house, not the contents or any ancillary items. Compare it to the estimate. Odds are the amount is below the estimate to rebuild your house. Then tell the agent that you're considering raising the amount of your Coverage A. Odds are you'll get an argument.

The accumulated miscommunications and misunderstandings about insurance that had developed in the years since the Oakland Hills fire became painfully apparent in late October 2003, when a lost hunter set off a flare in the tinderbox of the Cleveland National Forest northeast of San Diego, sealing the fate of 16 people and reducing 422 square miles of land and thousands of homes to cinder. Many of those homes were in the San Diego neighborhood of Scripps Ranch.

Terry and Julie Tunnell and their son Brian were at a Cub Scout campout with fifty other Scripps Ranch families when a park ranger woke them on Sunday, October 26, to say there was a fire elsewhere in the forest and they would have to evacuate. A Santa Ana wind had been blowing since the previous night, luffing the tent and giving Julie bad dreams. But the evacuation order produced no sense of panic. The ranger said the fire was far from the camp. Since the camp was more than a half hour's drive from their homes, it also seemed to be far from their community.

Erik and Judy Strahm were at home in Scripps Ranch reading the Sunday papers. With Judy seven months pregnant with the couple's first child, Juliana, there was not much else the couple could do. Erik decided to take a shower.

Bill and Karen Reimus were on a three-day getaway to Laguna Beach. Bill's parents were spending the weekend at the Reimuses' home, looking after the couple's son and daughter, then two and seven.

What happened next remains a mystery. Fire officials point to the winds and dry conditions and to the fact that much of their fire-fighting force had been sent north to fires around Los Angeles and so was not immediately available to respond to the local threat. But in the end they concede they don't understand how the flames from the hunter's flare could have traveled from his remote location to the very edge of San Diego so quickly. "The fire spread three times faster than anything we'd ever seen before," Cleveland National Forest fire chief Rich Hawkins said. "As fire professionals, we were in awe of this fire."

Julie Tunnell realized something was wrong when her family drove out of the mountains and onto Interstate 8; she used her cell phone to call a neighbor, who reported a commotion in the street, with people yelling and cars racing away. Julie remembers screaming at the woman to grab her preschool son and get out. When Erik Strahm emerged from the shower and heard his wife crying, he thought she was having another panic attack about the pregnancy— until he looked out the bathroom window to see a seventy-five-foot-high wall of flame rushing over the hills toward them. The Reimuses first heard of the firestorm in a tearful call as their in-laws and children, all still in their pajamas, barreled out of the subdivision.

Of the three families, only the Strahms returned to find anything left standing. Some 2,800 families found their houses burned to the ground, among them 45 of the 46 houses on Pinecastle Street, where the Tunnells and the Reimuses lived. Everyone turned to their insurance agents, and within days a pattern began to emerge.

When the Tunnells purchased their one-story 1,738-square-foot house in 1992, they had been extremely conservative. They'd bought small. They'd taken out a $220,000 fifteen-year mortgage so they would have it paid off by the time they were in their fifties and faced college tuition for Brian. They had kept their monthly payment low enough that they could cover it with Terry's salary alone. And they had purchased a "guaranteed replacement cost" insurance policy from State Farm, the nation's largest residential insurer. "We're pretty cautious people," said Julie. "There was a certain security to having a really small house and a really small mortgage and knowing everything was insured by America's most trusted insurance company."

But when the State Farm adjuster arrived at their destroyed home, he had bad news. Without their knowledge, the Tunnells say, the policy had been converted to an "extended" replacement-cost policy six years earlier, and the dollar limit on the "extended" policy was about $300,000 short of what they would need to pay off their old mortgage, rebuild their house, and replace its contents. That such a major change in policy could have slipped by the couple is surprising. Terry, forty-seven, is the chief financial officer of a San Diego company. Julie, forty-one, is an accounting professor at San Diego City College. They are trained in keeping tabs on matters such as insurance. With the couple's permission, State Farm provided a copy of the notice that it said it sent the Tunnells at the time of the switch. The document does carry a headline in red ink that reads, "IMPORTANT NOTICE about changes to your policy," and includes a section that says, "REDUCTIONS OR ELIMINATIONS OF COVERAGE. Guaranteed Extra Coverage. Guaranteed Replacement Cost Coverage."

The problem is that the four-page document points in so many different directions that it could leave anybody, even people with business training like the Tunnells, baffled. The document includes such statements as, "In an effort to provide protection for policyholders at an affordable price, we periodically make changes to your policy. Some of these changes broaden or add coverage. Some reduce or eliminate coverage." Besides listing reduction or elimination of guaranteed replacement-cost coverage, the notice also lists reductions for, among other things, "trading cards and comic books," "one or more volcanic eruptions," "wood fences," and "tsunami." It also includes a section headlined "BROADENINGS OR ADDITIONS OF COVERAGE" that expands coverage for items such as "stamps," which it seemed to have limited only the page before. And the document ends with this sentence: "This message does not change, modify or invalidate any of the provisions, terms or conditions of your policy." Asked why the company would clutter such an important announcement with so many mixed messages and comparatively minor details, State Farm spokesman Dick Luedke said that he believed the company had done a good job at notifying the Tunnells and that the firm regularly includes a variety of items in a single notice.

Despite repeated appeals, the Tunnells ultimately were able to collect only the dollar limits on the policy—about $220,000 for the house and roughly another $150,000 for contents and debris removal. That was enough to pay off their old mortgage and replace their belongings. But where was the money to rebuild?

In the case of the Strahms and the Reimuses, the problem wasn't guaranteed replacement but underinsurance. The Strahms had purchased their 2,100-square-foot house for $465,000 about two and a half years before the fire. Erik said the family's State Farm agent suggested insuring the structure for $200,000. When Erik objected that the amount was too low, the agent, according to Strahm, explained that the real value of the property was in the land. When Erik persisted, the agent agreed to raise the coverage to $250,000, plus about $50,000 for contents. However, in the wake of the fire, Strahm said that State Farm's own adjuster estimated that it would cost $407,000 to replace the damaged house and at least another $50,000 to cover the contents, leaving the couple more than $150,000 in the hole. Strahm accepted the company's $300,000 claims payment and promptly sued for the rest.

The Reimuses bought their $619,000 house just four months before the fire, so there could be little doubt about the value of the property or the fact that construction prices had been rising dramatically. According to Karen, when the couple purchased the house, they asked Liberty Mutual Insurance Company to sell them enough coverage that they could rebuild if the house was ever destroyed. In a demonstration of how serious the couple was about being ready in case of disaster, they also bought earthquake insurance, something only about one in ten Californians does. The Liberty Mutual agent recommended $225,000 in coverage on the house, or $100 per square foot of structure coverage. Only in the aftermath of the fire did the Reimuses discover that the going rate for reconstruction was between $150 and $175 per square foot. "I asked for a replacement-cost policy. It never even dawned on me to ask, 'Is this amount enough?'" said Karen. She is a commercial contract litigator, and Bill is general counsel for TaylorMade Golf, so they could negotiate a settlement with the insurer from a position of strength; the high cost of hiring lawyers and persisting in what are almost always protracted disputes deter many would-be claimants from challenging their insurance companies. Although they are prohibited by the terms of the settlement from giving the exact dollar amount, Karen said the couple's policy limits were "adjusted," presumably upward. She added, "It shouldn't take two lawyers to be able to reach an amicable resolution of a claim with your insurance company." Most families in America do not come equipped with two lawyers in case of trouble.

REWRITING INSURANCE POLICIES is a crude means for changing what insurers will cover. And as the outcries and lawsuits demonstrate, it has also turned out to be a recipe for repeated public relations fiascoes for the companies. But this method of altering the relationship between insurers and homeowners is quickly being supplanted by much more sophisticated techniques, the operation of which can be harder to spot and the effects of which can be more difficult to understand in advance. These new techniques may look like little more than sensible modernizing on the part of a traditionally hidebound industry. Insurers are applying the power of computers and mathematical techniques to learn more about their customers and the risks the firms have accepted in selling a particular policy. But the techniques are also dramatically changing the entire industry— and not just homeowner policies, but also health, disability, auto, and almost every other kind of insurance. In the process, they appear to be substantially reducing how much protection many people get when they buy a policy. To understand why this is so requires a brief excursion into how insurance has worked to date and how the new techniques are rearranging the industry's operations.

Traditionally, company actuaries have determined how often in the past bad events such as illnesses, accidents, or house fires have befallen members of a given risk pool and how costly those occurrences have been. Insurers have set their premiums based on these frequency and loss histories. One of the key characteristics of this approach is that it gives insurers an incentive to group together substantial numbers of people. That's because actuaries' frequency and loss numbers are more accurate when the pools are substantial in size. But the question has always hung in the air: What if insurers could know more in advance? What if they could outflank their actuaries, who rely on history and numbers, by finding ways to predict who's more likely to be hit with a setback in the future? What if they could charge those customers higher rates or, better yet, avoid those customers altogether? Wouldn't that boost profits, making shareholders and executives happy, and ensure that insurers had plenty of cash on hand to pay the smaller claims of the safer customers they do cover?

It is precisely this kind of advance knowledge that developers of the new computer techniques are promising to deliver on everything from fender-benders and fires to hurricanes and medical conditions. "We think we offer an alternative to actuarial science, which is fundamentally backward-looking," said an executive with Hemant Shah's Risk Management Solutions, Inc. (RMS), one of the most prominent of the new computer companies serving the insurance industry. "We provide insurers with ways to use science and engineering to make forward-looking predictions."

HEMANT SHAH is in the business of creating catastrophes. The computers at his Silicon Valley–based RMS contain mathematical models of every U.S. disaster from an earthquake that toppled chimneys in St. Louis in 1812 to the 9/11 assault that brought down the Twin Towers in New York. The computers also contain 100,000 synthesized "extreme events." RMS runs its disasters through your community—and sometimes right through your house—to see how you and your neighbors would fare in a hurricane, hailstorm, earthquake, epidemic, or terrorist attack. The firm sells its knowledge to insurance companies to help them decide whom to cover and how much to charge. Since Katrina, those decisions have been running pretty much in one direction. Many companies took one look at their 2005 losses and at RMS's predictions of still more to come, and bolted. Allstate, for instance, has gotten out of whole lines of coverage and announced it will exit big but problematic markets such as California. Other companies have spent two years dropping or paring back policies from Oregon to New York. Although initial predictions of widespread rate hikes have thus far proved unfounded, that is largely because of unexpectedly quiet 2006 and 2007 hurricane seasons. Most experts say that the combination of a new catastrophe and detailed studies by RMS and others showing that the dangers of disaster are far greater than previously thought could leave substantial parts of the country either uncovered or paying sharply higher premiums. "Between hurricanes along the East and Gulf coasts and earthquakes along the West Coast, it is an open question whether the private insurance industry will continue to insure the coastline at all," said University of Pennsylvania economist Howard Kunreuther, one of the country's foremost authorities on disaster.

Shah, forty, hardly set out to cause a revolution in insurance. He and a friend were simply trying to ace a business-school course at Stanford University in the late 1980s when they came up with the idea for the firm. During its early days, the company had only the simplest of techniques to offer its clients. At that point, for instance, when insurers—responding to a pair of moderately severe earthquakes in California—hired the firm to estimate how much risk the companies had taken on, RMS could do little more than map out where the companies had sold policies to see whether they had overconcentrated in one area or another. The young company's software then measured the distance between the properties and earthquake fault lines to find out how close to danger zones the insurers were covering. Today, with more than 1,000 employees and annual revenues reportedly reaching $200 million, the company provides far more elaborate services.

Despite its growth in size and sophistication, RMS—now majority-owned by the British media enterprise Daily Mail and General Trust—retains a college-bull-session atmosphere in many of its departments. There's also an ivory-tower insularity separating it from some of the consequences of its work. When RMS specialists gathered in a sleek company conference room a couple of years ago to discuss their analysis of millions of insurance claims from the Katrina period, they were particularly excited about the finding that big houses seemed to fare better in hurricanes than small ones. The group buzzed with ideas about why this might be. Until a visitor raised the issue, no one apparently considered the socially dicey implication that owners of big homes could end up being charged lower insurance premiums than those of small ones.

A similar insularity was on display in the spring following Katrina. Faced with two years of intense hurricanes that had resulted in higher-than-anticipated damage claims, RMS suddenly dropped its reliance on historical averages to predict storms in favor of the views of a four-expert panel. The panel concluded that the chance of big hurricanes occurring off the U.S. coast was substantially greater than previously thought; so, by implication, were the likely losses for RMS's insurance company clients. The conclusion set off an uproar. Insurers redoubled efforts to win big premium increases. Consumer advocates accused RMS of tailoring its results to help justify rate hikes. Some scientists complained that the firm's change of method violated a basic principle that, absent evidence to the contrary, the past is the best predictor of the future. Through it all, RMS remained unfazed. To do its job, Shah said, the firm must remain above the fray. "Our view of the world is that we try to under-

stand the risk," he said. "We try not to be involved in the consequences of our findings."

YOU MIGHT IMAGINE that giving insurers a huge new body of
knowledge about houses and their owners would help most policyholders, not hurt them. Insurers could, for example, notify homeowners of dangers that the firms and their computer whizzes had
identified. They could even help policyholders take steps to protect
themselves by providing loans to pay for fireproofing or structural
reinforcements to resist wind or earthquakes. Arguably, the result
would leave both homeowners and insurers better off—the former
because they'd be safer and the latter because they'd be less likely to
face expensive claims. In fact, although the advice is not always
warmly received, some insurers are doing just this sort of thing in the
drought-stricken West, where firms are notifying people that they
need to cut back brush or take down particularly flammable trees
near their homes in order to protect against wildfire.

But for the most part, the industry's technological revolution has
had the opposite effect. Instead of encouraging the kind of broad
risk-reduction measures that were once a hallmark of American insurance, the new computerized techniques seem to have discouraged
it. By providing so much information about individual properties
and policyholders, techniques such as RMS's have riveted insurers'
attention on how individuals' actions have helped increase risks and
therefore why individuals should bear the burden by paying higher
premiums. When it comes to disasters like Katrina, for example,
companies contend that one of the chief reasons the hurricane and
flood caused so much damage—and produced so many insurance
claims—is that Americans are rushing into harm's way by moving to
hurricane-prone coasts and earthquake zones like California. And
one of the chief reasons they are doing so, according to this argument, is that they're not being charged high enough insurance premiums. Higher premiums would send clearer messages about how

much risk such homeowners are taking on by living in vulnerable areas. The corrective "market" signal of higher rates is being blocked by state regulators, who insist on artificially low rates for political reasons, insurance company advocates say.

The argument has gained a wide following both inside the industry and out. In 2006, ten of the nation's top climate experts, including recently retired National Hurricane Center director Max Mayfield, issued a statement warning that "the main hurricane problem facing the United States is our lemming-like march to the sea." The experts laid much of the blame on "government policies that serve to subsidize risk" by holding down premiums. Former Allstate chief executive Edward M. Liddy had made a similar point in a San Francisco speech a few months earlier, saying, "The risks keep rising because people continue to flock to places that are exposed to catastrophe. Population in earthquake-prone and coastal areas is growing faster than the rest of the country, and the increase is by a wide margin." The solution, according to industry leaders and many policymakers, is to let insurers charge steeply higher rates in danger zones to discourage people from moving there, and to make those who live there pay for the additional risks they run.

The problem is that some key statistics don't seem to support the argument. Though government data do show various sorts of growth in the danger zones, they don't show it occurring at an appreciably faster pace than in the country as a whole. Census figures, for example, show that the population of counties located on the coast or in areas prone to earthquakes grew at an annual average rate of 1.56 percent between 1980 and 2006. They show that the U.S. population overall grew at a reasonably close pace of 1.24 percent. A variety of other growth measures show a similar pattern. Proponents counter that these averages mask spectacular growth in such vulnerable places as Miami-Dade County, Florida, and Dare County, North Carolina. But most of Miami-Dade's growth was in the 1980s and the early and mid-1990s; since then, its growth rate has settled back to the national average. And in the case of Dare County, the growth, though tremendous in percentage terms, has only involved an increase from 13,400 people in 1980 to just 33,900 last year.

What this suggests is that rising disaster damage and costs are less a function of insurance rates than of demographics and rising housing and construction prices. "You simply cannot make the case from the numbers that America's coastal counties have grown at a disproportionately faster rate than the country as a whole over the last twenty-five years," said Judith Kildow, who runs the largely government-funded National Ocean Economics Program at Cal State-Monterey. If anything, Kildow said, "the numbers show that growth is now greater inland."

In focusing on individuals and in calling for free-market solutions such as substantially higher, perhaps even unregulated, premiums, insurers certainly are following the pattern of overall U.S. policymaking in the past twenty-five years. But they are breaking with their industry's own historical record. When large portions of the nation's major cities burned during the nineteenth century, in large measure because of the introduction of electricity, the industry founded Underwriters Laboratories, Inc., to set safety standards for wiring and appliances. When highway deaths climbed in the mid-twentieth century, the industry created the Insurance Institute for Highway Safety to perform crash tests that helped pressure automakers into building safer cars.

Present-day officials deny that they have abandoned this tradition. They point to companies that offer premium discounts for coastal homeowners who install storm shutters. They note insurers' efforts to press for stronger local building codes. And they cite the industry's establishment of the Tampa, Florida–based Institute for Business and Home Safety (IBHS), which sets standards for disaster-proofing homes and runs a certification program. But most companies acknowledge that their discounts are too small to attract many takers. And except in Florida and California, industry lobbying for stronger building codes has produced decidedly mixed results. As for IBHS, it is utterly dwarfed by the magnitude of the problem that it has been assigned to tackle. Harvey Ryland, a former deputy director of the Federal Emergency Management Agency who retired in November 2007 as the head of IBHS, recently said that 100 institute-certified houses were available for purchase, with an additional 2,500 or so planned. This at a time when Census figures show that the number of housing units in the nation's coastal and earthquake counties is nearing 40 million.

GIVE RMS A STREET ADDRESS almost anywhere in the country, and it can pull up what's at the location and tell you when it was built and what it's made of. Then it can run hundreds, sometimes thousands, of simulated disasters across the structure. Those that bear up well are good bets for insurers; those that don't are bad ones. Then data miners come in with predictions about how a person will behave if sold a policy. Data miners use years of insurance company claims information to generate a computerized library of correlations between claims and such personal attributes as income, education, ZIP code, and credit score. Load an application for insurance into a data-mining program, and it will use its library of personal information to predict whether the applicant will file a claim in the future. Those the data miners identify as unlikely to file claims are good bets for insurers; those marked as likely to file claims are bad bets for insurance.

Regardless of the technical details, calculations such as these share three crucial similarities: They're only possible because of recent advances in computing power. They generate predictions about individual people and properties. And they have set off a mad scramble among insurers to slice their once-broad pools of policyholders into smaller and smaller risk categories.

From its base in Northbrook, Illinois, Allstate now sorts its home and auto policyholders into 384 categories, up from the 3 that it used until a few years ago. At State Farm in Bloomington, Illinois, the nation's largest auto and home insurer, the number of categories has increased 100-fold. At Mayfield Villiage, Ohio-based auto insurer Progressive, the number now runs into the millions. Insurance executives say that the rush to refine risk pools is producing uniformly positive results. It gives companies more detailed information about the risks they bear. That enables them to offer lower rates to, for example, homeowners who live in safe places. Firms can custom-tailor policies to fit each customer's needs. "It gets us closer to our customers," said an Allstate spokesman.

But the ever-finer slicing appears to be having other effects as well, effects that worry a variety of regulators and insurance theorists. States like California and Maryland have banned insurers from using credit scores, ZIP codes, and other such factors in deciding whether to cover someone, arguing that using such factors unfairly discriminates against the poor and minorities. Washington state officials complain that the proliferation of categories and risk factors has so confused policyholders that the state now requires a company to provide customers with written explanations whenever it gives them anything but its best rate. "If I have a lot of house fires, [insurance companies] should charge me more," said Washington state insurance commissioner Mike Kreidler. "But when insurers reach and grab information like credit or occupation or education, people say, 'Wait a minute. I thought we were talking about insuring my home or auto. What does occupation or education have to do with it?'"

Perhaps most broadly, the new techniques appear to be dismantling much of what insurance traditionally has been about. Until now, insurance of almost every type worked for both the companies and their policyholders because it has done two things. The first is pooling, which spreads a few risks over a lot of people. The second is providing cross-subsidies. Some buyers are more likely than others to get nailed by bad events because, for example, their genetic makeup leaves them prone to disease or their houses are not built to the latest code; other buyers are less likely to need help for mirror-image reasons. But for the most part, insurers have not known which policyholders fall into which category, so they have charged generally uniform rates. That meant those in a "more likely to file claims" category got a subsidy because they paid no more in premiums than those who were less likely to file claims.

As data mining and disaster models such as RMS's provide companies with increasingly detailed knowledge about individual policyholders, this veil of ignorance is being shredded, and there is less and less room for cross-subsidies. "Insurers are squeezing subsidies out of the system across the board, and they're going to carry it absolutely as far as they can," said Columbia University economist Bruce Greenwald. At first glance, that might seem like a good thing. It means, for instance, that policyholders with good genes and safe houses can enjoy lower rates. But at least in some cases, Greenwald and others argue, eliminating cross-subsidies spells big trouble. It strikes at the heart of the basic mechanism of insurance—in much the same way that being able to predict how jurors would vote could destroy the jury system. If lawyers could predict the verdict, they might be less willing to submit their cases to the system. In the case of health insurance, isolating high-risk individuals would mean that a substantial fraction of the nation could no longer afford coverage. In the case of homeowners' insurance, it might ultimately mean that large swaths of the nation's coasts will become unaffordable for all but the wealthiest Americans who can bear unsubsidized rates.

And this may not be where the dismantling ends. The same kind of modeling and data mining that's helping companies squeeze out cross-subsidies could end up eliminating much of the pooling as well. As insurers use the new techniques to get ever more refined estimates of what individual policyholders are likely to cost in the future, they may be tempted to charge people closer and closer to full freight for treating an illness or rebuilding a fire-damaged home. Then even those who benefited from the end of cross-subsidies could see their rates go up as they effectively are asked to pay their own way, rather than share the cost by pooling with others.

Industry executives argue that competition among insurers will prevent such eventualities. "I don't think you're ever going to get to the extreme of no pooling," said Greg Heidrich, senior vice president of policy with the Property Casualty Insurers Association of America, one of the industry's largest trade groups. But regulators are not as confident. "When you begin to tailor or refine policies," said Alessandro A. Iuppa, a past president of the National Association of Insurance Commissioners, which represents the nation's fifty state insurance departments, "you could end up with people basically covering their own losses." But that, of course, would not be insurance.

A FEW YEARS AFTER the Scripps Ranch wildfire, the insurance industry thought it had found an answer to accusations that it had been cutting coverage and leaving policyholders underinsured. A study by the *San Diego Union-Tribune* found that 96 percent of families who'd lost their houses in the conflagration had ended up building bigger ones, turning a neighborhood that the newspaper described as one of "medium to large tract houses into a collection of mini-mansions." Insurers jumped on the finding as proof that people had been generously, perhaps overgenerously, compensated by their policies. "It means the story of under-insurance has to be drawn into question," said Dan Dunmoyer, then president of the Personal Insurance Federation of California and now cabinet secretary for Governor Arnold Schwarzenegger.

But the real explanation for the larger houses may be quite different. Erik and Judy Strahm, who now have three children under the age of four, did indeed buy a bigger house. They moved from a 2,100-square-foot structure to a house with 3,200 square feet of living space. But they did not make the move because of a generous insurance settlement. They did it for just the opposite reason. They decided it was the only way to get out of the financial hole that the fire and the inadequate insurance payout had left them in. They decided to gamble that, in Southern California's fevered real estate market, the bigger house would grow in value faster than a smaller one and thus more quickly lift them back to where they had been before disaster struck. To buy the bigger house, they cashed in other savings and investments. Strahm said the couple now has an uncomfortably large investment tied up in their house: 75 percent of all of their assets, rather than the 50 percent they had before the fire. "Just because you see bigger houses doesn't mean people's insurance took care of the problem," he said. "It doesn't mean their finances are in good shape."

Terry and Julie Tunnell doubled the size of their house by having a two-story structure built where their one-story had stood. But they were able to do so only because a developer, Bob Cave of Stonefield Development, offered eighty-one burned-out families a package-rate deal for rebuilding and the couple tripled their $200,000 mortgage. As matters now stand, the loan they'd once hoped to pay off by the time Julie was fifty-two years old and Terry was fifty-eight will still be with them when Julie is seventy and Terry is closing in on eighty. The Tunnells hope that by building big, they, too, will be better positioned to ride the wave of the Southern California real estate market and—if they're lucky—replace in rising housing value what they lost to the fire and their fight with State Farm. They may well succeed, though the recent dive in the housing prices makes their decision look questionable. But even if their strategy pays off, it is a gambit that lies completely outside the realm of insurance. Instead of joining with others to pay a company to bear risk for them, they have taken a big gamble, and the risk is entirely on their own shoulders. "It's definitely a risk because of the higher monthly payments, and we don't know what's going to happen to real estate," Terry said before the recent market plunge. "But it's the only way we figure we can plug the hole in our finances."

8

EDUCATION

I F YOUR HOUSE IS THE BIGGEST ASSET you'll ever own, your college education—or the one you'll provide your children—is likely to be the most expensive service you'll ever buy. The sticker price for a good state school is around $15,000 a year for tuition, room, and board. If it's one of the premier colleges—an Ivy League school or the University of Chicago or Stanford, for example—you're talking three times that amount, or more than $45,000. By the time you throw in living expenses, the laptop, and travel, the full bill over four years can cost you close to a quarter of a million dollars per kid. That's the equivalent of running a luxury car into the ground annually. And those prices have been rising faster than any item in the Consumer Price Index, save gasoline.

What Americans believe they are getting for all of this spending is simple—a berth in the upper middle class or insurance against falling out of it. And a glance at the numbers suggests the money is often well spent. If you take the most straightforward measure of how those near the top and bottom of the educational spectrum are doing—the median hourly wages of college graduates versus high school dropouts—you'll find a huge and growing gap. At the crest of the early 1970s boom, Census figures show typical college graduates were making about two-thirds more than typical high school dropouts. By the middle of the 2000s, college graduates were making nearly two and a half times as much. And economists who generate more sophisticated comparisons that control for age, race, and gender say that in a true apples-to-apples comparison, the disparity is even greater.

But the story of college as economic insurance has grown more complicated over the past twenty-five years. You can think of higher education as both an investment and an insurance policy—an investment in the sense that it is a ticket to the upper-middle-class world of good jobs and affluence, and an insurance policy against losing your place in that world. But at least half of what you're getting is not as clear as it once was. The economic insurance that the degree confers is less certain. And, as the price of higher education has gone up and up, the increase has been largely borne by students and their families alone; that makes education a lot like many other kinds of investments and insurance turn out to be—cases of paying more for less certainty. And when you console yourself with the potential for higher earnings, don't forget that many of the extra dollars that college graduates expect to earn will go to pay down the mountain of student-loan debt that increasing numbers of graduates carry with them into the work world. For most college graduates and their families, that debt is the one thing there's no uncertainty about.

To begin to understand how things have changed, take the simple median wages for college graduates and high school dropouts. The median hourly wages of college graduates have climbed more than 16 percent since the early 1970s, much of it in the late 1990s. This is just what you'd expect if college is providing the skills required to cope with the modern economy—the human capital needed to succeed. But that's not the only reason the gap between those near the top and bottom of the educational spectrum has yawned open in these years. The other reason is that the median wages of high school dropouts *fell* more than 16 percent. And that had nothing to do with the skills being passed along to those at the top and almost everything to do with broader changes in the economy. It has been the combination of these two trends that has opened the gap as wide as it is and made college graduates such substantial economic winners.

The fact that there have been two trends, instead of just one, at work here is no argument against getting a college education. In fact, if the bottom is falling out of the economy, you'd better get a degree because you don't want to be one of those who falls with it. But it does mean that interpreting the gulf between your college-level wages and those of people who make less as being simply the payoff for acquiring the skills of the future oversimplifies your economic situation. If forces similar to those that came into play at the bottom of the economy begin to creep up the educational spectrum, the goal of ensuring oneself a favored earnings position through higher education could be threatened.

Which brings us to globalization. America prides itself on having the best system of college and university education in the world. Its reputation is so strong that nearly 600,000 foreigners flock here each year to study at U.S. schools. But the influx does not mean that the nation has the only good college and university system on the planet, and much of the rest of the world is catching up quickly. In doing so, other countries are contributing to a huge pool of college graduates who are willing to work for a fraction of what American graduates can afford to accept. In 1970, the United States accounted for 30 percent of university enrollments worldwide; today it accounts for less than 15 percent. The United States—responsible for producing 50 percent of the world's doctorates thirty years ago—is in line to produce just 15 percent of them by the end of this decade. The competition from abroad has already affected U.S. science and engineering PhD's, whose incomes have not grown as fast as they previously did or as fast as those of other U.S. professionals, such as lawyers, who do not yet face substantial global competition, according to labor economist Richard Freeman. "What we're seeing in science and engineering we're likely to see in a variety of other areas," Freeman predicted. "College-educated Americans are about to experience the kind of global competition that we've traditionally associated with high school–educated blue-collar workers." And in the absence of new government policies to change the outcome, "there is no reason to think the results will be all that different—downward pressure on wages, less job security, more turnover."

LEAH BRYNER, thirty, has tried just about every legitimate route available to a young person to get ahead in America. From carhop at the Peach City Ice Cream Company in Brigham City, Utah, at the age of fourteen, to press assistant at the White House in Washington at twenty-three, she has grabbed every opportunity that came her way. That has included a bachelor's degree from the University of Utah in 2002. But five years out of school, she has found herself in a $32,000-a-year administrative job with little opportunity for advancement and, by her own assessment, zero chance of landing what she is really looking for—a policy position in the state or federal government.

Bryner's own explanation for how she arrived at this career cul-de-sac is that for most of her life she didn't know what she wanted to do when she grew up, so she didn't make a beeline for a particular position. In this, she is no different from the vast majority of young Americans. In an increasingly competitive economy, however, such indecision can be costly. Young people are expected to make career calls early on, place large educational bets on those calls—usually with their parents' money—and suffer the consequences if the decisions turn out to have been wrong. If the student or the economy changes along the way, so that the career option chosen at a relatively early age has lost its luster, too bad. The alternative to not finding a career track at all may be far worse.

Bryner grew up in Brigham City, the youngest child of an engineer at Thiokol Corporation, the rocket maker, and a stay-at-home mother.

Both her parents had been married before, and there were nine children in the combined household. Bryner and one brother would end up being the only ones to finish college. That fact still seems to surprise her because she hardly spent her teenage years getting ready for college. She spent them preparing to do what all of her friends were planning to do after high school—get married and have kids.

Part of what sent her down a different path was that, with nine children at home, she needed to make her own money. That gave her the wherewithal to buy a car even before she had a license, and to achieve a kind of independence she would not otherwise have had. Another part of what turned her toward college was that things didn't work out with her boyfriend. When she broke off the relationship, she remembers thinking, "'I've got to come up with a plan B because I'm not going to marry my high school sweetheart.' I knew I needed to get some more education," she said.

The route to more education was not a direct one. After graduating from Box Elder High School in Brigham City in 1995, she moved to Salt Lake City. She went to the Fran Brown College of Beauty in nearby Ogden, and spent a few months working at a shopping mall "chop shop" in Salt Lake City before deciding the job "wasn't worth my time."

Her break came when she landed a position at Kwik Vending Service. The work consisted mostly of fielding calls from irate customers who'd lost their quarters in vending machines around the city. But the job provided her with the funds to take night classes at Salt Lake Community College. And because of it, she met the firm's owner, Robert H. Hinckley Jr., who talked up the Institute of Politics at the University of Utah, which his family had helped start. The result was twofold: The first was that she transferred from community college to the university to complete a four-year degree. The second was that through the institute she managed to land two separate positions in the Clinton White House, one an internship and the second a brief job. Both were low-level. But her stints in Washington while on leave from classes opened up the world to her. "Coming to D.C. made me see how small my world was," she said. "I saw other people doing exciting jobs that I hadn't thought were open to people like me. I never wanted to go back to Brigham City."

After graduating from the university in 2002, she landed a series of jobs—including one for nearly two years as assistant to Salt Lake City mayor Rocky Anderson. Each job promised to open doors to better positions, but ended up going nowhere. The city hall position proved a particular disappointment because it involved too little policy work and too many errands, like picking up the mayor's laundry. The result was that she found herself stuck living in a trailer in Salt Lake and at a work level far below what she was gunning for. "Right now," she said, "if I were looking for a job, it would be another administrative job because that's what I have experience doing and that is how I'm perceived by employers." But, she added, "that's not what I want to do with my life."

Most people would react to a story like Bryner's by saying she should give it some time. After all, here is a go-getter with a college degree; sooner or later, she'll land the job she wants. The reaction is suggestive of just how much faith we place in the power of going to college. Higher education has become America's chief sorter of those who'll get economic opportunities from those who won't. The power we credit it with, sometimes even when the credit is not clearly deserved, is suggested by the recent remark of a friend of mine, Bob Sipchen, the editor of *Sierra Magazine,* the Sierra Club's chief publication. A few months back, Sipchen was talking about the small fortune that he and his family had spent sending one of their three children through Wellesley. (The other two are still at equally expensive colleges.) The young woman had graduated and was working at an entry-level job, but had not yet decided what she wanted to do for a living. Sipchen's comment: "I just figure when she does decide, the degree will serve her well." What other service do Americans spend hundreds of thousands of dollars on with so little certainty about what they'll get for their purchase?

College is also the nation's principal jobs policy, the means that we use to determine who gets the most dependable employment openings that the economy has to offer. The dimensions of our enthusiasm for this policy can be seen in the fact that we've adopted it despite the fact that less than 30 percent of the workforce has bachelor's degrees. Efforts to create an employment education system for those without degrees have repeatedly failed, largely because they have been tarred as efforts to track people into lesser lives. The fraction of high school seniors in vocational education programs has steadily dropped from 24 percent in the early 1980s to about 14 percent, by one count.

Beyond its capacity to ensure our children's futures and determine who gets the good jobs, college is now the heart of the country's bipartisan strategy for helping those who have been laid off. Asked during a 2004 presidential debate what he'd say to someone who'd lost his job, President George W. Bush replied, "I'd say here's some help for you—to get an education. Education is how to help the person who's lost a job." Bush's opponent in 2004, Democratic senator John Kerry of Massachusetts, effectively endorsed his rival's answer by criticizing Bush for cutting spending on education. But this prescription has an incredibly mixed record of success. One major study, for example, found that only 15 percent of jobless benefit claimants ever turn to a college of any sort for help. Of those who do, less than half complete a single course. And of those who do finish, only one-quarter take courses proven to help people get reemployed. "You can't assume college and community college retraining is going to make workers who lose their jobs whole," said economist Louis Jacobson. "It sometimes happens, but not often."

That college maintains such a firm grip on our imagination despite its evident limitations as an economic cure-all is a product both of its fit with the basic arc of the American Dream and of "The Calculation"—the arithmetic that economists use to size up the payoff that comes from going to college.

In terms of the basic American Dream, there is arguably no other institution that does a better job of squaring the nation's egalitarian social principles with the wildly inegalitarian outcomes of its market economy. The logic that college applies goes something like this: All that homework we had to do and all those tests we had to take to get through school justify our favored place in line for the good jobs and the attendant payoffs that come with them. We earned our special privileges and unequal treatment. "We Americans welcome our increasing reliance on education as the arbiter of economic benefits because, at least in theory, it allows us to expand the pool of those who have opportunities without giving up individual responsibility. It creates the deserving successful," said education and job-training authority Anthony Carnevale.

As for "The Calculation," economists measure the dimensions of that success by comparing the cost of college to the lifetime of additional earnings over what a high school graduate or high school dropout would make. From that calculation, they conclude that the benefits far outweigh the costs. One recent calculation by Princeton economist Cecilia Rouse and a colleague suggests that college was such a powerful economic tonic that it would still be worthwhile at twice the current cost or even more.

But wait a minute! Something must be wrong here. If the economists' calculation captures everything that matters on this score and the price system works as advertised, then colleges should be charging two or three times what they now do and still be finding takers. People should be assessing benefits across whole lifetimes, rather than more manageable chunks of time, such as a year. And when it comes to something as beneficial as college, so the economists' logic goes, people should essentially be ignoring cost.

Of course, most people don't make decisions across lifetimes, and the substantial price increases that have already occurred have made a big difference both to families' finances and to what it means to go to school. They've helped turn college from an adventure in early adulthood to a big—and highly risky—investment. And that risk rests almost entirely with students and their families. The sticker price of an average private four-year school has gone up nearly eightfold in the past three decades, and that of a public four-year school has climbed nearly sevenfold, according to the College Board, the organization that administers the SAT and just about every other exam that is crucial to college and graduate school and represents higher education nationally. This, at a time when the incomes of families in the economic middle have risen just 23 percent, according to our panel study sample, and even those of families at the 90th percentile, where only one in ten does better, have increased only about 50 percent.

Colleges say these figures don't give a full picture of what is going on because they have boosted student aid in tandem with these price increases so that the net cost to students has not been as great as the sticker prices suggest. But much of the aid that the colleges talk about has not really been aid in the traditional sense of the word—assistance that is given to someone. A huge part of what colleges count as aid has come in the form of loans made by private lenders to individual students or their families. Schools have been little more than middlemen—often self-serving ones at that, collecting fees and other rewards for steering customers to preferred lenders. Loans accounted for fully one-third of the $130 billion in tuition, room, board, and fees paid for four-year undergraduate educations in 2006, the last year for which full figures are available, according to College Board analysts. That was up from less than 15 percent only twenty years ago. Although the majority of these loans were made by the government, many at a subsidized rate, the fastest-growing sector of student lending has been in private bank loans, which have jumped from essentially nothing in the mid-1990s to $17 billion by 2006 and are typically made at commercial rates of 8 percent or higher, according to the analysts. The increase in lending means that students and their families—not the institutions or government—are bearing most of the burden of escalating college costs. The trend toward borrowing has been further spurred by the fact that with costs rising so rapidly, many families have given up trying to save for them in advance; they simply borrow and hope for the best. Meantime, millions of students have become guinea pigs in what amounts to a new economic experiment—starting their work lives with adult-size debts even before they've landed their first adult jobs.

The combination of higher college tuition and other charges and the use of student debt to meet them means that, for college to make sense financially, there has to be a huge payoff economically. That, in turn, means students have to make the right decision about careers and fields of study that will result in good employment. They also have to complete their degrees: Numbers show that students who take courses but never finish—the "some college" category—end up doing little better economically than high school graduates, even while bearing many of the costs of college. And after graduation, degree holders have to land positions that pay—very, very well. As college budget authority Jane Wellman put it, "This isn't your parents' degree. You can't work your way through college anymore."

ALTHOUGH HARDLY BY DESIGN, Leah Bryner managed to run through just about every educational option that this country has to offer for how to prepare for adulthood. Her experiences illustrate the strengths and weaknesses of each. They also show how rising college costs are changing what college is all about.

Bryner hated high school and, by her own account, made no effort to make much of her experience there. But by senior year she'd begun to worry that she had better emerge with some marketable skill, so she signed up for beauty school. Her first stop was a holdout of the old vocational education system, one of Utah's "applied technology" centers. But the school required her to provide her own clients on whom to practice, something she was unable to do. So she transferred to the commercial Fran Brown beauty school, which provided clients. The school cost $2,000, which her parents paid. It landed her a state cosmetology license and a job at Haircuts Plus in the ZCMI mall in downtown Salt Lake. The position provided no security, however, because most of her compensation was to come in the form of commissions, and she wasn't bringing in enough business. As a result, she said, "I always had to worry about not making the rent."

Bryner's next stop was night classes at Salt Lake Community College. She knew she was no longer interested in cutting hair, and she hadn't been very good in high school. So she figured that community college would let her shop around for a new interest and find out whether college would be any more tolerable than high school. To her surprise, she liked the courses and did well at them. Her second semester she took American National Government and seemed to find what she'd been looking for. "It was taught by an attorney who was really passionate and showed how it related to the work he was doing," she said. "I grew up around politics in my home—although not ones I agree with—so it fit."

Bryner made one other discovery: She could afford the $700-a-quarter cost of tuition and books on the job she'd found with Kwik Vending. In the end, she spent $4,900 and almost two years attending classes. In many ways, her description of that time is what college used to be for many people—an affordable, open-ended exploration of the world of ideas aimed at allowing people to discover where they might fit in. Combined with the beauty school costs, her educational tally to date was $6,900.

Bryner's switch to the four-year University of Utah was not entirely smooth. The university was not organized around people like herself who were trying to go to school while holding down full-time jobs. Finding night classes proved a challenge. But her involvement in the school and the Institute of Politics put her in line for a series of internships and part-time positions that seemed to promise an exciting career ahead. She landed a Washington internship in the White House gift-mail office, chronicling everything that people sent the president. She subsequently landed a low-level job in the White House press office working on the early-morning press clips. She worked as an assistant for the University of Utah's vice president for legislative affairs for health sciences. She got a one-month gig with NBC Sports at the 2002 Salt Lake Winter Olympics. And in August of that year, she graduated with a bachelor's degree in political science. From babies to a bachelor's degree, cosmetology to a college graduate, it was quite a transition!

But the accomplishment came with one drawback—the price. Bryner's time at the university, one of the least-expensive state schools in the country, had still cost nearly double what she'd paid for community college. And taking advantage of the unpaid internships and temp positions had disrupted her full-time work, leaving her about $12,000 in debt. Her student borrowing had been in the form of so-called Stafford loans, a government loan program. About half of her debt carried a subsidized interest rate, but the other half did not. Her educational tally to this point was $18,900. "It bothered me a lot to have the loan. Up until the university, I was able to be debt-free," she said. She set about doing something about the problem, running through a series of jobs aimed at earning more money and eventually landing the position as the Salt Lake City mayor's assistant. She also took in a roommate to help cover her rent. But the costs that she was trying to pay down would turn out to be peanuts compared to the full load of educational debt that she would eventually take on.

THE ECONOMISTS' ARGUMENT for college education remains a strong one even in the face of heavy debt. The gap between the wages of high school dropouts and graduates and college graduates is undeniably large and still growing. The effects of globalization, although showing up in some specialized areas such as science and engineering, seem more threat than reality for the time being. A degree seems like the best investment a parent like Bob Sipchen or young person like Leah Bryner can make to improve the chances of getting into the upper middle class and staying there.

The question, especially as college costs have risen, is whether the investment benefit has been growing stronger or weaker. Does a college education provide as much economic protection as it used to? To tackle that question involves going back to the kind of measures discussed earlier in the book of how often people take steep financial falls and how much risk even those who have not taken big plunges bear. The numbers are not encouraging.

During the early and mid-1970s, generally no more than 2 percent of college-educated families suffered 50 percent income plunges in any two-year period, according to young scholar Elisabeth Jacobs. By the middle of the present decade, that fraction had tripled. Between 6 percent and 8 percent of college-educated workers were seeing their incomes cut in half during any two-year period. True, the odds of taking such a fall were comparatively small in both periods. But the way that most people assess a danger is not simply by asking how big are the chances of a bad thing happening but also by asking how bad it will be if it does happen. And it's hard to imagine the circumstances under which a 50 percent drop in income would be considered anything but very bad, especially if you are carrying a substantial student-debt load. It's true also that during the same years, the odds of 50 percent income falls were even higher for high school graduate and high school dropout families than they were for college families. But they did not rise anywhere near as much. And in any case, the economic point of college is to open the way for graduates to land higher incomes, then protect them against losing those gains. "A college degree certainly provides some insurance against income instability, but it does not offer anywhere near as much security as it once did. Moreover, the increment of protection over what a high school degree provides has narrowed over the last decade," said Jacobs.

As with the measures in the third chapter, these measures of big income losses refer to bad events that have actually befallen families. And as with the earlier numbers, the frequency with which these events happen—though higher than it used to be—remains relatively low. But what we'd like to know is whether the risk of these and other similarly bad economic events has increased. It also would be nice to know in advance of the events happening. And as students and families who are about to spend huge sums of money trying to ensure bright futures, we'd like to look at whether getting a college degree ensures against these risks and to the same degree that it used to. We're not likely to turn thumbs down on higher education even if it turns out to be a bigger gamble than in times past; the risks of not getting an education are too great for that option. But if we're not getting as good a deal as before, even though we're paying so much more, we'd like to know that. For one thing, we might want to think about how to get a better deal for our money.

To look at these questions, we need to return to the idea of the volatility of families' income and ask whether, even for families that have not taken big hits, their incomes have changed in ways that leave them more prone to trouble. We're especially interested in the income of families where one or both parents have gone to the trouble of getting a college degree or even something more, like an MD, JD, or PhD. The numbers show two things for these families. The first is that income volatility has risen for college-educated and advanced-degree families along with the income volatility of families headed by parents with only some college or high school diplomas or no degrees at all. As the economy has become competitive, the income stability of all families has been shaken. The second finding is that, although college-educated and

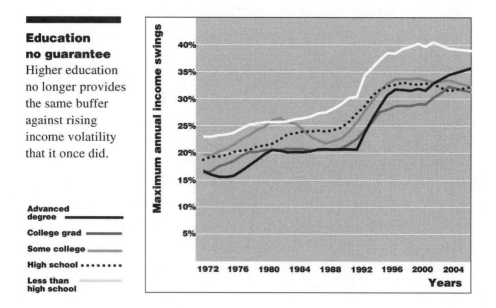

Education no guarantee
Higher education no longer provides the same buffer against rising income volatility that it once did.

Advanced degree
College grad
Some college
High school ••••••••
Less than high school

Maximum annual income swings

40%
35%
30%
25%
20%
15%
10%
5%

1972 1976 1980 1984 1988 1992 1996 2000 2004
Years

advanced-degree families have had less volatile incomes than other families for most of the past three decades, that appears to be changing. In the past few years, the volatility of these better-educated families has surpassed that of families headed by high school grads. That doesn't mean the incomes of these two kinds of families are converging; the earnings gap between the college- and high school–educated remains large. But it does mean that the stability of these various families' incomes—and so the economic risks they bear—has become more nearly equal. In practical terms, that suggests getting an education, though it may still be a good investment as far as better earnings are concerned, doesn't provide as much insurance as it used to against the possibility of seeing the higher income it produces plummet. As before, the idea behind using swing or volatility as a risk measure is that, the more a family's income swings, the greater the chance that family will be caught in a downdraft when a crisis—such as divorce or illness—strikes, and the harder it will be for the family to work its way back to firm financial ground.

Last fall, after interviewing repeatedly for policy jobs, Leah Bryner came to the conclusion that having a college degree was not going to serve as her ticket into the world of adult work as she'd expected. So she quit her administrative position in Salt Lake City, packed up her belongings, and headed east to Philadelphia to enroll in Temple University Law School. "I saw that the mayor [whom she'd worked for] is a lawyer and a lot of the people in government are lawyers, so I'm fairly certain that with a law degree I'll be doing something more than answering somebody else's phone," she said.

She's taking a big risk with this step. She's financing the entire undertaking—tuition and living costs—through the federal Stafford loan program and a second federal program called Graduate Plus, with some of the money carrying an 8 percent interest rate. She figures that by the time she graduates from Temple, she'll have ten times the debt she had when she finished at the University of Utah, or about $120,000. But she can't wait any longer. "I want to get started with whatever work I'm going to do in life. I want to have projects that I can own as my own, that are not 'Did you get the cleaning picked up by five o'clock?'"

IN A SURPRISE move in December 2007, Harvard University announced it will make it less expensive for families with incomes up to $180,000 to send their children to the school. In quick succession, many of the nation's other prestigious schools followed suit. Unfortunately for Leah Bryner, neither Temple nor its law school was among the group.

The institutions were not moved solely by altruism. Washington lawmakers had begun grumbling about setting a fixed minimum that schools with big endowments must spend on student aid, or else risk losing their tax-exempt status. But long-time observers such as Anthony Carnevale believe that elite institutions are genuinely concerned about pricing themselves out of financial reach of most Americans.

The problem is that no more than a few hundred of the roughly 4,500 colleges and universities in the nation can afford to expand aid and reduce rates in the way Harvard did, and only a fraction of qualified students will be able to gain admission to those that can. For the rest, the balance of risks and rewards associated with going to college and the forces eroding the economic insurance value of a degree continue to play out much as they did before the recent announcements.

The elite schools "are doing what they can," said Carnevale. But in the end, he added, "they're kind of spitting in the wind."

9

HEALTH

THERE ARE NO DANGERS TO THEMSELVES or their families that worry Americans more than the possibility of serious injury or illness. One way or another, we manage the small stuff. Colds, flu, babies with colic, kids with skinned knees—the minor medical plagues of everyday life may spoil a few days or disrupt our work schedules, but we take them in stride as part of life's basic deal. What scares us are the big events—the telephone call that informs us a teenager has been in a car crash or heralds the arrival of a disease that we previously thought happened only to others. These are the events that can dash your hopes or steal away your life or that of a beloved spouse or child. In an instant, they can wipe away everything you took for granted, erase every plan you'd ever made. And they can come with unimaginably large costs in tow. I know. In the fall of 2007, as I started writing this chapter, which happened to be the final uncompleted piece of the book, I got a call from my wife, Robin. She had gone to our family doctor for what seemed like a pulled muscle—a stitch in her side that wouldn't go away. Come to the doctor's office quickly, I was told. They've found something.

The gray film of the CAT scans showed what we were told was ovarian cancer. So with the help of our doctor, Michael Newman, we headed for the best center for ovarian cancer treatment that we could find: Memorial Sloan-Kettering Cancer Center in New York. In little more than a week, Robin was undergoing surgery. But halfway through the operation, the surgeon emerged to tell me that they'd found something besides what they'd expected, a different kind of cancer and a far more difficult one to treat. We returned home to Washington, D.C., to come up with another plan. This time, Robin would go to Georgetown University Hospital every two weeks for large doses of chemotherapy, then for the next forty-eight hours wear a fanny pack that would inject still more chemicals into her body.

As the new treatments started, envelopes began to arrive at our house, each containing a form with a huge dollar figure attached to it. The operation at Sloan-Kettering had cost $45,000, and it's not clear yet whether that price includes the fees of the surgeons, anesthesiologists, and other specialists who were involved. The sticker price for the compounds in Robin's biweekly chemotherapy would be $13,000 per treatment. Per treatment! Thankfully, the spaces at the bottom of these forms that read "You owe" have so far shown zeros or only a few hundred dollars. That's because we are lucky enough to have very good health insurance through Robin's employer, *The New York Times*. Absent that coverage, I figure my family could underwrite Robin's treatment for a couple of years before we'd go broke. Then I would be unable to do anything to help my wife, the mother of our children, survive.

About 162 million other Americans, or 62 percent of the nation's working-age population, get health care insurance through their employers. Health insurance is one of the vital struts that holds up our families and our lives. Along with our jobs and the other benefits that come with them, along with our houses, communities, education, and provisions for retirement, medical insurance brings a measure of stability to our lives. Statistics show that people with insurance who suffer major medical events such as the one my family is going through typically pay no more than 15 percent of the total treatment cost themselves. Without such protection, every day would be shadowed by the possibility of unpredictable and uncontrollable expense or even financial ruin. Without such protection, planning and carrying forward a typical middle-class life would be very nearly impossible. That's why, despite the rising cost, so many American workers sign up for their employers' health care plans. Making sure that you are not crushed by medical costs is part of the basic pact that most couples make with each other—a promise to be around in the good times, bear what you can in the bad times, and ensure that crushing financial burdens don't fall on you and your family.

Unfortunately, there are signs that the current employer-based system on which I'm depending cannot continue, and that if it fails, health care will look an awful lot like what has happened to the nation's retirement system. In short order, most traditional pensions were supplanted by 401(k) investment plans, and the primary responsibility for making retirement arrangements was shifted from employers to individuals and their families. As we shall see in the next chapter, those responsibilities have proved too much for many people to handle well.

Among the warning signs that something similar may be happening to health insurance: The fraction of the working Americans and their families covered by employer-provided medical insurance has shrunk from more than 68 percent to 62 percent in the past seven years; that's equivalent to the 16 million people who would have had insurance in 2000 going without it now. The fraction of large employers offering retirees health benefits to supplement the retirees' government-provided Medicare has dropped from 66 percent to just 33 percent in only twenty years. Surveys show that even big, financially healthy companies that have been the backbone of the employer-based system are searching for ways to reduce their health obligations to employees. Increasingly, corporate leaders in the United States argue that they can no longer compete with foreign firms that don't bear such costs because the competitors' governments bear the burden, or workers in poorer countries simply do without. Statistics show that about 40 percent of small firms—those with two hundred or fewer employees—are not providing health insurance at all, and such firms constitute a growing proportion of all U.S. employers.

In the summer of 2007, there was an additional sign that change was on the way, and it came from an unusual quarter: the health care proposals unveiled by presidential contenders in both political parties. Predictably, the Republican proposals tended to resemble those of the Bush administration, emphasizing personal responsibility, private enterprise, and market mechanisms. What was more startling were the proposals of many of the Democrats. To a person, they said that they had learned from the mistakes of the overambitious Clinton health care effort of the early 1990s, which ended in failure. Most said they would seek to bolster existing employer-based insurance, rather than upend it as the Clinton plan proposed to do. They would also have government provide some other form of coverage for those who are now uninsured, coverage that would operate alongside the employer-based system.

But two characteristics of the widely varying proposals stood out as worrisome. The first is that, for those who don't have insurance or lose it, most of the proposals would place primary responsibility for getting new coverage on the individual. Because the responsibility for ensuring coverage is placed on the individual instead of on employers or the government, where virtually every previous reform proposal has placed it, this approach is called an "individual mandate." The approach is not unheard of. In most states, you're required—"mandated"—to have auto liability insurance in order to drive a car. But it's a new idea—or at least a newly popular idea—when it comes to health insurance. The second worrisome characteristic of the new crop of Democratic plans is that many contain elements that some experts say could have the unintended effect of convincing companies that now offer health insurance to drop their coverage, which would leave many employees fending for themselves. The result would be to make the individual mandate and individual purchase of insurance coverage a vastly more prominent feature of the American health care system than it is now. What started out as an ancillary method for protecting a minority of workers could fast become the chief means by which most of us would get our coverage.

What makes the possible spread of "individual mandates" worrisome is that the current market for individual health insurance is beset by many of the problems that scare the living daylights out of people—high costs that rise even higher if you actually file significant claims and coverage that can vanish just when you need it most. This chapter will describe just one example involving Blue Shield of California, but that ought to be enough to convince you of the kind of trouble that could lie ahead.

Of course, the presidential candidates understand these problems. Most of the major Democratic contenders have responded by promising to create buying pools and impose sweeping regulations that they say would give those without employer coverage the same dependable protections that come with job-related health insurance. In other words, the candidates promise to fix or replace most of the current market for individual policies. The danger is that the country could end up with only "half a loaf" of reform—the half that shifts all responsibility to individuals, but not the half that helps people bear their new burdens.

The political parties and their most fervent supporters are deeply divided. Even if the Democrats were to win the White House and strengthen their majorities in Congress, they are unlikely to have the power to push through drastic change. The idea of the individual mandate plays to broadly agreed-upon values like personal responsibility; that's why Democrats—hoping to attract middle-of-the-road voters—are turning to the idea. And that's why Republicans will likely be more than happy to sign on to the idea. The danger is that individual mandate will win wide acceptance while the politically contentious regulations needed to make such a mandate work fairly could end up on the cutting-room floor.

Given the current fondness for deregulation, and the undeniable economic benefits it has brought us in many fields, why would that be such a bad outcome? Would not market mechanisms force insurance companies to provide better medical coverage just as they have forced Detroit to make better cars? The answer is that deregulated markets don't always produce the best results. Whatever the theory, buyers and sellers do not always have equal market power in the real world, and therefore the results are sometimes neither fair nor efficient. And the evidence is overwhelming that, when it comes to health insurance, the balance of power is heavily tilted in favor of the seller of insurance. If responsibility for getting coverage is to be shifted from employers to individuals in the same manner that other kinds of protections from job security to retirement have been shifted, then the change must be accompanied by substantial assurances that insurers will do what they say they are going to do—leave no one uncovered, no legitimate claims unpaid, and no policies pulled when expenses start rising. And the only institution strong enough to insist that such assurances are honored is the federal government.

AMERICA'S CURRENT employer-based health insurance system is regularly portrayed as a fluke of history—an arrangement no one would choose if they were designing a coverage program from the ground up. Until the first third of the twentieth century, medicine was pretty primitive and comparatively cheap. People generally paid for it out of pocket or relied on charity. As recounted by Jonathan Cohn in his recent book *Sick,* the focus on employers started eighty years ago with a cash-strapped Baylor Hospital in Dallas, Texas, and its new administrator, Justin Kimball. The hospital had expanded rapidly during the booming 1920s, but found itself in the Great Depression of the 1930s saddled with patients who couldn't pay. Kimball struck on the idea of turning to his old employer, the Dallas public school system, and making it an offer. In return for a fifty-cent-a-month contribution, the hospital would promise any teacher twenty days of care so long as at least three-quarters of the teachers signed up.

The three-quarters figure was crucial because that was the fraction that Kimball estimated would produce enough revenue from healthy teachers to cover the medical expenses of the unhealthy ones who needed care. The figure, in other words, ensured a wide-enough mix of healthy and unhealthy customers that it would be easy to spread the costs of the unhealthy few across the healthy many. Selling Kimball's proposition turned out to be a snap. Within a few years, first hospitals and then doctors across the country launched similar plans. In 1934, the founder of a hospital plan in St. Paul, Minnesota, started running advertisements illustrated with a blue cross on them. Plans offered by doctors soon adopted a similar blue symbol. Thus was born Blue Cross and Blue Shield, the first and for many years the only giant health insurers. Virtually all of the early Blues concentrated on groups, especially employers. The focus was reinforced during the Second World War, when federal price administrators prohibited wage hikes to control inflation but allowed benefit increases, including health benefit increases. And it was reinforced immediately after the war when the government decided that the money that employers spent on health insurance would be exempt from taxation in what has by now become a $150-billion subsidy for employer-provided insurance.

The tax break reflected the huge public purpose that insurers, especially the Blues, served for much of the postwar period, which was to spread health insurance far and wide. The Blues did so by charging policyholders a "community rate," the same premium no matter their age, sex, or medical condition, and, in many cases, by instituting so-called guaranteed issue, promising coverage to anybody who would pay. In these respects, the Blues' coverage came to resemble that of government social insurance programs like Social Security and unemployment compensation that were available to all comers at similar rates. The resemblance was reinforced by the fact that for years the Blues were nonprofits, rather than commercial enterprises. By 1980, most full-time workers at the nation's large companies were insured through their employers, and in many cases through the Blues, in a trend that seemed to promise near-universal coverage in short order.

But the happy trends did not continue. Wider insurance coverage encouraged heavier use of medical services and prompted investment in new technology, which had the unfortunate side effect of driving up health care costs. Meanwhile, the long postwar boom, which had provided American employers with an interest in hanging on to their employees and the wherewithal to pay for the benefits to keep them, stumbled to an end in the 1970s and early 1980s. With it began the breakdown of the tie between employer and employee. "Just as cheap health premiums and tight labor markets once created pressure on all employers to provide their workers decent coverage," Cohn wrote, "now expensive premiums and loose labor markets created pressure not to provide coverage."

IF THE NATION's employer-based health insurance system was a fluke of history, the system of health insurance purchased by individuals independent of their jobs is even more of an anomaly. Individual insurance starts at a cost disadvantage to its employer-based counterpart. Insurers have to sell policies to one person at a time, usually through an agent who demands a commission, instead of being able to sweep up hundreds or sometimes thousands of people through a single deal with a big employer. The insurer also has to deal with each policyholder's payments and claims separately, as opposed to turning bundles of them over to employers' human resources departments to handle. Both of these problems have declined in importance as the power of computers has grown, reducing clerical costs. But that still leaves a third problem with individual policies that doesn't seriously trouble most employer and group insurers, something called "adverse selection." Big groups, such as all the employees of a good-size company, tend to be a varied lot; the share of healthy and unhealthy workers can be predicted fairly accurately by actuaries. By contrast, people who buy individual policies tend to be people who are sick or expect to be sick. Otherwise, they wouldn't go to the trouble and expense of buying the coverage. That means sellers of individual policies tend to attract the sickest and therefore most expensive clients in a trend called "adverse selection." For many years, the only thing that individual insurers could do to cope with this problem was go through the expensive process of carefully screening—or "medically underwriting"—each potential customer. Even then, it was not a sure thing; insurers could end up with an imbalance of sick people that would send their finances into a tailspin.

Adverse selection proved such a difficult problem, in fact, that it kept commercial insurers out of the health insurance business altogether for decades. That left the field almost exclusively to the Blues. But insurance companies eventually figured out a way to offer individual policies without risking financial damage. Instead of charging a single "community rate" as the Blues generally did, for-profit insurance companies began to charge people different rates depending on their health conditions and to adjust those rates as people's health conditions changed. Once they settled on this new pricing policy, called "experience rating," they were able not only to enter the individual market but to begin undercutting the Blues for the choicest employer business as well. Along with the breakdown of the employer-employee tie, the advent of experience rating helped put an end to what had once seemed an inexorable march to universal health coverage.

WHATEVER THE DIFFERENCES between employer-provided and individual insurance, and however much insurance has changed from the days of community rates, the purpose of a health policy has remained pretty much the same for policyholders: to make sure that if serious illness or injury strikes, the dollar costs rest with an insurance company, which can bear the financial burden more readily than a family. My own family did not have a clue until last fall that my wife would be diagnosed with cancer. We'd had our normal share of health concerns and were conscientious about having the tests and taking the steps that Dr. Newman told us were necessary if we were to stay well. But we did not suffer any financial worries because we knew that if a problem arose, our insurance would cover it. Now that the crisis is upon us, we are counting on that coverage to provide the necessary treatment and shield us from financial ruin. So far, our confidence has been well placed. But not everyone with health insurance is so fortunate. Sometimes insurance doesn't work the way it is supposed to. That can be especially so with the individual health care policies that are being held up as something of a model for where health coverage should be headed.

REBECCA J. ROWLANDS started her work life managing an almond farm in the San Joaquin Valley of California. She was a chambermaid and, later, assistant manager at the Vagabond Hotel in Palmdale, where the only real excitement was the occasional arrival of a space shuttle at Edwards Air Force Base. She was a receptionist at a day spa in the fancy Brentwood section of Los Angeles. But the jobs she liked the best were always the medical ones.

Her first was as a receptionist in the early 1990s with the Conejo Medical Center in Lake Sherwood. The position paid twelve dollars an hour and came with employer-provided health insurance. She was responsible for making sure that patients' records were up-to-date for a five-doctor practice. She moved from there to a neurologist in Thousand Oaks, where she was given more responsibility. She got to check patients' blood pressure, take their medical histories, and conduct a kind of triage where she'd make an initial call about a patient's condition before the patient was seen by the doctor. She kept that job until a few years ago. "I found it fascinating, just how the body worked," Rowlands remembered in a conversation in the summer of 2007. "People would come in with a mole on the toe, and it would turn out to be a malignant melanoma. One woman had a breast cancer so large it was coming through her skin." Another complained of such terrible headaches that Rowlands rushed her in to see the doctor, who had her airlifted to a hospital because of a rare and potentially fatal malformation of the nerves and blood vessels in her brain. The woman credits Rowlands with saving her life.

However, it was not the diseases but the patients, especially the older, cantankerous ones, that were what touched Rowlands's heart. There was a man named Lou—she's not sure of his last name. He'd clearly been handsome in his younger days. He still was, though his bright green eyes were failing him. "He'd hit a curb, and they wanted to take away his driver's license," she remembered. "It was humiliating for him." There was Henrietta, who worried incessantly—and loudly—about what would happen to her birds if she were hospitalized. Nobody could stand her—except Rowlands. "The patients are the reason you stay at work, especially when the job is not that great," Rowlands said. "You fall in love with them."

In 1988, when Rowlands was still at the Vagabond and before she'd started at Conejo, she was living with a boyfriend, Doug Whittington, who had his own contracting company. The two were making enough that she got a new Honda CRX and he bought a Ford Ranger. They talked about buying an A-frame house that overlooked a lake and getting married, something they subsequently did. At a company picnic that summer, she began to experience vaginal bleeding, and Whittington had to take her to the hospital. There, doctors discovered a large benign cyst on her left ovary. She was operated on, and to her surprise both the cyst and the ovary were removed. The procedure was covered by her employer-provided health insurance through Vagabond and appeared to put an end to the problem.

Rowlands's marriage to Whittington lasted just over five years. When it failed in the early 1990s, she quit her hotel job and began her career as a medical receptionist and office manager. At the time, California's market for individual policies was undergoing a sea change. At first, the change made little difference to Rowlands because she continued to receive the same kind of employer-provided coverage that she'd gotten at the hotel. As a result, she barely noticed what was happening. In time, however, the change would catch up with her—with disastrous results.

Individual insurers had dealt with the problem of adverse selection, or the greater tendency of sick people to buy individual policies, either by careful scrutiny of applicants to make sure they didn't sell too many policies to the sick or by staying out of the business altogether. But now in addition to these techniques, companies increasingly engaged in another one as well—so-called post-claims underwriting or rescissions. Under this method, insurers sold policies, collected premiums, and even sometimes paid small claims. But instead of carefully scrutinizing an applicant in advance, the insurer would wait until a policyholder filed a big claim, then sometimes cancel the policy and refuse to pay. Insurers asserted that they took this drastic step only in cases of fraud, where policyholders lied to them about their medical condition so that the insurer couldn't make a proper underwriting judgment about whether to cover them. But recent reporting by *Los Angeles Times* reporter Lisa Girion found that some companies engaged in rescissions even in many instances where there was no real evidence of fraud. She showed that firms latched onto honest mistakes, inadvertent errors, and minor inconsistencies in policyholders' applications and used them as a pretext for cancellations. The move saved the insurers both the cost of doing expensive prescreening of applicants and the cost of paying big claims. But it left the policyholders floundering in bills and unable to pay for their medical care.

It is hard to overstate how using rescissions except in the rarest of instances turns the very logic of insurance on it head. Insurance, after all, is all about bad events that haven't happened yet and about who will bear the financial consequences if they do. People buy policies precisely to make sure that if something goes wrong, the insurer will pay and most of the cost will not fall to them. They rely on the promise to pay in planning their lives even in the absence of the bad event. But if a company can go back on the deal after the fact of the event, the protection that an insurance policy is supposed to provide vanishes, and all of the plans that policyholders made relying on that protection turn out to rest on quicksand.

"People pay insurance companies thousands of dollars a year for nothing but a promise," said Cindy Ehnes, director of California's Department of Managed Health Care, which regulates much of the market for individual insurance. "With rescissions, the companies essentially rip up that promise, leaving patients terribly exposed and physicians and hospitals unpaid." Ehnes and California state insurance commissioner Steve Poizner are now trying to ban the practice. But their effort is not the first by California officials to tackle the problem. The fact of the earlier effort—and its apparent failure to make a serious dent in the problem—suggests just how hard the current generation of individual-mandate advocates will have to work to regulate the new insurance markets they propose to create in order to make sure that people don't get stuck with something that's worse than no insurance at all: the promise of coverage that disappears when you need it.

Much as it is today, health insurance was a big issue a decade and a half ago, in the early 1990s. Costs were climbing, insurers were trying to protect profits by getting tougher with policyholders, and the number of people without health insurance was on the rise. Also like today, states were out in front in trying to wrestle with the problems. In California, a big health overhaul measure went down to defeat on the very day that Bill Clinton was elected to the White House in 1992. California's plan was a victim of many of the same arguments about saddling business with crippling costs that would eventually sink the new president's own reform plan. In addition, the state slipped into recession, driving the state budget deep into the red and ending any immediate chance for a sweeping and potentially costly overhaul of health care. State legislators tried to pick up the pieces by proposing a series of incremental measures. "We were seeing a lot of abuses in the health insurance market, but there was absolutely no chance to advance a broad reform, so we were being pragmatic and taking small steps," said Burt Margolin, a former assemblyman from West Los Angeles and at various times chairman of the California State Assembly's health and insurance committees. One small step proposed by Margolin was to ban rescissions on policies covering very small groups of employees. The measure eventually became law. A second proposal offered a year later by then-Assembly Speaker Willie Brown would have imposed a similar ban on policies covering individuals. It, too, was enacted, but only after being watered down.

As originally filed, the Brown measure could not have been more straightforward. It read, "No insurer issuing or providing any policy of . . . insurance covering hospital, medical or surgical expenses shall engage in the practice of post-claims underwriting." It went on to define post-claims underwriting as "the practice by an insurer, following a claim by an insured, of rescinding a contract or denying benefits based on an alleged misrepresentation on the application or enrollment form."

The insurance industry jumped all over the proposal. Michael Arnold, a lobbyist for Blue Shield of California, was among those who warned that the proposed legislation would cripple companies' ability to fight fraud. "This may not have been the intent . . . but the provisions are written in such a manner that [insurance applicants] may be encouraged to commit misrepresentation," he said. The criticism had its intended effect. As it finally emerged from the legislature, the measure redefined post-claims underwriting to mean rescinding a policy "due to the insurer's failure to complete medical underwriting and resolve all reasonable questions arising from . . . an application be-fore issuing a policy." The arrangement left it largely up to insurers to say whether they had failed in this fashion, and in the years to come they won a series of court regulatory cases based on this language that gave them wide latitude in how they handled individual health policies.

IN THE LATE 1990s, after having been divorced and on her own for several years, Rebecca Rowlands began dating a doctor she'd met while working at the Conejo Medical Center, Iranian-born Moham-mad Shamlou. Although Rowlands was closing in on forty years old at the time, the relationship spurred her hopes of having children. And those hopes were only raised when the pair got married in 1999. But something not as happy was also going on during those years: A cyst like the one that had forced her to have an operation in the 1980s and had claimed her left ovary was beginning to grow on her right ovary. At first, the new cyst was small. Rowlands's medical records show that it was regularly labeled as benign, not cancerous. The records show that she was advised simply to keep an eye on the prob-lem. But by the time of her marriage, the cyst had reached significant size. Her physician at the time, Dr. Nancy Taylor, urged her patient to have the growth removed as a precaution. Rowlands resisted, worried that what had happened in the 1980s would happen again—namely, that the surgeons would take not just the cyst but the ovary as well, ending her chance for having children. Taylor continued to press for removal. The records show the two women sharply disagreed about the matter.

In the spring of 2000, less than a year into her marriage to Sham-lou, Rowlands agreed to become her new husband's medical office manager. At the time, she was still working for the Thousand Oaks neurologist and still had her employer-provided health insurance. Thinking that they would need new insurance coverage, the couple applied to Blue Shield of California for an individual policy. As part of the application, Taylor sent Blue Shield her records on Rowlands and the cyst problem. Ultimately, nothing came of the application. Rowlands decided to keep her old job and her group coverage and to handle the work for Shamlou on the side. But as a subsequent court case would reveal, the application and the medical records remained tucked away in Blue Shield's files.

Rowlands's marriage to Shamlou didn't last. When she left him in April 2002, she decided she needed to put some distance between herself and her ex-husband, so she moved forty miles southeast to Venice, California. Unfortunately, the move meant that she had to give up both her Thousand Oaks job and her employer-provided health insurance. Over the next few years, she held a series of medical office jobs, most of which did not come with health insurance, as she sought to build a new life for herself. Although she dated some, no prospects for a new partner turned up. Unmarried and by now forty-six years old, she decided that it was time to do something about the cyst problem. In the spring of 2005, while working as a receptionist at the Brentwood day spa Lili Beau Visage, she complained about needing health insurance, and the spa's owner, Lili Pope Hunt, set up an appointment with an insurance agent, Jeffrey Adler.

What happened next is a matter of considerable dispute. Hunt says that Rowlands and Adler met at the front of the pastel-pink spa one day in early April but that the get-together lasted "only a few minutes." Rowlands says that the only real question that Adler asked was for the name of her doctor. She answered Dr. Taylor. She saw nothing unusual in the fact that Adler did not ask other questions, especially about her health, but simply wanted her to sign a form. This was the procedure she'd gone through whenever she'd signed up for employer-provided insurance. Adler refuses to comment. Blue Shield executives decline to talk about what transpired between Rowlands and Adler, saying Adler is not their employee, but an independent agent, and therefore they have no control over him.

Whatever was said, the result was an application for health coverage that contained almost no information about Rowlands's health. Every box on the medical history page of the form, save that she menstruated and smoked, was checked "No." That included a question about whether Rowlands had sought treatment or medications at any time in the previous twenty years for matters involving the female reproductive system, including "problems of the ovaries." Rowlands said that she never saw the application when Adler was filling it out. And the document was not attached—as required by state law—to the policy that she eventually received from Blue Shield. But receive a policy she did, and by May 1, 2005, Rowlands was back among the medically insured.

She immediately put the coverage to use, seeing at least four doctors over the course of the summer, seeking and winning Blue Shield preapproval for a pelvic CT scan, and, once she'd run through the policy's $2,000 deductible, filing and receiving payment on a number of comparatively small claims. Several mention a diagnosis of "unspecified ovarian cyst." In October, she got preapproval for an operation, and on November 14, she underwent surgery at St. John's Health Center in Santa Monica for cyst removal and a hysterectomy.

There was one piece of information in Rebecca Rowlands's 2005 application for health insurance that might have helped Blue Shield do as California law suggests an insurer should—"complete medical underwriting and answer all reasonable questions" before issuing a policy: the name of Dr. Taylor. If in fact Rowlands had been doing what the insurer subsequently accused her of doing—lying about her true medical condition in order to win coverage—it seems unusual that she would have provided Adler with Dr. Taylor's name. After all, it was Dr. Taylor who had expressed the gravest concerns about Rowlands's cyst problem, and it was Dr. Taylor's records describing those concerns that were sitting in Blue Shield's files when it processed Rowlands's 2005 application.

WHEN ROWLANDS underwent the operation to remove the cyst, surgeons found a medical disaster. A pathology report on the results
read, "Sections from the right ovary show a malignant epithelial tu-
mor. . . . There is invasion of the cyst wall. . . . Sections from the right
fallopian tube also show . . . carcinoma in situ as well as foci of invasion of the fallopian tube wall." Rebecca Rowlands had cancer.
Within weeks, she started chemotherapy. And by early January 2006,
less than eight weeks after the surgery, her medical bills had already
mounted to $60,177.65, according to subsequent court papers.

It was at this moment—*after* Rowlands had incurred her first major expense under the policy with the surgery and chemotherapy—
that Blue Shield chose to begin asking questions about her
application and her coverage. Records in a subsequent lawsuit show
that on November 17, the very day Rowlands was being discharged
from St. John's Health Center following the operation and having
just been told she had cancer, Blue Shield dashed off an "URGENT
MEDICAL RECORDS REQUEST" to at least three of her physicians. The request asked for just about everything under the sun—"Dr's notes,
referrals . . . testing, admit/discharge summaries, labs/X-ray results,
health questionnaires, surgery notes & findings, etc. from 2002 to the
present." It insisted on receiving the material at no charge, and said
that it could not consider paying any bills until it got the records.

By mid-December, with Rowlands less than a month out from
the surgery, Blue Shield also began writing her, asking for increasingly detailed information about her medical history. It warned
that "failure to provide Blue Shield with this information . . . would
leave us with no choice but to conclude that there was material information that was not disclosed on your application and will
therefore result in termination" of coverage. Rowlands responded
with a letter listing the doctors she'd recently seen. She also got the
physician overseeing her chemotherapy to send Blue Shield a special form intended to switch on a clause in her insurance that requires the company to cover policyholders facing critical medical

conditions. Under the list of critical conditions, the doctor checked "Life-Threatening Cancer."

None of this made any difference. On January 9, 2006, Paula Wells, a senior underwriter with Blue Shield's Underwriting Investigation Unit, wrote Rowlands. "We have reviewed medical information received after you submitted your application," the letter began. "Based on this information, we determined that you did not provide complete and accurate information on your application. . . . If we had known this critical information at the time of underwriting, your Health Service Contract would not have been approved. Therefore, we are terminating your contract as having never been in effect." Two months out from an operation, unable to work, with a cancer diagnosis, Rowlands no longer had insurance.

In the months that followed, Rowlands signed up for Medi-Cal, California's version of Medicaid, the big state-federal health insurance program for the poor. But her chemotherapist refused to accept Medi-Cal as payment because it pays less than the doctor's normal fee. Rowlands tried to convince the doctor to continue treating her by paying $2,300 out of her own pocket, but the amount was a tiny fraction of the cost of the treatment, and three rounds into what was supposed to be a six-round cycle of treatments, she was told that she would have to go elsewhere. She ended up at Santa Monica UCLA Medical Center, which agreed to administer the treatments for the Medi-Cal fee.

But after completing the chemotherapy, she went for more than a year unable to find anyone willing to perform an MRI or CAT scan in order to find out whether the chemo had stopped the cancer. By the time a UCLA oncologist, Dr. Saeed Sadeghi, agreed in May 2007 to complete the paperwork necessary for Medi-Cal to pay for an MRI, Rowlands was suffering from a bloated abdomen and showing new signs of trouble. She had hired a lawyer and sued Blue Shield, but it would take more than a year for the company to agree to an undisclosed settlement. By then, Rowlands had seriously deteriorated.

Blue Shield executives discussed Rowlands's case with me after she signed a waiver freeing them from privacy restrictions. Company vice president Tom Epstein and communications director David Seldin acknowledged that Adler, the agent, filled out Rowlands's application, a practice that they described as standard. They said they didn't know whether he asked her any of the health questions, but suggested that this was not the company's concern. In part, that's because Adler is not a Blue Shield employee. In part, it is because whether or not he did, Rowlands signed the application, which meant she attested that everything in the document was true. "For someone to sign an application and not review it is quite negligent, if not reckless," said Epstein. At the time Rowlands applied, the company did not do its own review of the application or ask for her medical records, again a practice they described as standard. In particular, the company did not contact Dr. Taylor or look for the physician's records on Rowlands that were in the firm's files. Asked whether the company paid some claims, including ones that mentioned Rowlands had an ovarian cyst, the pair did not know. They asserted that the investigation that led to the rescinding of her policy was prompted by her October 2005 seeking of preapproval for an operation and was under way well before the November discovery that she had cancer. But the documents they provided me to support their claim suggest the very opposite. The investigation was launched three days *after* the cancer diagnosis.

In an e-mail to me, Seldin wrote, "We don't dispute your . . . point about health care's place as an example of how risk has been shifted onto individuals and families to a greater degree than it should be. But we think it is unfair to single out a particular company for criticism—particularly a company that has worked to change the system—when we are simply doing what the realities of the marketplace require."

Blue Shield, although a nonprofit, has amassed a surplus of nearly $2.5 billion since it "restructured" its strategies in recent years and is thought by many to be preparing to switch to for-profit status in the same way that Blue Cross of California did in 1996.

In December 2007, California state insurance commissioner Steve Poizner announced he was seeking to fine Blue Shield $12.6 million after the agency said that a market-conduct examination of the company's operations in 2004 and 2005 uncovered 1,262 violations of law, half involving improper cancellation of policies. "Blue Shield committed serious violations that completely undermine the public trust in our healthcare delivery system," Poizner said in a statement. "Rescissions can be devastating to sick patients. Let this be a message to all health insurers that we will not tolerate irresponsible rescissions and shoddy claims handling." Blue Shield has vowed to fight the charges.

Whoever wins, the world is changing on health insurers. And that change will come quickly if any of the 2008 presidential campaign plans that put the coverage burden on individuals gain favor. There simply is no way to have real insurance if the system operates as it has in too many instances in California—where insurers have had the right to promise financial protection against a medical crisis but then take the protection away if a policyholder's claims grow too large. And, as the state's experience illustrates, it will take more than a simple law to end the practice. The state had approved a law intended to prohibit post-claims underwriting fifteen years before Rebecca Rowlands found that the policy she just purchased and was relying on to pay for much of her cancer treatment had been rescinded. The measure did almost no good.

My family and I are ready to fight. We have the doctors we need. We have the support of our employers. And most important of all, we have good insurance. For Rebecca Rowlands, however, it may be too late to fight. She has been hospitalized continuously since August 2007 with a series of increasingly severe medical problems. Even if she survives, and even with her settlement with Blue Shield, it is likely she would emerge to face a six-figure medical debt that it is hard to imagine she'd ever be able to pay.

Calling for an individual mandate as a means of attracting a broad coalition to health reform may be politically wise. But unless that call is accompanied by stiff regulations that ensure people are not entirely on their own in obtaining and keeping coverage, the result will be a cruel hoax. Having insurance to cope with a health crisis is one of those protections that no one except those in that all-too-brief period of healthy young adulthood—or those who are very, very rich—can afford to do without. Our risk of being struck by serious illness or injury must be pooled with those of others, and the costs must be spread across a large group of both sick and healthy. Insurers cannot be counted on to assemble those groups on their own; the financial incentives to take the healthy and avoid the sick or likely-to-be-sick are simply too great. If employers are no longer to play the role they have traditionally played of assembling these groups, there is only one alternative—government. Unwelcome as many Americans may find the idea of government playing a bigger role in health care—and as much as we may object on philosophical or other grounds—we must not fool ourselves into believing there is some simple alternative. Certainly, the notion that an individual such as Rebecca Rowlands alone can arrange for her own protection is not an option.

Health care insurance, like jobs, housing, education, and retirement, is one of those things that is fundamental to the welfare of both individuals and societies. It is one of those things we must have some certainty about in order to lead stable and productive lives. It is one of those things we must take up together.

10

RETIREMENT

Y OU MAY NEVER HAVE HEARD of an economist named Harry
Markowitz, but back in the early 1950s he made a discovery that
transformed the way economists and financial managers look at investment and managing the associated risks. Today, politicians and
policymakers implicitly embrace Markowitz's insight as the key to
helping you make sure your "golden years" are truly golden. As a
twenty-five-year-old graduate student at the University of Chicago,
Markowitz had what's been described as "the most famous insight in
the history of modern finance." So revolutionary was the insight and
so far-reaching was its impact that, in 1990, Markowitz received the
Nobel Prize in Economics. Among other things, Markowitz's work
helped recast the stock and bond markets, the brokerage business,
banking, and insurance. It's probably not too much to say that almost every decision financial strategists make today owes a debt to
Harry Markowitz and his insight.

In oversimplified terms, what Markowitz saw boiled down to this:
When people make financial arrangements for the future, they

should not put all their investment eggs in one basket. Instead, they should diversify. Obvious as this may seem now, it was not obvious in the past; most economists thought it made sense to pick a good investment and bet the farm on it. And even after Markowitz proved that was a bad strategy, it turned out that implementing his approach was quite hard to do. That's because of another part of Markowitz's insight—namely, that to be successful, diversification requires more than mere variety. Putting your eggs in two baskets instead of one does little good if the same person is carrying both baskets; one slip and all the eggs still break. The trick is to offset the inherent risks of one investment with the inherent strengths of another—balancing investments that would prosper in boom times, for example, with others that would gain strength in leaner times. It's also wise to invest in enterprises that are not dependent on each other the way, for instance, the steel and auto industries are. Markowitz's genius lay not just in seeing the importance of diversification but in designing complex mathematical models to help choose the right combinations of different investments. Over the past fifty years, his strategy and the mathematical successors to his complex models have become the conventional wisdom of sophisticated financial management. No modern-day banker, Wall Street portfolio manager, or corporate financial officer would dream of operating without the benefit of Markowitz's thinking.

Yet as great as the impact of his insight has been on modern-day economics and business strategy at the professional level, the idea may be even more critical for the average American family because such families are now expected to become masters of their individual financial destinies—most especially, the part of the financial future known as retirement. This application of the idea of individual responsibility is at the heart of the great transformation that has occurred in American society over the past quarter century—the shifting of the burden of ensuring financial security away from large institutions such as government and business corporations and onto individuals and families. Nowhere is this risk shift more complete or potentially devastating than when it comes to retirement. With the rise of 401(k) plans and other defined contribution arrangements, the sine qua non for a secure and comfortable retirement is successful management of one's savings and investments over the forty or so years of a typical working life. And, given the inevitable economic ups and downs during such a long period of time, no single strategic principle is as important as sophisticated diversification.

The idea of individual responsibility as a justification for risk shift rests on the assumption that people can and will make the kinds of shrewd financial decisions that experts are expected to make. After all, if ordinary people can't manage their own finances, including the critical challenge of retirement, it would be irresponsible folly for the institutions that have the necessary resources and capabilities to do the job to thrust that responsibility onto those who don't. If people cannot become skilled financial managers, diversifying their investments to protect against future shocks and setbacks, then the approach to retirement that's now in vogue could turn out to be a disaster for millions of people. It also could be a disaster for the country as a whole. That makes the shift of responsibility for retirement to the individual one of the biggest policy gambles of the modern era.

So how is the great roll of the dice going? Are people stepping up to their new responsibilities? Are they showing that they can acquire and apply the expertise necessary for successful long-term investment? Well, the early evidence is not reassuring. A great many people don't seem to have any interest in becoming active players in the new game; quite a few seem to ignore the whole thing. Among those who do take an active hand, a great many don't seem to be very good at it. Mastering the art of long-term money management seems to be a lot harder than the politicians and policy theorists who brought us this new system suggested it would be. (That shouldn't come as a surprise: Professionals, who work full-time at it, have a lot of failures, too.) Finally, the notion that individuals can use the diversification strategies and tactics that big investment firms employ to ensure long-term financial success has a fatal flaw: The biggest factor in most people's finances is their own work. It's what we earn by our labor that makes investing for retirement possible—along with just about everything else in our lives. And, in an age of increasing specialization, how can we diversify our labor? The manager of a stock portfolio can diversify his holdings by putting some of his money into manufacturing, some into service industries, and some into high tech. But how can an individual do the equivalent of that with his work? Can I, for example, cover my flanks by having simultaneous careers as a writer, a doctor, and a computer programmer?

IN LOOKING DEEPER into the new theory of individual responsibility as it applies to retirement, let us start with the question of whether people are in fact willing to take on the job. And, since we've been talking about Harry Markowitz's insight into the importance of diversification, let us begin with him—not as a Nobel laureate, but as an individual who's supposed to take financial responsibility for his own golden years. Surely, if anybody should be ready to step up to the plate, it should be the father of modern finance. When it came to investing his own retirement savings, however, Markowitz concedes that he barely managed to practice what he preached. Today, he laughs at the primitiveness of his diversification decision. "I either had in my head or had just written down the most revolutionary theory of investment the world had ever seen, and here I was asked, 'How do you want to invest your retirement?' and I said '50:50'"—a rudimentary split of his old-age savings between a stock fund and some conservative low-interest bonds. "I'm twenty-four, twenty-five. I'm never going to retire. I'm never going to die. I had other things to think about," the now eighty-year-old economist said of the young man who made that simpleminded decision. "In retrospect," his older self reflected, "I should have done something more sophisticated."

If there's anything that economists, policy experts, and political leaders are sure is true about America over the past twenty-five years, it's that its citizens have become financially sophisticated. The inflation of the 1970s weaned us of our pedestrian fixation on ordinary passbook savings accounts. The market boom of the 1980s and 1990s showed us where the real money was, and money market accounts, mutual funds, and discount brokers let us go after it. When the market lost its glow after the bust of 2000, mortgage refinancing and home equity loans let us get the game going all over again, this time with our houses. Americans, we are widely told, have turned their families into financial portfolios; they've gotten their own piece of the action.

But with the exception of a few at the very top, the idea that America has become a nation of mini–J. P. Morgans simply doesn't bear scrutiny. Virtually all of the financial wealth we've gathered has come not from wheeling and dealing but from buying houses and signing up for employer-sponsored savings plans. Essentially, we don't save in any other way. When it comes to nonfinancial house wealth, there are few signs that most people traded their way to the real estate top; we just happened to be living in houses whose values rose as part of a broad phenomenon that extended across almost the whole U.S. economy and now seems to be coming to an abrupt and painful end. As for our business acumen, there is a growing body of evidence that a substantial fraction of Americans, even many spectacularly educated and accomplished ones, can't get the most elementary investment decisions right.

None of this would represent a terribly serious problem were it not for two developments, both having to do with how Americans are expected to pay for their retirements. The first is that the nation's employers, who not only provide us our jobs but also serve as conduits for our wealth accumulation, want out of the retirement business. For more than a generation, by offering traditional pensions, employers have played a central role in ensuring that much of the nation had enough to live on in old age. But they don't want to play that role any longer. "Employers are no longer interested in having the responsibility for and bearing the risks of their employees' retirement saving," said retirement authority Alicia Munnell.

The second development is that the 401(k)s, individual retirement accounts (IRAs), and other accounts that are supposed to be the free-market replacements for the fading employer-based retirement system and crucially depend on individual investment savvy have stumbled badly and are recognized by a wide variety of policymakers as having done so. Indeed, quietly and without renouncing their public commitment to President George W. Bush's vision of the "Ownership Society," leaders in Washington and some parts of the business community have begun to reverse course. As we shall see, they have begun adopting policies that take some financial freedoms away from people by making it harder for workers to neglect their retirement savings plans and making it easier to automatically enroll new employees in 401(k) programs unless those employees go out of their way to object.

The switch from traditional pensions to individual retirement accounts may be the clearest example of the risk shift that this book argues is occurring in nearly every corner of Americans' lives. And it illustrates how big changes can occur with little fanfare. The shortcomings of individual accounts and the efforts to shore them up are a lesser-known story. The story shows that for all our pretensions, most of us are not—and at some level cannot be—the financial sophisticates that the new retirement investment system presumes we will be.

Traditional pensions are designed to provide their recipients with a guaranteed income in old age almost no matter what. Because employers promise to make fixed payments to retirees, these pensions are known as "defined benefit" plans. Because those payments are usually so far in the future, grow with an employee's tenure with a firm, and must continue from retirement until a person dies, employers are expected to save and invest funds to ensure that they can meet their obligations. The risk of investing and the responsibility for paying are entirely theirs, not the employee's.

The old system was not foolproof. People who left their jobs before they'd put in the requisite number of years with a company got nothing. And some employers simply reneged on their promise of a pension. But in the latter case, the government stepped in. The federal Pension Benefit Guaranty Corporation collects premiums from companies and acts as a pension insurer. The combination of a company-provided, government-guaranteed pension and the federal government's two giant defined benefit programs, Social Security and Medicare, made for a powerful bulwark against financial trouble in old age.

By contrast, individual accounts such as 401(k)s involve no similar promise of income. Instead, what these accounts offer is a tax break for people to put aside money for retirement out of their own paychecks. Employers may contribute to the pot, which is why these kinds of accounts are called "defined contribution" plans. But that's the limit of their obligation. The risks and responsibilities are all on the employee.

America changed from a defined benefit society to a defined contribution society over the past two or three decades, and did it with barely a ripple. Half the nation's private-sector workforce had non–Social Security retirement plans in 1980, and half had them in 2004, the latest year for which numbers are available. But beneath this placid surface, the retirement system was turned upside down. In 1980, 62 percent of private-sector workers belonged to plans promising defined benefit pensions. By 2005, that number had dropped to just 10 percent, while 63 percent had defined contribution arrangements.

Explaining how such momentous change could have occurred— and with barely a peep of objection, or even debate—is a challenge, especially when you consider that it has occurred at the very moment when the job of accumulating enough money for a secure retirement has gotten harder. Rising life expectancy, rapidly escalating medical costs, and Washington's gradual increase in the retirement age for Social Security, which effectively reduced benefits, have all boosted the amount of money retirees need in order to be sure their resources last as long as they do. One reason for the lack of fuss over the change was the stock boom of the 1980s and 1990s. At some point during the past two decades, many people seem to have concluded that the market had slipped the bounds of mere finance and become something grander—a reality show more engrossing than any yet devised by the networks and an unsinkable vessel for carrying on the American Dream. Individuals seemed to lose sight of the fact that the market could go down as well as up. Perhaps equally important for those who reached retirement during a trough, it could stay down for long periods. Many behaved as if they were on an up escalator to wealth that had no "off" switch.

Another big factor was probably the changing view of many mainstream economists, social theorists, and public policymakers. Since at least the Great Depression, many of these people had distrusted the market as prone to unfairness and self-destruction. But as the century came to a close, the doubters became convinced that the market offered the country its best—perhaps its only—way out of a series of excruciating challenges: how to pay for generous past promises of benefits, how to compete with foreign rivals who seemed to face no similar costs, and how to cope with the coming crush of the baby-boom retirement. The idea was that, left to play their free-market roles, individual Americans would invest their own way to retirement security and thus relieve business and the government of the job.

Finally, by the time employers began rewriting their pension plans, millions of workers had so little leverage that protesting was practically impossible. For a host of reasons, labor unions—the most active negotiators in creating the old pension system—had withered away. More and more workers held the kinds of midlevel white-collar jobs in which employees had never bargained over benefits, and there was no shortage of reasonably well-educated workers. When employers sent out notices announcing the new defined contribution system, expressions of concern or unhappiness rarely went beyond the water cooler.

FROM THE VERY OUTSET, the question hovering over the new approach was how well people would do investing on their own. A mid-1990s *Wall Street Journal* story put the problem this way: "By the year 2000, employees will be managing $1 trillion of their own money in 401(k) retirement plans. [By the first half of 2007, the latest period for which figures are available, that number was $2.97 trillion. If you count IRAs, which are mostly filled with rolled-over 401(k) money, and other types of defined contribution accounts, it was $9 trillion.] What if they goof up?"

The answer, it turns out, is that enough people have goofed up enough of the time that the shimmering promise of an on-your-own, free-market 401(k) retirement system has largely proved to be a chimera. Until recently, more than two decades into the do-it-yourself experiment, one out of every five people eligible for employer-sponsored 401(k)s failed to sign up for them, according to the Federal Reserve. More than half of those who did sign up pumped their money either into overly conservative or overly aggressive investments, according to the industry-financed Employee Benefit Research Institute. Nearly half put a substantial chunk of their money into the stock of the company they worked for, a big mistake because it leaves people dependent on a firm's success for both their paychecks and their retirement benefits—the classic eggs-in-one-basket error. Only 10 percent contributed the maximum amount allowed. Almost no one changed investment choices, even though experts harangue that investments must be regularly adjusted to accommodate people's age and market conditions.

Even more disconcerting, recent research suggests that many people don't behave anything like the economically savvy men and women that the on-your-own, free-market system requires in order for them to succeed. They shut down in the face of multiple choices. Offered the same investment, but with low and high fees, they go for the high ones. In effect, they walk away from free money. It is not a confidence-inspiring set of behaviors.

The mistakes have taken their toll. In 2004, the last year for which figures are available, the median balance of 401(k) accounts for households closing in on retirement with adult members fifty-five to sixty-four was $83,000, according to the Federal Reserve. That may seem like a reasonable amount, but it is only enough to buy a monthly benefit payment of about $570. The general rule is that a family's personal retirement savings should be enough to make up at least half of their preretirement income. This would barely be enough to keep a couple above the poverty line.

In committing the kind of investment errors that have produced these results, ordinary Americans are not alone. Many Nobel Prize winners admit to similar errors. Some of the nation's most prestigious educational institutions have built the mistakes right into the way they operate their retirement systems. Markowitz won the Nobel for devising elaborate methods for handling investment risk. But he admits that he didn't take on enough risk when he was young by pumping more of his money into stocks. He explains his decision this way: "If I'd gone too high on the [risk] frontier, I would have gotten ulcers."

Douglass C. North won the prize in 1993 for work on the importance of institutions in fostering growth. But when it came to investing his $400,000 share of the prize money, he trusted his gut, rather than institutions. He decided the stock market, which, as it would turn out, was only halfway through its long bull run, had peaked, so he pumped the money into low-interest municipal bonds. As a result, he said, "My wife spent years berating me." Still, he stubbornly hung on to those bonds, and stocks eventually reversed course and plunged. The chief benefit, he said, was "my wife quit berating me."

Joseph E. Stiglitz, who won the Nobel Prize for his work on how "imperfect information" affects economic decisions, was studying investment in the mid-1970s when he decided to put all of his retirement money into stocks. The problem is that he then went on to study other things and left the money right where he'd parked it. That looked like a brilliant decision right up until the 2000 stock bust, which he said anyone could see coming. "If I'd only listened to myself," he laments, "I would be considerably better off than I am today."

George Akerlof, who shared the prize with Stiglitz for his analysis of the mismatch of information between sellers and buyers of used cars in an essay titled "The Market for Lemons," put a substantial chunk of his retirement savings into money market accounts, which until recently were a lemon of an investment because of historically low interest rates.

Markowitz, North, Stiglitz, and Akerlof are hardly alone among Nobelists in making mistakes. In interviews with a majority of the twenty-five U.S.-based prizewinners in economics, I found many who acknowledged slipping up, either by making faulty decisions or by failing to pay attention to their own retirement arrangements. Nor is the Nobel fraternity atypical of the nation's educated elite. In a survey of several premier universities, including Harvard and Stanford, I discovered that roughly half of the faculties and staffs of these institutions failed to make any decision about retirement at hiring. The result, at least until recently, was that they allowed their retirement savings to be funneled into low-earning investments. The same forget-about-it approach shows up among the 3.2 million members of TIAA-CREF, the Teachers Insurance and Annuity Association-College Retirement Equities Fund, which oversees the retirement investments of most of the nation's college professors and research scientists. One study suggested almost three-quarters failed to make a single adjustment to their retirement accounts during the long course of their careers, despite repeated urgings of experts to change the mix of their investments as they age.

What this record of slipups and inattention suggests is that the policymakers who launched the nation's quarter-century experiment in free-market retirement investment were operating on a faulty assumption. Most families, it seems, *don't* want to be active investors. Clearly, some do. But a huge number of people—both Nobel laureates and normal citizens—find the rest of their lives plenty demanding and can't or don't want to spare the time that their 401(k)s require. "I think very little about my retirement savings," said 2002 Nobel Prize winner Daniel Kahneman, "because I know that thinking could make me poorer or more miserable or both."

"Investment is not something you can do with your left hand, so I decided I should not do it at all," said 1987 winner Robert M. Solow.

"I would rather spend my time enjoying my income than bothering about investments," said Clive W. J. Granger, a 2003 winner.

IN THEORY AT LEAST, this record of resistance and lack of interest could change in the future. But what about the question of whether it's realistic to think that people are capable of doing the job once they decide it's necessary? Can people actually learn enough about managing their retirement investments to be secure and reasonably comfortable after they stop working?

One reason for concern is that retirement investment is more complex than almost any other kind of financial task that individual Americans are expected to perform—including financing a house or paying for college—because it is spread across such a long period of time and involves so many imponderables. "You can't know whether you've done it right and provided yourself with an adequate retirement until it's too late," said Stiglitz, "and you can't do it over and over and learn from your mistakes."

Moreover, there's not much accrued collective wisdom about how to manage retirement investment. That's almost inevitable because retirement is a problem of such recent vintage that society has had comparatively little time to figure out how to deal with it. In earlier times, relatively few people lived long enough to face extended retirement. And those who survived usually kept working, often at less demanding tasks. Most also accepted very modest standards of living. For much of the nineteenth century, three of four post-65-year olds still worked. Many of those who didn't, owned property or the tools of a trade that could be sold or leased for income, or they relied on their families. But as urbanization broke up extended families and industrialization removed production from farms and village shops to factories in big cities, individuals increasingly came to rely on wage work. As they did, they faced the question of how to survive when the work stopped.

The answer was savings, but of an extraordinarily complicated kind. "The problem of vision was especially acute," economist Steven Sass wrote about the changed circumstances in which people found themselves in the new industrial economy. "The very concept of 'unemployment'—of which modern old age retirement is part—did not enter the popular consciousness" before the end of the nineteenth century, Sass said. The idea that people would invest their retirement savings in anything more than passbook savings accounts barely made it into the culture before the end of the twentieth century.

Seeing retirement investment as a task that has been thrust on most people, one that's incredibly hard to learn and one for which society offers few guideposts, helps explain the findings of recent research. This research focuses on Americans' actual investment behavior, as opposed to what the models say people should do. The findings appear to document outbreaks of economic irrationality: 401(k) investors, for example, regularly demand more investment options from their retirement plan, but as the number of account choices goes up, the number of choices that people actually make goes down. "People say they want more choice, but when they're given it, they get overwhelmed and use it as a reason to opt out of deciding," Columbia University researcher Sheena S. Iyengar said.

On costs, a Harvard-Yale research team recently asked a test group to allocate $10,000 among four mutual funds, all of which were invested in the same stocks and differed *only* in the fees they charged. In the first round of the experiment, 95 percent of participants failed to choose the least-expensive option. In a second round, the fee differences were specifically pointed out to the test participants, but 80 percent still failed to select the lowest-cost fund. Analysts said that participants seemed intent on figuring out which of the funds offered the greatest return, even though the four offered essentially the same annual return. This appears to be a case where the investment task appeared so complex that it left people confused about what to focus on.

Concerning economic self-interest, analysts have long wondered why so many 401(k) investors fail to put enough in their accounts to get their employer's full matching amount. The reason people most often give is that they don't want to tie up their money, then have to pay government-imposed tax penalties if they need to withdraw it. But when a Harvard-Yale team studied people who had reached an age where the penalties no longer applied, they discovered that 40 percent still failed to put in enough to get the match. "It's astounding. These people are doing the economic equivalent of leaving $100 bills on the sidewalk," said Harvard economist David Laibson, one of the researchers.

During the early years of 401(k)s, policymakers downplayed the significance of the new accounts by describing them as mere adjuncts to traditional pensions. "The law that created Section 401(k) of the Internal Revenue Code was designed to resolve a bureaucratic dispute between the IRS and companies, not to set off a financial revolution," said Daniel Halperin, a Harvard law professor who was deputy assistant treasury secretary for tax policy when the law was passed in 1978.

As the accounts became more widespread, policymakers explained the fact that many Americans had low balances—or no retirement savings at all except Social Security—by saying that the
system hadn't been in place long enough; it was not yet mature. As
for the evidence that people were making mistakes, advocates said
that would be handled by financial education. "The idea was that you
could educate people to be economic geniuses," said David C. John, a
senior analyst with the conservative Heritage Foundation, a strong
advocate of the 401(k) revolution.

But the investment aberrations—freezing up in the face of choice,
going for high-priced investment instead of the low-priced one, and
so forth—did not look like they would be easily amenable to education. And then the 2000 stock bust occurred. Although the market
has since recovered, the size of the drop and its damaging effect on
those who retired in the midst of the decline rattled policymakers. So
has the market's erratic behavior since 2007.

One estimate sought to gauge how "perfect" new retirement investors would have fared if they had put substantial savings into
401(k) accounts and finished their work lives at various points during the boom that ended in 2000 and subsequent bust. What this
study found was that those who retired at the peak in 2000 could
have enjoyed one and a half times their preretirement income, while
those who retired a few years later in 2003 would have had only a little more than half as much income as they had before they retired.
The sheer size of the swing meant that there could be no errors;
people had to start saving at the very outset of their work lives, make
no mistakes along the way, and be very, very lucky at the end.

Quietly, companies began to change their approach. They did not
return to defined benefit programs, but they did begin to move away
from the idea that everything could be left up to the individual. Some
big companies, convinced that employees needed to save and fearful
about how long educating them to that need might take, began to enroll new employees in 401(k) plans automatically; to avoid investing

for retirement, employees had to take affirmative steps to opt out. By 2006, even many conservatives had become convinced that such automatic savings provisions were necessary. In the summer of 2006, Congress quietly approved provisions that will mean millions of Americans arriving at new jobs will find that if they do not choose to invest in a 401(k), their employers will "automatically default" them into one, unless they say otherwise. They will learn that if they don't make a decision about where the money should be invested, it will automatically flow to one of several "default" investments, among them a "life-cycle fund" that will change in composition as they age. And they will discover that instead of the amount going into the account being something minimal, like 3 percent of their paychecks, the amount will ratchet up to 10 percent or more unless they object. "This is the free market on cruise control," said former Bush administration assistant labor secretary Ann L. Combs. "We put people in the driver's seat and found a lot of them didn't know how to drive. They went too fast—or even too slow."

Of course, some Americans don't need cruise control. Retirement investment has been their ticket to a world that was once the exclusive domain of financial titans. They have snapped up stocks, bonds, mutual funds, and sometimes more exotic investments, and learned to tap the rising values of their homes. They have complied with Markowitz's message about diversification better than he has. As a result, they have assembled comfortable nest eggs that are available to them not just in old age but even before. Indeed, the 401(k) experience has convinced many people that they are as financially competent as any individual or business in today's economy, as capable of using free-market tools to hedge against dangers such as illness or unemployment and grab for the good life.

In thinking this, people may not fully appreciate how much has changed since Markowitz had his famous insight about diversification, how almost infinitely flexible the new financial thinking that Markowitz helped spawn has allowed the business and investment

worlds to become, and how people who must work for a living operate at a disadvantage when they try to rely on individual accounts
and investments to secure their families' futures. To understand why
this is so requires looking a little more closely at what Markowitz discovered, examining the advantages and limits of his discovery for
families, and then looking at one person's not-altogether-successful
attempt to put the Nobel Prize winner's theory into practice.

THAT MARKOWITZ would decide to study the stock market and investment as he began an academic career was a surprise. In the early
1950s, the wreckage of the Depression was still so fresh in the minds
of most economists that the market was not thought to be an entirely
legitimate topic of scholarly inquiry. And actually making an investment seemed even less legitimate; there was no telling whether you'd
win or lose. Markowitz and his successors invented mathematical
models that revealed an order behind the chaos of the market and
provided business and professional investors with tools to shape,
limit, and control the risks they took when they made investments.
The ideas transformed Wall Street, the financial operations of corporations around the world, and, to the extent they helped spur creation of diversified mutual funds, the options open to working
Americans investing for their own retirements.

   But in several important respects, these ideas were—and are—
off-limits to the majority of American families. In many cases, families don't have the financial assets to participate in the markets where
the ideas hold sway, so they can't benefit from them. Far more important, their biggest asset, bigger in some ways than their houses—
their own labor and that of their family members—doesn't fit the
models. A company can diversify its financial arrangements or business lines to protect against setbacks in any one area. But managers
for that very same company must basically depend on their work to
make a living and rely on whatever they can save after daily expenses
to tide them over should they face trouble. The result is that many

of the tools available to shield Wall Street and Corporate America from economic danger are not available to working America. And many of the safety nets that are specifically designed to redress this imbalance between business and individuals—such things as unemployment compensation and disability insurance—have been skimmed back, leaving working Americans more exposed to financial setbacks.

At the time Markowitz proposed his study, his professors knew so little about the stock market that they had to send him to the library to read up on the subject. Markowitz zeroed in on a book that explained that investors should value a stock by projecting its future dividends, deciding how confident they were about those projections, then picking the one with the highest expected payoff. The problem, as Markowitz quickly spotted, was that this implied that they should pick *only* the preferred stock. After all, why invest in anything with a lower payoff? As he thought about this approach, the young graduate student quickly realized that investors would be spending far too much time focused on the reward or return of a stock and not enough on the risk of it. He also realized that they were devoting too much effort to picking single stocks and not enough to assembling groups or portfolios that would allow them to spread out or diversify their risk of losing on any one.

In focusing on risk and diversification, Markowitz was flying in the face of the conventional wisdom of the time. Peter L. Bernstein, in a book that's in part about Markowitz and his insights called *Capital Ideas,* quotes the economic giant John Maynard Keynes arguing in favor of putting all of your eggs in one basket—just the right basket. "To suppose that safety-first consists in having a small gamble in a large number of different [companies] . . . , as compared to a substantial stake in a [single] company, strikes me as a travesty of investment policy," Keynes said. Wall Street broker and pundit Gerald Loeb was similarly dismissive, labeling diversification "undesirable" and "an admission of not knowing what to do and an effort to strike an average."

Beginning with the assumption that all finance involves a trade-off between risk and reward, Markowitz devised methods for constructing diversified portfolios that would do better than single or concentrated investments for the same risk. Such portfolios were not simply big collections of stocks, because some sets of stocks all do well or poorly together and so provide no protection against each other. Instead, he devised methods of assembling collections of stocks or other investments whose values moved at counterpoint to each other, like the valves of an engine. If one was sinking in value, another was rising. Such finely tuned mechanisms offered Wall Street investment managers and the chief financial officers of major companies the means to achieve the highest likely reward for a given amount of risk, or the lowest risk for a given level of return. That constituted a substantial improvement over Keynes or Loeb, who might succeed in making an investment with a higher payoff, but only at the risk of a bigger loss.

WHY CAN'T DIVERSIFICATION WORK the same wonder for families? It *can* for some parts of their lives (for example, for their retirement accounts); although Markowitz's models are not readily adaptable for individual use, it is possible to find investment funds that make good use of his ideas. But in the current competitive economy, where safety nets that once offered protection have been removed or weakened, we are effectively being asked to think of our families as free-standing businesses that shield themselves much as corporations or investment houses do by measuring and apportioning the risks they face, by building in hedges against dangers, by diversifying investments or operations. And this is where the trouble starts. Even if a family could be persuaded to accept the challenge, even if it could save a lot, acquire sufficient expertise, and make none of the mistakes humans typically make, it would still face the task of diversifying away from its single biggest asset—the earning power of its members. And that's nearly impossible.

I am a "mainstream media" journalist. If—as is happening—the mainstream media business starts plunging, I can't suddenly turn myself into a heart surgeon. Nor can I buy an insurance policy against mainstream-media failure. I could invest in Internet stocks, which seem to be going up as the mainstream media goes down. But I'm already bearing a lot of risk because of what's happening to my profession; this hardly seems the time to pump money into risky stocks. In any case, it's hard to imagine being able to afford enough shares to offset my loss if I have to take a pay cut or if I lose my job.

The situation is not totally bleak. If I am laid off, I can tide myself over a short period by collecting unemployment benefits. If my job truly has become outmoded, I can go back to school and train for a new kind of work, although this option fades with age simply because there's less time left to complete the training, find the new job, and pursue the new career long enough to make a significant difference at retirement. On the other hand, something that could improve with age is that my family and I could have more savings and therefore have less of our total assets tied up in our earnings power. Young people, on the other hand, have almost nothing but their earning power.

The most striking aspect of this problem is the conflict between what the economy seems to tell workers they should do and what it rewards them for actually doing. It asks families to operate as little businesses and handle a wide array of dangers just as regular businesses and investors do—by diversifying. Yet it rewards workers for doing the very opposite: concentrating on a particular profession or trade. In fact, specialization and concentration are at the heart of the modern economy, the very things that distinguish it from the early nineteenth century. In that era, before the emphasis on specialization and maximum output per worker, older people could find some productive activity until late in life, and retirement was not a big problem. But we're not about to return to that world, and it wouldn't solve our current problem if we did. Even in the eighteenth and nineteenth centuries, workers who did not specialize were almost always at the bottom of the earnings ladder. A skilled cabinet-maker earned more than a rough carpenter who framed barns and outbuildings. Tool and die makers, whose intricate skills were essential to most industrial operations, made more than assembly-line workers even after the advent of unions.

The notion of a family as a business that can handle a wide array of problems with the aid of various individual accounts such as 401(k)s; health, dependent-care, and commuter tax-saver accounts; and health savings accounts—the idea at the very center of the "Ownership Society" agenda—is not the product of modern finance. It is a nostalgic throwback to a previous, perhaps simpler, era in American history. Working families cannot play the roles assigned them in an Ownership Society, not simply because of the shortfalls in their investment skills or because their time is consumed by more pressing matters such as raising children, but because they can't escape their reliance on paid work, most often specialized work. In the parlance of Markowitz and modern finance, they cannot diversify against their largest single asset—their jobs.

The only working model I know about of someone who seems to have tried such a diversification is a fellow who recently painted a house for me in Ipswich, Massachusetts. He is a house painter. He is also a clam digger. He plows out driveways after winter storms. It's a near-perfect example of Markowitzian diversification—income streams from completely unrelated and mutually reinforcing activities. Clams in summer, snow in winter, house painting in between. But adding all the streams together doesn't yield enough to make my house painter a model that many middle-class American parents would recommend to their children. That's because about the only people who can diversify their labor are people with relatively little specialized skill or training. And in our society, that's not where the money or the good life can be found.

The story of one family that tried to apply Harry Markowitz's ideas at a higher skill level illustrates the limits to what working people across most of the economic spectrum can do.

For more than two decades, Lowell Seibert made a living driving pile and working as a highly skilled millwright erecting huge pieces of industrial machinery across the Midwest. But with mortgage payments, college tuitions, and, most important, the prospect of retirement looming, Seibert traded in his outdoor job seventeen years ago and went to work for the Packard Electric division of auto-parts giant Delphi Corporation in Warren, Ohio. He was offered nineteen dollars an hour (eventually raised to thirty-two), good benefits, and the promise of a solid pension and old-age health insurance. "Heavy construction is a rush," he said of his old position, "but Packard was a sure thing."

Fifty-nine-year-old Seibert is a precise man. He can still describe in minute detail his last job before going to Delphi. He oversaw the installation of something called a continuous caster at WCI Steel, Inc., in Warren. The device, 10 stories high and 500 feet long, swallows liquefied metal at one end and spits out immense steel slabs at the other. It had to be assembled to tolerances of only a few thousandths of an inch, or about the thickness of your fingernail. It ran like a charm on its maiden run.

The same kind of precision is apparent in the plan Seibert assembled for his retirement and that of his wife, a nurse named Christine Ferranti. Although he doesn't know Markowitz from Adam, Seibert understood the idea of not having all of your eggs in one basket, especially in an economy like the Midwest's, which has been in decline almost from the moment Seibert went to work straight out of high school in 1968. He devised what seemed like a foolproof financial arrangement that relied on no single source for retirement security.

The way Seibert figured it, after he retired, he could precisely match his top monthly wage at Delphi by drawing about $1,300 a month from his millwright union's pension and like amounts from his Delphi pension, his Delphi-sponsored 401(k), and Social Security. The goal was to retire at sixty-two, he said. "I thought I was pretty much set."

Seibert's plan wasn't perfect. It would not have met Markowitz's exacting requirement that the elements of a perfectly diversified portfolio vary in value completely independently of each other and at perfect counterpoint. Seibert's union, Carpenters and Millwrights Local 171 in Youngstown, Ohio, depended on the steel industry, which, in turn, depended heavily on the auto industry. Delphi depended on the auto industry. That meant the fates of the union and the company, although in no way formally tied to each other, were likely to fluctuate in sync, which is not good for diversification. In addition, like nearly half of individual retirement investors, Seibert felt that he knew his own employer better than he did other companies, so he directed that *all* of the money he saved through his 401(k) be invested in Delphi stock, which further tied his fate to the auto industry.

Compared with most Americans, however, the Seiberts were in spectacular shape, having arranged for so many sources of retirement money, having put together enough to replace 100 percent of his top wages, rather than just the 80 percent most retirement experts say should be the goal, and having secured through Delphi the promise of retiree health benefits to supplement the government's Medicare.

With this kind of comfortable retirement income at their disposal, the couple made big plans for old age. Seibert took up golf. The pair mapped out trips to Europe and Las Vegas, and regular visits to Disney World with their new grandson, Anthony. And they planned to put the finishing touches on the two-story Dutch colonial that Seibert built for his family in the early 1980s but never quite finished. Among the items on their to-do list: new siding, landscaping,

an enclosed back deck off the kitchen, and new furniture and carpeting for the family room. A key item was to be an extra-wide La-Z-
Boy recliner so that Seibert could tuck in with future grandchildren
to read them stories.

Then Delphi declared bankruptcy.

In October 2005, Delphi's newly installed chief executive, Robert
"Steve" Miller, citing global competition and crippling "legacy costs,"
ushered the nearly $30 billion-a-year company into one of the largest
industrial bankruptcies in U.S. history. Miller immediately began saber-
rattling about slashing workers' pay, voiding the company's union contracts, and dumping the firm's pensions on the federal government. In
doing so, Miller drew from a playbook that he had already used at Bethlehem Steel, to damaging effect for workers like Ron Burtless, the steel
company electrician who was injured on the job.

Miller's actions were widely seen as corporate guerrilla warfare.
His aim was to push Delphi's unions, the United Auto Workers and
the International Union of Electrical Workers-Communications
Workers of America, which represents workers in the Packard division, to the verge of strike. By doing so, he hoped to force the company's former parent and largest customer, General Motors, to step
in to pick up some of the costs of turning the long-troubled company around by shuttering plants and buying out workers. After almost two years of on-again, off-again bargaining, Miller got just
about everything he wanted.

The effect on the Seiberts came in stages. When the company
declared bankruptcy, shares of its stock immediately plunged from
a twelve-month high of $9 a share to just 33 cents a share. That
drove the value of Seibert's 401(k) from $85,000 to $5,000. The
money is gone and will not come back. Next came a waiting game
as the company and the unions hurled insults at each other while
negotiating a deal. Miller once described Delphi workers as little
better than overpaid lawn cutters. UAW president Ron Gettelfinger
returned the favor by calling Miller and his aides "hogs slopping at

the trough." Finally, the buyout offers and voluntary severance packages began to appear.

Seibert was offered $140,000 to walk away from the job, benefits, retirement and all. But that would have left his family without any health insurance. So in a complicated deal, he accepted a pared-back retirement under which he is paid the original amount he expected, but only until he is sixty-two and eligible for Social Security. Then the amount will drop from $1,300 a month, which is what he'd expected to receive under his neatly diversified plan, to $752. In return, he has been promised he will keep his family health benefits. He will still get his millwright's pension and, of course, Social Security. The way he figures it, "I missed my mark by $1,500 [a month]." What that means is that most of the trips, the siding, the landscaping, and the back deck go, as does the carpeting. Instead of a La-Z-Boy, Seibert has purchased a cheap knockoff. He has put away his golf clubs and begun looking for a job.

Because Miller cited foreign competition in taking Delphi into bankruptcy and because much of the auto-parts business has now gone overseas, Seibert figured he could get trade-adjustment assistance under a federal program to aid workers who lose their jobs because of imports. So he applied and was admitted to a program leading to an associate's degree in civil engineering from Youngstown State University. He even got some of the credits accepted that he'd earned when he'd attended classes thirty-five years earlier. But in June 2007, Washington said he doesn't qualify for the aid because he's collecting a pension. So he's applied for a maintenance supervisor's job at a local manufacturing plant, a position that will pay about half of what he was making at Delphi. If that doesn't work out, there are jobs at a lumberyard and the local Home Depot. One way or the other, he said, "I'm not going to be retiring anytime soon."

IF ONLY IT WAS THAT SIMPLE. If only we could solve the problems of investor blunders and market plunges by tacking a few extra years onto the end of our work lives. After all, most people are not just living longer but also staying healthy and vigorous longer; today's 65-year-old bears little resemblance to the 65-year-olds of our grand-parents' day. Moreover, there's evidence that continuing to work may be good for older people; it keeps their minds active, helps them stay engaged with the world. Congress has embraced the idea as part of a solution to the Social Security problem; it's begun to ratchet up the age at which workers can retire with full benefits.

Unfortunately, continuing to work will not solve the core prob-lems of having not saved enough or paid enough attention to our in-vestments or having retired during a market downturn. And it will not cope with the danger of outliving our retirement funds. For one thing, it's unlikely that many workers can stay on the job long enough to do more than modestly augment their 401(k)s and other savings arrangements; the mismatch is simply too great between what can be set aside in a few years and how much is needed to sup-port decades of retirement. Moreover, a substantial number of work-ers will encounter medical or other problems that make continued, full-time work impossible. And in case you hadn't noticed, most em-ployers are not clamoring for older, more experienced employees; they're pushing for younger, cheaper ones.

Working longer also does nothing to resolve the fundamental contradiction between the notion that we can invest our way to re-tirement bliss by employing the precepts of diversification and risk-reward trade-offs and the fact that most of us can't diversify our most valuable asset—our own labor. Like it or not, we are in a work world that increasingly expects us to specialize. That leaves us hos-tage to how the economy chooses to treat the specialty we pick and makes it hard to turn our families into the kind of financial portfo-lios that successful retirement investment requires.

Of all the elements of modern American life affected by the shift of risk from business and government to families, providing for your own old age may be the one that makes the most unimaginable demands. The lengths of time involved are so long—the thirty, forty, or fifty years of a work life. The uncontrollable factors such as health and economic change are so great. There are no "redos"—you don't find out whether you've successfully executed your retirement arrangements until it's too late to do much about them. And the demand for success is extraordinarily high; if even one-third of working people are inadequately prepared to retire, as many experts believe, that could spell a very different, and distinctly less humane, America than that of the past half century. The combination suggests that people are going to have to engage in a level of savings vastly greater than anything most have shown the resources or inclination to do to date. Or we are going to have to find ways to get the big institutions of society that have been sloughing risk onto families to resume some of the roles that they played until recently and pick up a substantial share of the retirement burden once again.

11

NEW ORLEANS

Laurie Vignaud and Nicole Mackie face double dilemmas: If either restores her wrecked house in the great suburban expanse north of downtown New Orleans, will her neighbors do the same? And even if they and the neighbors do, will that be enough to ensure that their Gentilly neighborhood doesn't end up an isolated pocket in a diminished post-Katrina New Orleans?

For now, the two women—colleagues, members of New Orleans' African American middle class, and housing experts with Capital One, one of the nation's largest financial institutions—have come down on opposite sides of the questions. Forty-eight-year-old Vignaud, who escaped the 2005 hurricane with her two teenage daughters and her aging parents, has purchased a townhouse in Houston and set down roots there. Although she has had her flooded New Orleans ranch house gutted to stop the rot, the place remains boarded up. She doubts her old neighborhood will ever fully recover. By contrast, thirty-six-year-old Mackie, who dodged the storm with her husband, Earl, and the couple's young son and daughter, has returned to the city. With a

$100,000 insurance settlement and most of the couple's savings, plus Earl, a contractor, to do the work, the Mackies have patched up their flooded one-story and tried to resume their former lives.

Neither woman is entirely comfortable with the decisions that she and her family have reached, so each has left herself an out. Vignaud recently renewed her Louisiana driver's license and displays Louisiana plates on the Lexus RX 330 she purchased at Sterling McCall Lexus in Houston. The Mackies have agreed on what they will do if disaster strikes again. "We will go and never come back again," said Nicole.

MUCH OF AMERICA'S new prosperity is on vivid display in luxury cars such as Vignaud's Lexus and in the proliferation of such amenities as stainless-steel appliances and home electronics centers. But many of the country's new economic perils are invisible—problems with jobs, health care, and insurance that individuals must handle privately, without the help of, or even discussion with, friends and neighbors. There is, however, one example of a peril that combines in garish fashion how much less most Americans can expect from their employers, insurers, government, and fellow citizens, and, conversely, how much more has been placed on their shoulders alone. And that example is New Orleans in the months and years immediately following Katrina.

What Katrina did was to take trends that had been under way in an unseen or uneven way for a quarter century and cause them to play out in concentrated, rapid-fire—and therefore floridly obvious— fashion. In effect, the storm turned New Orleans into a giant petri dish for how contemporary America approaches the challenge of what kind of country it is and wants to be. "All of a sudden, time sped up in New Orleans," said former Tulane University School of Architecture dean Reed Kroloff. "Time sped up, and both the problems that were slowly destroying the city before the storm and the social and economic changes that were slowly remaking the nation took on a physical form that everybody could recognize. It's rare anyone gets to experience this kind of thing, and not always good," said Kroloff. "But," he added, "it offers an incredible, once-in-a-lifetime chance to recalibrate where we are headed."

Katrina was a tragedy for most of America's Gulf Coast. It visited death and devastation on Biloxi and Gulfport, Mississippi; Mobile, Alabama; and hundreds of towns and rural communities along the coast. What sets the New Orleans area apart is the scale of the destruction there. The storm generated not only wind and rains but a surge from Lake Pontchartrain to the north that overwhelmed the venerable levees, pumps, and drainage canals that were supposed to protect the city. By the time it was over, more than seven hundred people had died in New Orleans alone, many of them nursing home patients and other elderly and infirm persons who were among those left behind in the bungled evacuation. The infrastructure that is the cardiovascular system of a modern city scarcely existed as the floodwaters receded—from sewer, water, and power services to hospitals, schools, and police and fire protection. Survivors were scattered from West Texas to the Upper Midwest; more than two years later nearly half of New Orleans' pre-Katrina population still had not returned. Michael Chertoff, the secretary of the Department of Homeland Security, called it "probably the worst catastrophe, or set of catastrophes," in the country's history.

In order to see New Orleans—which is so often treated as a strange flower and not really part of the rest of the country—as a case study of economic trends occurring nationally, it is necessary to step away from the Mississippi River, leave behind the preciously preserved French Quarter and antebellum Garden District, exit the tourist city, and head north into Lakeview, Gentilly, and New Orleans East. There, you will find suburbs that could be almost anywhere in the nation, coping with problems that would crop up after almost any catastrophe. Indeed, for all its reputation as the exotic exception, New Orleans after Katrina offers a much better example of what an

American community would look like after the kind of terror attacks that Washington now says are quite possible—more so than post-9/11 New York City, where the damage, though awful, was localized and society never really stopped functioning.

In order to realize that, despite the billions of dollars in public assistance, New Orleans' comeback has become a largely private affair among families and neighbors, you need to focus on the sheer number of double dilemmas of the sort Vignaud and Mackie are struggling with. Consider these, for example: More than two years after the disaster, the city's tottering electric utility, Entergy of New Orleans, still can't restore power to some neighborhoods because not enough people have moved back to foot the bill. But the people can't return until power has been restored. The Army Corps of Engineers, which has rebuilt its failed levees, says it can't guarantee the structures won't fail again. But absent a guarantee, insurers are reluctant to insure, lenders are reluctant to lend, and homeowners are reluctant to restore the very houses that the levees were repaired to protect. Many chain stores won't reopen until their customers are back. But the customers won't come back until the stores reopen. Many schools won't resume classes until their students return. But families can't return until there are classes for their children.

Officials portray these dilemmas as painful but entirely predictable parts of the recovery process. And they *are*—for a certain kind of recovery, one that relies almost entirely on individuals to decide where and how to rebuild, that depends on neighbors negotiating with neighbors over the terms and timing of return, that leaves families to foot the largest bills and shoulder the biggest burdens of a comeback. It's reasonable to expect these problems, in other words, when the recovery is largely a free-market affair.

By now, the free-market approach seems to have been all but inevitable from the get-go. But it was not the only option available to New Orleans in the immediate aftermath of Katrina. It was not the only one considered by national and local leaders. And it was not the one followed by many other communities along the storm-damaged Gulf Coast. Indeed, if government policy prior to Katrina had been any guide, if the post-storm proposals by even conservative Republicans had gained any traction, if President George W. Bush's call for a great national undertaking on behalf of New Orleans had enjoyed any follow-up, the city's rebuilding would likely have been faster, more complete, and troubled with far fewer double dilemmas.

It's not that free-market strategies can never work on social problems. More than two hundred years of American history testify to capitalism's extraordinary capacity for stimulating energy, ingenuity, and sheer hard work. But the same history demonstrates that free markets do their jobs best when they operate within the framework of organized society, the kind of framework that only government can establish and maintain. "There are classes of problems that free markets simply do not deal with well," said Thomas C. Schelling, who won the Nobel Prize in 2005 for his analysis of the complicated bargaining behavior that underpins everything from simple sales to nuclear face-offs. "If ever there was an example, the rebuilding of New Orleans is it."

PROSPECTS FOR A SPEEDY, publicly led comeback peaked about two weeks after Katrina, when the president used the backdrop of St. Louis Cathedral in the city's historic Jackson Square to promise a national television audience that Washington would respond to the hurricane with "one of the largest reconstruction efforts the world has ever seen." He said, "There's no way to imagine America without New Orleans, and this great city will rise again." Although the speech included a large dollop of political damage control—it had taken Bush several days to recognize the extent of the devastation Katrina had caused and almost a week to get troops and substantial aid to the city—the president's words embodied a public policy that had been hammered out in legislation during the seventy-five years since the Depression and especially the thirty years since the late 1970s, and that still seemed firmly in place as recently as a decade prior to the storm.

Until the adoption of this policy, ordinary Americans typically treated natural disasters as people had throughout the ages—that is, as tragedies visited upon them for no apparent reason, coped with through the help of family and friends, but otherwise accepted as inevitable parts of the human lot. As the country grew, however, society became more integrated and the economy began to operate first on a national and then on a global scale—and such local, ad hoc responses proved increasingly inadequate to the task for bringing back damaged areas. Also, as signature notions about America being the author of its own fate combined with insurance notions about being able to predict and prepare for bad events, the idea of passively accepting setbacks became increasingly repugnant. In place of these approaches, according to economic historian David Moss, the federal government "increasingly emerged as the insurer of last resort, offering limited compensation for a wide range of uninsured and uninsurable dangers affecting not just public facilities such as roads, but also private firms and, most importantly, individual citizens."

A House report on a 1970 law expanding Washington's role in disaster relief concluded that "not only do private individuals who are suddenly and totally deprived of the means of providing for themselves . . . require emergency assistance . . . but also longer-term assistance must be provided to such individuals, the sources of their employment and the communities in which they live." One of the measure's key sponsors, Representative Harold T. Johnson, a California Democrat, explained that only such assistance could ensure full recovery in "a complex twentieth century such as [that in which] we now live." By the early 1990s, the government was going beyond simply providing aid in place and sought to engineer comebacks that reduced the chances of disasters recurring. When the Mississippi River jumped its banks in 1993, Washington began buying up thousands of homes in flood-prone areas and arranging for their owners to move to higher ground. After the initial lethal delay following Katrina, it looked as if the government was ready to play a similarly aggressive role in New Orleans.

The president sought first one, then two emergency aid bills totaling $62 billion, a figure that has since nearly doubled. The Army Corps of Engineers signed $3.7 billion in contracts to bring back the levees to their pre-storm strength. In late 2005, FEMA announced it would provide thousands of households with up to $26,200 in financial aid to help them get back up and running. By mid-2006, Washington and Baton Rouge settled on the even more ambitious "Road Home" program that was intended to compensate tens of thousands of homeowners for uninsured losses of up to $150,000.

The only problem is that none of these aid efforts came off at anything like the scale that was initially described—nor with anything like the necessary organizational firepower. As recently as the spring of 2007, more than $20 billion of the initial amount of emergency funds remained unspent. Subsequent congressional investigations found that the typical aid grant under FEMA's late-2005 program was closer to $2,600 than $26,000, and that when Road Home delivered any money at all, it was less than one-third the suggested maximum, not enough even to begin repairing a deeply damaged house. Perhaps as striking, the federal, state, and local governments repeatedly demurred when it came to engineering the recovery, or even providing broad direction. To an extent barely conceivable in the months immediately following the storm and Bush's speech, the central actors in New Orleans' comeback drama have been individual homeowners operating largely under their own power, using mostly their own money, and negotiating returns on their own terms.

To an outsider, this may sound like just about the right result. After all, when a family's house burns down, we expect them to have their own insurance and the strength of character to put their own lives back together. When people get sick, we expect them to get themselves to the doctor. We don't think that the government should step in to help. In the years since Katrina, a surprising consensus has grown up among key political leaders that something similar is true for disasters. Government can inject some money. But it's up to individuals—not Congress or city hall—to decide whether, when, where, and how New Orleanians return. It's now thought to be up to the market to tally these individual decisions in order to see which neighborhoods prosper, which wither, and what shape the post-storm city takes.

When asked why the Lower Ninth Ward had failed to come back, New Orleans mayor C. Ray Nagin shrugged off the question, saying, "That's just the way citizen investment has gone." The problem with Nagin's response and, more generally, with the idea of a parallel between a single family's setback and a calamity befalling an entire city is that they overlook a simple fact: Virtually everything needed for the kind of one-at-a-time, free-market recovery that is touted by those who endorse the notion of a parallel was demolished by Katrina. "What's missed [by the market advocates] is that it wasn't a single house or business that was destroyed by the storm, but the entire region," said former representative Richard H. Baker.

Baker is a deeply conservative Louisiana Republican who nevertheless authored one of the few comprehensive rebuilding proposals to be put forward in the wake of the storm. His plan called for a government-financed corporation to orchestrate recovery by offering displaced homeowners a deal: either sell their damaged properties to the firm at 60 percent of pre-Katrina value or retain ownership and by doing so reserve themselves a spot in a revived community. The corporation would then clear tracts of land, hire a contractor, and rebuild communities all at once. Baker's idea was gaining considerable momentum in early 2006 when it was effectively killed by Bush recovery chief Donald Powell, who announced he would resist any effort to "put the government in the real estate business." In a parting shot, Baker warned that the White House approach of leaving it to individuals, perhaps with some government aid, to negotiate their own ways back was the wrong strategy. "It does no good to stand up just one person or one family because there is nothing left where they once lived—no schools or grocery stores, doctors or banks, police stations or fire trucks," Baker said. "We've got to go into the business of restoring whole communities." Communities that people like Laurie Vignaud and Nicole Mackie helped to finance, and that others like Vignaud's 76-year-old father, Leroy, and Mackie's husband, Earl, and her 67-year-old father-in-law, James, helped to build.

THE YOUNGER VIGNAUD grew up a few miles from her now wrecked home at 1249 Granada Drive, the only daughter of four children of a plastering contractor and his wife. In the mid-1960s, Leroy Vignaud began snapping up buildings to repair, then rent or sell. By the mid-1970s, he was landing top-dollar jobs like restoring the ornamental plaster inside St. Louis Cathedral that would later become the backdrop for Bush's address on Katrina.

With the money he made, Vignaud was able to move his family into a big house with a circular staircase in a then largely white section of town. He also bought himself a blue Mark IV Lincoln Continental, which still sits in the carport out back. "I busted some ground there," he said proudly of his economic and racial climb. His daughter had a debutante party when she turned seventeen.

After a brief marriage to a U.S. Air Force officer that produced two daughters, Ashley, now twenty-one, and Lindsey, eighteen, the younger Vignaud went to work for black-owned Liberty Bank. By the late 1990s, she had moved over to historically white Hibernia. The bank was purchased two years ago by Capital One, and Laurie Vignaud was promoted to senior vice president. Her job gave her the wherewithal to send her girls to private school, drive a Lexus ES 300 sedan, and hire an interior decorator for Granada Drive.

If the elder Vignaud busted racial ground and his daughter broke financial barriers, they were nothing compared to the social and economic distance traveled by Nicole Payton, now Mackie. She grew up in "The Fisher," a public housing project so dangerous that after spending millions for renovations, the government blew it up a few years ago. She is the oldest of seven siblings and half-siblings brought up by a disabled single mother and a grandmother who drilled her in these simple standards: "You have to do better. You can't have children without being married. You have to go to college. You have to make me proud."

Mackie delivered on all four counts, having her own debutante party, graduating cum laude from New Orleans' Xavier University, landing a white-collar job with Premier Bank in Baton Rouge and later Hibernia/Capital One, and marrying Earl Mackie, whose family— in the contracting business, like the elder Vignaud—had already moved up to its own big house in the suburbs. The couple bought their first house at 2259 Filmore Avenue a few months before the arrival of their son, Jason, in 1999. Their daughter, Jazmyn, followed shortly in 2001. "She's proud of me," Mackie said simply of her grandmother, Theresa Porche.

Although the elder Vignaud and the elder Mackie had both done well, they kept largely to their own circles. Leroy Vignaud's club, the Viking Krewe, for example, never paraded at Mardi Gras, but quietly sponsored an invitation-only—and almost entirely black—ball. On weekdays, he wore work pants and drove a beat-up pickup truck, rather than his Lincoln, on the theory that "if you got it, you don't have to show it; otherwise, somebody might try to take it." Unspoken is that the "somebody" was apt to be white. It was left to Laurie and Nicole to learn to move smoothly back and forth across the racial divide.

For several years, the division of labor between the two women was that Laurie would work within the bank to organize the financing for affordable housing developments and get them built. Then Nicole would help low- and moderate-income families work out the personal finances necessary to buy into the developments. One of

Vignaud's first projects was an eighteen-house development called Delery Square in the Lower Ninth Ward. She and Nicole worked together on a program designed to ensure that New Orleans police officers and firefighters could afford to live in the city. And they put together a separate program to help the city's cash-poor jazz musicians own their own homes. By mid-2005, they had a dozen projects at various stages of completion.

Then Katrina struck.

Besides flooding Vignaud's Granada Drive home to the roofline and depositing eight feet of water in the Mackies' raised bungalow, the hurricane and flood wrecked scores of bank-financed affordable housing units in the city. In the case of Delery Square, the shells of the houses still stand, but everything around them has been washed away. The storm also flooded the five properties that Leroy Vignaud had been hanging on to for retirement income. More than two years later, he has been able to restore and sell only one.

To get some sense of what greeted returning homeowners, consider the scene from the doorstep of Vignaud's 1249 Granada Drive house a few weeks after the storm. Inside, floodwater had flipped Laurie's black upholstered sofa, snapped her rolltop desk in two, and rammed her washing machine through the laundry room ceiling. Moisture had gotten under the glass of a hallway poster, clouding its printed message: "Turning Point. The Harlem Renaissance." Humidity had caused the wooden blades of the ceiling fans to wilt like rotten palm fronds.

The only orderly thing in the house was the mold. Each spore that had grown in the steamy interior had sent out spokelike tentacles called "hyphae" that bloomed into furry "fruiting bodies" at regular intervals. The result where a single colony had won dominance on a wall or a ceiling was a startlingly symmetrical pattern of a bull's-eye. Overlapping bull's-eyes in garish pinks, blacks, milky whites, and greens had covered absolutely every surface. "Conditions are optimal for the fungi," marveled University of Colorado mycologist Mervi

Hjelmroos-Koski, who visited the city shortly after the hurricane to take mold samples. "They are just doing their job," Hjelmroos-Koski said in defense of the mold. Their job, she explained, was to digest whatever surface they landed on. They did it so effectively that Vignaud's house, which survived the storm structurally intact and at first glance appeared untouched, was effectively consumed from the inside out. A few weeks after Hjelmroos-Koski's visit, a work crew had to strip the building down to its two-by-four-inch studs and toss everything from pasty wallboard to Laurie's dresses into a heap on the curb. A trash crew from the Army Corps carted the mess away. Outside, you could look in any direction: Every structure for miles and miles was in essentially the same shape.

DESPITE THE DIMENSIONS of the destruction, two factors contributed to the adoption of a private, free-market approach to the recovery. The first is that, unlike many major cities, New Orleans does not have powerful ties to Corporate America, so the national business lobby had relatively little incentive to work on the city's behalf. The second is that, outside the immediate area, public attention became—and has remained—fixated on what essentially is a red herring.

On the business side, in contrast to Chicago at the time of the Great Fire of 1871, San Francisco when the 1906 earthquake hit, or 9/11 New York, New Orleans was not a boomtown when disaster struck. The private sector had been in decline for decades. And as it happened, those few industries that had remained strong were surprisingly disconnected from the city and thus had relatively little reason to fight for its recovery. The ports of New Orleans and South Louisiana, for example—which local officials repeatedly claimed would help spur reconstruction—are actually self-contained and largely independent of the city, according to Port of New Orleans president Gary LaGrange. Although the port handles vast quantities of steel, rubber, plywood, grain, and frozen poultry, for instance, vir-

tually all of it flows straight through without stopping to be processed or purchased locally. The ports bounded back quickly, but
their revival did little to rekindle the New Orleans economy. "New
Orleans is the biggest through-put port in the country," LaGrange
said. "It doesn't need the city." That meant there has been relatively
little economic muscle—and attendant Washington clout—behind a
government-coordinated recovery effort.

The second factor that facilitated the shift away from some kind
of public approach has involved the continuing, intense focus on the
poor and almost entirely black Ninth Ward. To be sure, Ninth Ward
residents suffered a disproportionate share of the deaths owing to
Katrina because they didn't have the physical and financial wherewithal to escape. They endured some of the most visible hardships—
crowded into the overwhelmed Superdome or stranded on rooftops
and highway overpasses where reporters and camera crews could
record their plight but authorities apparently could not rescue them.
And it was from among the poor that the unsettling reports origi-
nated of criminal gangs looting fellow storm victims and stores. In
the nearly three years since Katrina, haggling over what will become
of the Ninth Ward has dominated much of the debate over the future of the whole city. The result is that the recovery effort has gotten
tied in knots, and the whole process has been deeply injurious to
the city.

As real as the Ninth Ward's problems were and are, it is not New
Orleans, any more than Wall Street is New York or Hollywood is Los
Angeles. In the case of New Orleans, however, equating the part with
the whole has created the impression that mending the city requires
overcoming a set of obstacles that have daunted the nation for more
than a century—race, poverty, and their accompanying social disin-
tegration. And the resulting paralysis of public decision-making has
created a painful contrast between New Orleans as a city both physi-
cally and socially below sea level and America's image of itself as a
city on a hill. That in turn has fostered a tendency to let matters take

their own course—a tendency that has even infected the city's own leaders.

Ray Nagin, an African American Democrat and former $400,000-a-year Cox Cable executive, was first elected New Orleans' mayor in 2002. He won as a fresh face with a shaved head, a technocrat's cool manner, and a promise to bring business discipline to a notoriously unruly city. But as New Orleans descended into chaos during the August 2005 storm and people began to die, Nagin dropped his business cool and lashed out at federal officials to "get off your asses and let's do something [to] fix the biggest goddamn crisis in the history of this country." Even months later, his private-sector sentiments seemed to have been shelved as he stumped for a recovery plan both heavily government subsidized and publicly led. He told the *Los Angeles Times* that without a clear plan and substantial federal financial help, it would be "unfair to ask people to pump their already damaged savings back into their homes and businesses."

However, when a Nagin-appointed blue-ribbon panel, the Bring Back New Orleans Commission, ran into a racial buzz saw in mid-November 2005 by suggesting that low-lying—and largely black—areas of the city might have to be abandoned as part of the rebuilding, the mayor skipped the group's meeting and was later found to have gone to Jamaica on vacation. The commission quickly retreated and by January had come up with a more modest proposal. This time, it suggested a four-month moratorium on construction to give neighborhoods time to show that they could bring back at least half of their pre-Katrina residents. If half the people in a neighborhood returned, it was thought, an area would become a viable community, not an isolated outpost.

This time, Nagin briefly, if gingerly, backed the proposal. But the moment that it, too, was derided as a scheme to rid the city of its poor and minority residents, he quickly reversed himself, blasting it as heavy-handed and explaining, "I'm a property-rights person." Since then, he and his aides have generally taken the position that it's up to individuals to decide when and where to rebuild, and up to the market to decide who wins and who loses. He was unenthusiastically reelected in May 2006.

With no top-down plan or, for that matter, any clear signal at all from any public or private authority, New Orleans is almost entirely dependent on a bottom-up process in which a viable community is reborn only if enough individuals decide to take a chance on rebuilding their own property. In theory, virtuous cycles such as these are at the heart of every market economy and, once under way, should lead to the city's full revival. But a close look at some of the uncertainties that remain nearly three years after the storm suggests how daunting such a one-at-a-time, on-your-own approach is. In the face of these uncertainties, the fact that *any* displaced New Orleanians—rich or poor, black or white—have come home seems little short of miraculous.

According to Thomas C. Schelling, the Nobel Prize winner, the key to making almost any kind of human activity work is "credible commitments." Buyers must make them to sellers. Governments must make them to citizens. Nations must make them to each other. In New Orleans' case, credible commitments are crucial to ensuring those who want to return that they will not be alone if they rebuild. "It's essentially a problem of coordinating expectations," said Schelling of the dilemma facing people like Vignaud and Mackie. "If we all expect each other to come back, then we will. If we don't, we won't."

The only way to achieve such coordination is either by one neighbor making a credible commitment to another that he or she will rebuild or by government making broad commitments to whole neighborhoods. From the very outset of the recovery, the credible commitment that virtually every New Orleanian wanted more than any other was a pledge from the Army Corps of Engineers to rebuild the levee system bigger and better than before Katrina. But the corps has gone to extraordinary lengths to avoid making such a commitment.

For most of the fall and winter after Katrina, corps officials said they had to focus exclusively on what became a $3.7 billion job of repairing damaged levees in time to provide the city with some protection for the 2006 hurricane season. The job proved considerably bigger than initially expected because outside investigators, and later the corps itself, concluded that much of the Katrina flooding had been caused not by the raw power of the storm but by design defects in the levees. "The flooding caused a breakdown in New Orleans' social structure, a loss of cultural heritage and dramatically altered the physical, economic, political, social and psychological character of the area," and the corps was largely to blame, an agency-sponsored investigation concluded in mid-2006. "Call it a mea culpa, or call it a dry recognition, or admission, or whatever—but we're not ducking our accountability and responsibility in this," said Lt. Gen. Carl Strock, at the time the corps' commander and chief engineer.

But "not ducking accountability" apparently did not mean what most people thought it meant, and the corps was not doing what most people—including most officials with other federal agencies— thought it was doing during this early phase of work. All the corps was doing was restoring the levees to something close to their previous condition, rather than to the much higher level of protection most people were expecting. That fact emerged when FEMA asked the corps to certify that its repaired levees could withstand the once-in-100-years flood that the structures were supposed to have been able to handle pre-Katrina, and the corps abruptly refused. Corps officials first said that achieving 100-year protection would cost an extra $6 billion. Then they reduced the estimate to $2.5 billion. Then they announced they would commission a study to determine just how much protection the levees would provide. The extra money appears never to have been provided, and the study was still under way more than a year after it was launched. As a result, New Orleanians like Mackie who have returned to live in their below-sea-level city have essentially no idea whether and to what extent they are protected against another Katrina or even a lesser storm. "They're taking complete flyers," Robert G. Bea, a former corps official who is now one of the agency's sharpest critics, said of returnees. "At this point, they have absolutely no concrete information about what kind of dangers they face."

If city residents aren't getting what they need from the Army Corps, they're not doing much better with the government's national flood-insurance program. In theory, the FEMA-run program should make it easier for people to decide whether to rebuild because the government promises to cover up to $250,000 in flood damages. And because FEMA requires that the buildings it insures be built above the projected level for a 100-year flood, the program seems to set a standard of safety that people must meet.

In the immediate aftermath of Katrina, the agency promised to issue new flood maps laying out where people could and could not build, or how high off the ground they would have to raise their new houses in order to qualify for the government insurance. But when the corps refused to certify the levees, FEMA officials reacted by delaying release of the maps. Instead, the agency announced that for the time being, all new houses in most of the city would have to be built three feet above the highest nearby ground. But the agency couldn't say how it had come up with the three-foot figure or how long it might be operative. City officials sought to reassure homeowners by promising that anybody who built to the three-foot standard would be grandfathered in and would not have to change their homes if the standard changed. But FEMA hasn't offered any similar assurance. That means homeowners could find themselves in the impossible position of having to jack their homes up five or ten more feet above their current levels, or else go without flood insurance.

The combination of no real city recovery plan and behavior like this by federal agencies has made a mockery of the notion of the "credible commitments" that people like Schelling say are so important. In the process, it has enormously increased the stakes for residents facing the double dilemma of whether, if one rebuilds, his or her neighbors will do the same, and, even if they all do, if that will be enough to ensure their neighborhood's survival.

As a work crew gutted her Granada Drive house the November following the storm, Vignaud suddenly realized that the only evidence she had that any of her neighbors had been back since Katrina was the heaps of dank furniture and smashed plasterboard outside their houses. But did the piles mean that they were getting ready to rebuild or simply picking through the wreckage on their way out of town? "I keep looking at all this stuff and wondering whether they're coming back or not," she said, standing outside her front door. "It's crazy, like a riddle I can't solve."

But solving the riddle is crucial to deciding whether it is safe to return. As Craig Colton, a Louisiana State University geographer, put it: "In essence, what we've said to people is, 'Go out and be a pioneer, but if not enough other people follow you, then we'll leave you stranded.'"

THROUGH IT ALL, some residents actually have managed to solve the riddle and, by doing so, set their wrecked neighborhoods on the road to recovery. Free-market advocates have snapped up these successes as evidence that markets and individual initiative alone can revive societies like New Orleans from the ground up. But a close look at the most widely cited examples suggests that the very opposite conclusion is warranted. In one way or another, what each of these neighborhoods has found are ways of making the credible commitments that neither the public nor the private sector seemed capable of providing. They have done so not by piling one individual commitment atop another as the market advocates would have it, but by leaning heavily on community ties that predated the storm and survived it, or by creating entirely new organizations to replace those that so badly failed them. The results in neighborhoods that have not been able to pursue one or the other of these strategies and, by default, have ended up as petri dishes for one-at-a-time comebacks are strikingly—often frighteningly—different.

On the northern edge of the city, close to Lake Pontchartrain, is New Orleans' 500-family Greek Orthodox community and its church, Holy Trinity Cathedral. As warnings about Katrina grew more ominous in the days leading up to the hurricane, church leaders helped arrange for the community's exodus from the city, focusing especially on the elderly and infirm. In the days immediately following, they turned around and mobilized to bring everyone right back home again. "We organized everything," said John D. Georges, a former president of the parish council and chief executive of Imperial Trading Company, a regional supplier for convenience stores. Fr. Anthony Stratis worked the phones and the e-mail lists, trying to locate parishioners scattered across half the country. Parish council member Dr. Nick Moustoukas followed up by wiring money to the neediest. Ten days after the storm, Georges and council member Christ Kanellakis helicoptered in to rescue the church's chalice and tabernacle. Operating independently, a Greek Orthodox chaplain on a Coast Guard cutter dispatched to New Orleans to help with rescue and recovery assembled a group of National Guardsmen to slosh their way to the church and begin mopping it out.

Part of what attracted community members back following the storm was the sheer weight of history. Holy Trinity, founded during the Civil War, is the oldest Greek Orthodox community in the Americas. "Our forefathers didn't establish a church in New Orleans just so we could pick up and move when there's a hurricane," said Stratis. "If they established it here, it's our job to keep it here." But by acting in concert, the community effectively provided members an immense self-insurance policy. It solved the double dilemma by ensuring that a substantial fraction of the community would come back together and that the jobs and services on which it had relied before the storm would be there after the storm. The parish council organized bulk purchases of appliances for homeowners who had lost stoves and refrigerators in the flood. It acted as a broker for construction crews, some Greek, to repair community members' homes. It provided money to those who couldn't pay for the work themselves. By the time the patriarch of the Eastern Orthodox Church traveled from Istanbul to New Orleans four months after Katrina, Trinity's marble-carved walls had been scrubbed, its lawn had been resodded, and more than 1,000 people were home to attend the service at which he presided.

Five miles away from Trinity is Lakewood, a white upper-middle-class neighborhood that was destroyed by the same levee break that flooded the cathedral. Lakewood did not have the ethnic and religious ties of the Greek Orthodox community to fall back on after the hurricane and flood. What it had instead was Denise Thornton. Thornton is a 49-year-old businesswomen whose husband, Doug, manages the Superdome, the sports arena, which normally hosts the Saints and the Hornets but ended up as the city's principal public shelter during Katrina and site of some of the most horrific scenes of deprivation. Starting with two slim advantages—that she stayed through the storm and that she was a member of a neighborhood property owners' association—Thornton almost single-handedly invented a new institution: the Beacon of Hope center. And she turned it into a stand-in for city hall, FEMA, and the kind of quasi–public agency that former Representative Baker's plan envisioned to orchestrate the recovery. "We're doing government's job for them," she said.

Thornton started by renovating her two-story brick home. By February 2006, six months after Katrina, 5475 Bellaire Drive had a lush green lawn, pink and purple petunias lining the driveway, and a pair of evergreens out front. In a landscape of brown muck, dead shrubs, hanging gutters, and shattered trees, the place became a magnet for people. She capitalized on that fact by convincing the cable company to restore phone service, scrounging up a desk and fax machine, and turning her living room into a "resource center." In May, she sponsored a "Parade of Homes" where those considering a return toured the houses of the eight or ten families already back. Real estate agents opened up the properties of those who wanted to sell out. And contractors vetted by Thornton offered their services. When people would volunteer, she would assign them to hound the public works department to unclog the storm drains; follow FEMA, and later city trash-hauling crews, to make sure they did their jobs; or track down the owners of deserted properties and find out what they needed in order to decide whether to return or sell. She developed a stock answer for questions about the levees: "Well, I can't do anything about that. What can I do?" She and the local property owners' association redirected money for beautification projects and hired a security guard. By mid-2007, eight "Beacon of Hope" centers were operating in an area stretching from the Thorntons' house almost to Holy Trinity Cathedral, and nearly 8,000 families—close to 70 percent of the area's pre-Katrina population—were either back or renovating to come back.

OUTSIDERS CAN DIFFER over exactly how much to make of the Greek Orthodox community's experience or that of Lakewood. Thornton portrays the "Beacon of Hope" centers less as a stand-in for government or a means to community action than as a refuge, a lifeline, or a resource for individuals coming back under their own power. That suggests that what's occurring in Lakewood is simply a variation of the free-market theme for which the city has become the unwitting testing ground. But if that's true, then how to interpret what's occurred in neighborhoods where there are no beacons or ethnic and religious ties to galvanize activity and where the free market appears to be operating in its purest form—with recovery proceeding literally one family at a time? Here, the market has so far produced very different results. These communities seem to be coming back, not as their old thriving selves but as "jack-o'-lantern" neighborhoods, with one or a few families returning to live amid what otherwise remains ruined and desolate terrain. One of those neighborhoods is Vignaud's and Mackie's old home: largely black, middle-class Gentilly.

NICOLE MACKIE was perfectly happy where she landed after Katrina—in a house in Baton Rouge purchased by her in-laws. Her kids were in school, and her job had relocated to Capital One's office in the Louisiana capital. But for Earl Mackie it was a different story. Encouraged in part by his father, who remembered making a fortune in roofing in the wake of Hurricane Betsy in 1965, he began commuting the two hours from Baton Rouge within a month of the storm. He finally convinced Nicole to move back to New Orleans after more than a year of arguing that the family's roofing business, the couple's Jehovah's Witness congregation, some rental property, and Earl's tiny rap music label, Take Fo', were all there. In any case, he added, the couple's house was on a major cross street, Filmore, and close to one of the city's main drags, Eleysian Field, so they would not be isolated. As it turned out, living conditions, at least initially, were considerably more primitive than they'd bargained for.

Although streetlight service had been restored shortly before they moved back in October 2006, there were still no traffic signals. That didn't matter much since, after dark, there was no traffic. "It used to be [before the hurricane] there were cars all the time," said Earl. "Everybody knew where we lived, and they'd be yelling up, 'How you doin'?'" But now, he said, "you see maybe one or two a night." Only two other families had returned to live on the block when they got home, and even now the number is discouragingly small. The result during the first few months was that the family would lock themselves in after seven o'clock, and they all slept together on a mattress and box spring in the front room. Even now, when one parent makes a nighttime run to the store, the other keeps watch to make sure the errand runner makes it to and from the car safely. The city estimated that 16,000 of the area's 44,000 pre-Katrina residents, or only about one-third, had returned by late last year. But the Mackies' estimate the fraction is one-quarter or less. "Basically, it's still a ghost town," said Nicole. The couple appears ready to stick it out for a few years, but they acknowledge that if there is any other major setback, especially another big storm, they're gone.

DURING A RECENT VISIT to New Orleans, Laurie Vignaud swung by Granada Drive. The neighborhood was still empty except for two neighbors who'd moved back, one next door and another across the street and down a ways. Vignaud pounded a "For Sale" in the front lawn of the boarded-up shell. Then she headed on to visit her father and mother.

At seventy-six and legally blind, the elder Vignaud has written off most of his five rental properties as losses. He focuses his attention on getting the big house with the circular staircase back in shape. Many days are spent waiting for contractors who don't show, which leaves him fuming about the fact he can no longer do the work himself. Asked why he keeps pushing to repair every last detail of the place, he can't quite find the words to explain. He admits he'll probably never move or sell it. Still, he says, "I can't walk away from my resources."

KATRINA AND THE RESPONSE TO IT by political leaders and policymakers in Washington and elsewhere represented the culmination of economic changes that have been under way since the late 1970s. Until the storm, those changes had occurred largely out of public view in the quiet confines of corporate human resource departments, the Supreme Court conference room as the justices debated ERISA, and the executive suites of the nation's major insurers as they contemplated cutbacks in disaster coverage. One might argue that, like Leroy Vignaud, the decision-makers did not walk away from New Orleans. But the parallel is only superficial. Vignaud assumed that his properties were so much a part of his life that he had to take responsibility for them himself. By contrast, the insurance companies, government agencies, and others who shaped the national response to New Orleans did something very different. They stepped back and waited for the market to put a price on the city and determine how and what parts should be restored. And that made all the difference in the world.

Powerful as markets are, there are some decisions they do not make well—at least unguided. Among them is restoring ruined cities and building or rebuilding society from the ground up. Their use in this situation is simply cruel. It leaves individuals to stitch together on their own a world that they were told would be revived by the nation as a whole. To turn the problem over to markets is to force families to handle imponderables such as the strength of government-built levees or the return of municipal services and businesses—factors that are beyond their ability to assess. Katrina and its aftermath revealed the limits of the market. It was a lesson that had been a long time in coming.

12

CONCLUSION

E VERY IDEA HAS ITS TIME, and for every idea that time passes. The idea to emerge from the late 1970s, the idea that the United States had become ossified by regulation and trapped by stagflation, proved a powerful insight. And the suggested cure, a new reliance on free markets, has been a powerful tonic. The free-market principles put in place over the past quarter century reinvigorated the U.S. economy and restored American global dominance at a time when both seemed to be fading. But like so many ideas played out over a long period, the notion of market mechanisms as the solution of choice for every problem has produced some unexpected and un-wanted results. Chief among them, it has left working families up and down much of the income spectrum living with fewer economic protections, bearing more economic risk, chancing steeper financial falls. Free-market advocates portray what's going on as a trade-off of less security for more prosperity. For the past twenty-five years, they say, most of us have been getting more than enough of the products and services that make for good, even affluent, lives. Many people have blinked at the risk, focused instead on the benefits, and concluded the trade-off was fair.

Recently, however, we've begun to hear that we may have been getting more of our already-diminished protections than the economy can afford or than we can reasonably expect. In a rhetorical anomaly that somehow has passed almost unnoticed, we have been told that the U.S. economy is the most bountiful and productive in human history, yet we, as individuals and families, will have to make do with still fewer economic backstops. In tomorrow's America, it's said, the task of meeting life's inevitable challenges and setbacks will rest even more firmly with us, rather than being shared broadly by the community. In other words, we will be expected to spend our lives making this the richest, most dependable economy on earth, but both government and business will pare back the responsibilities they take for our well-being. Offered in this fashion, the trade-off has begun to look considerably less fair, which has led to the uneasiness that many Americans now feel about their lives.

The advocates say that the change is perhaps unfortunate, but inevitable. They say the fact that people's lives may have been more secure in the past is irrelevant: Times have changed. The furious pace of technological progress, the global doubling of the workforce in the early twenty-first century, the emergence of such giants as China and India with their huge and well-educated legions of workers have rewritten the playbook. The old world in which business and government promised working families reasonably stable lives can never be restored. But the advocates of this view slide almost seamlessly from the notion that past promises can't be restored in their old form to the idea that there can be no promises at all. And the notion of no promises at all simply cannot stand. Because what we've done in recent decades is more than simply cut a few social programs or tighten up some business practices. We've rewritten the deal under which most working Americans conduct their lives. And the rewrite leaves today's workers exposed to economic forces well beyond their control and with almost no leverage. Among other things, the result has been a sharp decline in working people's ability to get a fair portion of the gains they helped create, a situation that has left even many college-educated workers doing little better than treading water while their employers and the economy as a whole have lifted off.

The change is apparent in a simple set of numbers. As pointed out by economists Frank Levy and Peter Temin, during the twenty-five years from 1980 to 2005, business productivity—the measure of output per hour of labor that is considered the Rosetta stone of economic improvement—climbed almost 70 percent. Over the same period, median weekly earnings of full-time workers rose only 14 percent. Meanwhile, median weekly compensation—wages plus benefits such as health insurance—climbed only 19 percent. That gap between productivity growth and wage and compensation growth is among the widest since the end of World War II. "It's hard for me to believe that a generation of Americans with more education, more resources, and no less sense of fairness than those that preceded them would accept a situation such as this," said Levy.

For a time, advocates may continue to find an audience for their free-market credo. That may be especially so among a generation of young people who have grown up with almost no faith in Washington's ability to improve economic conditions and a conviction that market-driven technology, not government, is the ultimate arbiter of society's shape. But the time is coming when unquestioning reliance on markets alone will give ground to a new politics of shared responsibility. It is coming because American history has been a continual effort to strike the right balance between markets and personal opportunity on the one side and mutual obligation on the other, and we've just spent an inordinate amount of time on the markets-and-opportunity side of the equation with only glancing notice at the mutual-obligation side. No one told working Americans that in embracing the auction-block ethos of the market, they were signing up for the consequences I have described in the preceding pages. No one told them that risks once borne by business, government, and the economy as a whole would end up smack on their doorsteps. And it is coming for another, perhaps even more powerful, reason: Although Americans are a striving people who want to get ahead, most of us consider our families and personal relations a private domain in which fairness and decency take precedence over market economics, and that domain has suffered substantially under the current balance.

An education, a job and benefits, health, a house, provision for retirement, and—as New Orleans illustrates—a functioning community: These are the foundation stones of our material lives, the rocks on which we build our futures. They are the stuff of practicality, not poetry. But without them, there would be no creature comforts, no opportunity to raise our children decently, no chance to advance in a career or from one generation to the next, no room to dream. The problem, as we have seen, is that for most of us, every single one of these foundations has been shaken, making the pursuit of better lives an increasingly risky venture.

The jobs and the job market on which all but a thin upper echelon of society depend have changed in ways that most people only vaguely understand and are powerless to control. Yet those changes have put them in greater danger of destructive encounters with unemployment, wage stagnation, and a breakdown of what has been—at least until recently—people's most important economic relationship: that with their employer. For several decades after World War II, the jobs and benefits built into the relationship between millions of Americans and their employers were protected by union contracts. Millions of other workers, though not union members, benefited indirectly from the benchmarks that unions established. When companies encountered financial setbacks or changes in market conditions, they tended to reduce working hours or take other temporary belt-tightening measures instead of cutting benefits or resorting to the mass firings that are common now.

Today, the average tenure for prime working-age men, those forty-five to fifty-four years old, has fallen by one-third, and with it the stable incomes that accompany stable jobs, just as the government has cut back on programs for workers who've lost their jobs and may need help, including retraining, to establish new careers. One result is that a small but growing number of working people are operating in a netherworld of "unjobs"—temporary work, consulting gigs, and chancy careers with often-ephemeral start-ups. A few choose this life, but many more find themselves stuck in it, and they find little comfort in the euphemistic suggestion that they are just going through "job transition."

Perhaps the single greatest response of families to these changes has been the rise of the two-earner household. Putting two people to work has undoubtedly helped families cope with increased financial pressures. But the way in which it has helped is nothing like the way most economists portray it. And the advent of the two-earner household has brought its own set of risks. The addition of a spouse into the full-time workforce has reduced the chances of a family facing the 100-percent declines in income that could occur if a single earner lost his job. But it has *increased* the odds for substantial losses by doubling the number of workers on whom the household depends for income and thus doubling the number who can be laid off or suffer an earnings setback. This new risk is often overlooked. First, economists interpret women's entry into the workforce as voluntary, rather than a response to stagnating incomes and the deterioration in employee-employer relations. Second, economists generally treat women's wages as something akin to a luxury, rather than an essential part of the family budget. But such an interpretation is not true to the facts of most people's lives. Ask almost any woman, especially one with young children, whether her decision to go to work was optional—just a matter of personal fulfillment—and you're likely to get an earful. Most will say they work because their families need the money. Ask whether the family can afford to set her earnings aside as mad money, and she's likely to laugh. Having both spouses work may have made life better, but it has also raised the danger of a serious reversal of fortunes.

The story is much the same when it comes to job-related benefits. For most U.S. workers, employer-provided benefits are their single most important safety net in times of trouble. Only after retirement—when we qualify for Social Security and Medicare—do the benefits that Washington provides come close to matching the importance of what employers provide during our working years. So-called fringe benefits were once considered necessary incentives to help persuade valuable employees to stay with the same firm for long periods, even entire careers. But as companies have grown less interested in cultivating worker loyalty, and as the cost of benefits has increased, firms' interest in providing health insurance, dependable pensions, and other such indirect but vital compensation has waned. And what's true of big corporations is even truer of the small, lean start-ups that create many of today's new jobs.

There is a second, more insidious story about health insurance and other benefits—one that substantially diminishes how reliable your coverage may turn out to be, even if you have coverage. Decades of court rulings have produced a quiet revolution in the federal law that gives employers increasingly wide latitude in how and when they provide benefits, or whether they provide them at all. More and more Americans find themselves in Kafkaesque paperwork duels over whether they are eligible for one kind of benefit or another. During these lopsided battles, which are often resolved only after endless calls, letters, and sometimes legal action, the employees must put their own money, good credit, and well-being on the line. Some unlucky people find themselves with no benefits at all—just bills that are wildly beyond their ability to pay.

The trend away from employer responsibility for benefits, and toward individuals bearing the burden, may be at its most critical stage in health care. The premiums that companies charge employees have gone up 125 percent in the past nine years alone. That's well ahead of general inflation or wages during the same period, and represents only part of the cost shift in which companies are engaged. Firms also are raising deductibles and co-payments and are limiting the range of products and services that are covered. Most small businesses, which make up an increasing share of all employers, offer no health insurance or only the most minimal protection—frequently for only the employee, not the family. Even among large firms that continue to offer traditional medical insurance, the scope of coverage has been trimmed through policy changes or employers' use of the court-reinterpreted benefits law. Health care is a classic example of an employer benefit that once seemed to promise coverage for all—thus playing a major role in meeting one of society's most critical needs—but now threatens to be dumped on employees, who are ill-equipped to bear the burden. Many can handle routine costs. Without insurance, however, one serious illness can exhaust the resources of all but a tiny fraction of Americans.

The same pattern of shifting risks can be seen in what, for most people, is by far their single largest financial asset—their home. The ability to sell a house or pull funds out of it through home equity loans is the most significant source of money most people have in an emergency. As with jobs and benefits, however, houses are providing less protection than they used to. That's not just because, as we are being reminded by the recent slump, the value of a house is not guaranteed to rise over time, or even to remain stable. It's also because, as our families in Oakland and San Diego discovered when wildfires destroyed their homes, what's protecting a family's equity in its house—bought-and-paid-for homeowners' insurance—often provides less protection than it once did. Insurance industry experts assert that the bevy of exclusions, riders, and coverage limits imposed in recent years merely clarifies what is covered and thus makes insurance a more certain protector. But in many cases policyholders are not aware of the practical effects of the changes, and therefore not aware of the risks that have been shifted onto them or—in the case of disasters like floods and earthquakes—onto the government.

Even a college education, which once seemed to come with an ironclad guarantee of a prosperous and secure career, has become an investment carrying significant risks. Only the exceptionally gifted student who identifies a clear and remunerative career from the get-go and pursues it relentlessly is still ensured entry into the world of white-collar affluence. For many others, college has become a way station to seemingly interminable internships and the purgatory of life suspended between studenthood and adult self-sufficiency. As the price of college has climbed, many young people enter this struggle carrying big debts. And the risks and burdens do not end with the winning of a bachelor's degree. As the job market demands more specialized skills, newly minted college graduates face the prospect of spinning the education roulette wheel all over again, this time for graduate school.

As for the other end of life, at least until the 1970s, it looked as though most working Americans would have a double layer of protection in old age: Social Security from the government and an employer-provided pension managed by professionals and guaranteeing a specific level of benefits for life. The risks of investing the money and making sure enough was set aside to last as long as needed were shouldered by employers. No more. As employers have become less interested in maintaining career-long ties to their workers and more concerned about being able to shed financial obligations quickly, they have stopped offering defined benefit pensions and frozen those they've already promised. The 401(k) system that has replaced traditional pensions shifts virtually all of the risks onto the individual. And the evidence is that perhaps one-third of Americans, including some spectacularly well-educated ones, are not doing a very good job handling their new responsibilities.

Finally, there is the matter of community. When the survivors of Katrina faced a devastated New Orleans, the nation rejected the idea of mutual obligation in the form of a federally organized and financed redevelopment plan; survival of New Orleans as the vibrant if troubled community has been left largely to markets and individuals. The result thus far has been "jack-o'-lantern" neighborhoods and a diminished city. Exactly what and where to rebuild in an area as environmentally vulnerable as the Mississippi Delta is a complicated question. Dumping the issue onto a scattered population of battered individuals seems unworthy of a great country.

The rough new realities facing American families may not show up in the statistics for the overall economy, but they do register in various measures that look at the world through the lens most families use in gauging their situations: their own incomes. They register in the fact that, though small, the fraction of families that lose half or more of their income from one year to the next has roughly doubled from the early and mid-early 1970s to the early and mid-2000s, rising from 5 percent to about 10 percent. They register in a similar increase in the number of families that have suffered big financial setbacks after experiencing any of a list of common but potentially destabilizing blows—such things as unemployment or divorce or separation. In the case of unemployment, for example, the odds of a 50 percent income hit have gone from roughly 1 in 6 to 1 in 4. And they register for a nationally representative sample of families, some of whom have suffered such blows but most of whom have escaped personal misfortune but nevertheless have seen their incomes taking increasingly wild leaps and plunges. For sample families in the middle of the income spectrum, the annual swings up and down have climbed from as much as 17 percent to almost 26 percent, or by half.

Increased volatility and instability have hardly been confined to the middle; those near the bottom of the income distribution and, perhaps most strikingly, those near the top also are experiencing greater income swings. The greater the swing, the greater the danger that you'll be caught in a downdraft when something like unemployment strikes, leaving you in a financial hole.

What's important in each of these measures is not the precise numbers but the trend over the past quarter century toward greater volatility in families' finances—toward greater swings up and down. Just as volatility is the chief measure of the risk in the stock market, so, too, here it is a measure of the risks that families are bearing—and by these measures they are bearing greater risk than they did ten or twenty or thirty years ago.

Which brings us back to the paradox with which we began the book: How can the United States as a nation be growing more secure in its prosperity—as it has been doing until recently—even while many, perhaps most, Americans are becoming less so? The easy explanation for this seeming contradiction is rising income inequality—the fact that most of the new wealth is going to those at the pinnacle of affluence. That does not, however, explain everything. It's true that income has become more and more unequally distributed. But that doesn't mean prosperity is not widespread. The median size of new houses has grown from 1,505 square feet to 2,227 square feet—an increase of nearly 40 percent since 1985. The median number of cars has increased from two to almost three. The amount of food that typical Americans eat in a day—not wealthy gourmands, but people like you and me—has climbed by more than 10 percent, which may not make us healthier, but certainly indicates greater spending power.

If income inequality explains only part of the paradox of both widespread bounty and greater personal precariousness, what accounts for the rest? The answer, as we have seen, is a substantial shifting of life's risks—and the burden of dealing with them—from government and business to individuals and families. The pattern is not a new one for the nation. As the original colonies grew beyond the communal villages with which they began, as hamlets turned into towns and towns into cities, as small patches of crops gave way to larger farms and local artisans were replaced by industrial-scale manufacturing, both farmers and urban workers found themselves left alone to deal with the ravages of fire, flood, drought, and man-made disasters such as unstable currency and repeated financial panics. Slowly but surely, however, over decades of political struggle, Americans redressed the balance with government programs like unemployment compensation, community groups like fraternal organizations, and new products like insurance. In the process, they demonstrated an understanding of Franklin Roosevelt's insight that society had so changed from its pastoral roots that it had become virtually impossible "for individuals to build their own security single-handedly."

That is all the more true in our latest transition—from an industrial to a service and information economy. It runs against everything else that's happening in the economy to suggest that we must become our own experts about some of the most complex facets of our lives—planning pensions, managing investments, matching wits single-handedly with insurance companies and others to protect our interests. Increasingly, both the economy and American society compel us in the opposite direction—toward becoming more specialized. It is no longer enough to be competent in a broad field such as electronics, medicine, business, or law. We must become experts in one particular segment of a field. And we are expected to fit into not just national but global webs of work that leave us ever more dependent on others as they are dependent on us. We can't possibly hope to be self-sufficient and also be engaged in the economically integrated world of today's global village. And it's not like the 1970s or 1980s, when the pain of change would land on particular regions like the Rust Belt or specific industries such as steel and auto. Now, a marketing executive like Bruce Meyer or a high-tech exec like Allan Hess can take a steep financial fall almost as easily as anybody else. Upheaval is occurring across the economy, leaving just about every working person vulnerable to being uprooted.

My purpose in the preceding pages has been to follow the common thread that runs through the lives of working Americans at all but the very top in hopes that outlining the pattern will help point to a way out. I do not propose now to offer an agenda or definitive fix. But it might be useful to demonstrate in some concrete way that people need not accept the recent loss of security as their inevitable lot, something they are as powerless to control as the weather. There are things that we can do.

Let's start with jobs. No one is going to outlaw layoffs or bring back long-lived jobs by legislative fiat. But if these problems are not going to go away, we need to decouple employment from many of the safety-net programs that employers have provided since at least the Second World War—and for which they have been handsomely compensated with tax breaks. The most important of these is health care insurance, but there are others as well. For example, we have depended on wages to provide broad distribution of the fruits of economic growth. However, if the economy keeps growing but wages do not, then maybe it's time for some other distribution mechanisms. One suggestion is for something called "baby bonds" or "individual development accounts." These are funds that the government would raise through taxes on those who do reap the fruits of economic growth. The resulting revenue would be set aside for every American child; an account would grow until a person reached adulthood, when the money could be used for college tuition or as the down payment on a house.

When it comes to the benefits that people continue to receive through their employers, it is time to make the existing federal benefits law live up to its own stated purpose—to "protect participants in employee benefit plans and their beneficiaries." That most likely means people have to be able to sue for consequential damages when they are wrongly denied benefits—whether by going to court or submitting claims to neutral arbitrators. Companies and their benefits administrators cannot be treated—as the courts now generally do—

as dispassionate experts in benefit cases. With the prospect of saving or losing money depending on whether they deny or approve claims, the companies are very clearly interested parties with conflicts of interest. The Supreme Court or Congress must pare back the sweeping claim that only federal law, and not state law, can apply to benefits. Otherwise, we will stifle the very state of experimentation that has resulted in so much good in America, including—at least initially— passage of the federal benefits law.

As for protecting most people's biggest asset—their homes— insurers can't be ordered to take risks they don't want to take. But that doesn't mean they can cherry-pick which risks or areas they will cover and which they won't, or have the right to shift the highest risks onto state-created agencies or homeowners alone. If an insurance company doesn't want to offer broad coverage to a large area such as a state, then it should be told to leave all the business in that large area to somebody else. That way, risks could be spread, not unloaded onto hapless individuals or underfunded government bodies. More generally, companies that provide all sorts of personal insurance and that are engaged in a technological arms race to spot the least-risky client and charge all the others steeply higher rates or not cover them at all should be told that enough is enough. Government needs to step in and tell firms which of a few "rating factors" they can use in marketing and pricing their coverage and which they cannot, or else insurance will soon stop functioning as insurance.

Given the rapid changes in the U.S. economy, it's hard to see how any plan could make college education the reserved-seat ticket to the good life that it used to be. But there are things we could do to better balance the risks. As matters now stand, colleges and universities are essentially forcing students and their families to finance exorbitant cost increases largely through student loans. There are two problems with this. First, one of the biggest debt burdens in most people's lives—the average college graduate now leaves school with some $21,000 in loans—comes at the beginning of workers' careers. That's when their prospects are the least certain and their earning power is at its lowest, rather than later, when they are established and better able to pay. Second, students must take on this debt before they have any realistic way to measure what they will earn. No investment banker would pour money into a business venture without having any idea how profitable it could be. But that's what we now require college students and their families to do.

An interesting idea, once championed by Nobel laureates Milton Friedman and James Tobin, a conservative and a liberal, advanced at least tepidly by President Bill Clinton, and recently revived by David Moss, the Harvard economic historian, is something called income-contingent lending. College students would pay for education with long-term loans similar to thirty-year home mortgages. And interest payments would be deferred or forgiven for any year in which a graduate's household income fell below a specified level. That way, the debt burden could be made to correspond at least somewhat to the dividends that the individual investment in higher education turned out to yield. Such a system would have to deal in some way with the fact that some forms of training lead to better-paying careers than others, even though society needs many of those that are less remunerative. But the Friedman-Tobin-Moss proposal at least begins to fix a problem that, though little recognized by those who don't have kids in college, could gradually erode the skill levels and competitiveness of the American workforce.

Health care is an expense that can go from minor to massive in an instant and so is nearly impossible for all but the richest families to bear by themselves. That's why we invented health care insurance. But the very expenses that give rise to insurance give insurers a powerful incentive to "slice and dice" potential customers, distinguishing between those who are unlikely to file claims and those who are likely to file big ones, then going after the former and doing nearly everything possible to avoid the latter. For half a century, we avoided this problem by funneling most coverage through employers. An aggregated workforce formed a big pool of policyholders, each of whom could kick in comparatively small amounts—along with moderate contributions from their employers—in order to cover the large costs of the relatively few who become ill. But that system is, at a minimum, fraying. With jobs becoming more unstable, companies coming under greater competitive pressure, and medical advances prolonging life ever longer while simultaneously raising the cost, companies are moving to get out of the game. What's needed is a new system that better meets the needs of all concerned—employers and workers alike.

One proposal would give families a tax break but otherwise leave it up to them to get themselves covered. This seems like an unpromising solution, given the dimensions of the costs involved and the mismatch in market power between an individual family and an insurance company. A second idea is to replace employer pools with a national pool and create a single-payer system run by the government. This is how much of the rest of the advanced world handles health care. But that would effectively mean legislating the nation's current health insurance industry out of existence, something that is not going to happen. A third proposal is to try to maintain as much of the old employer-based system as possible for the time being, but to set up a parallel system of group purchasing of insurance outside of the employer system. Given recent insurance trends, such a system would require a great deal of government regulation—to define comprehensive coverage; prevent cherry-picking of healthy, low-cost consumers; to create a fair bidding process so that costs were no higher than for other insurance. It would, however, have two great advantages: It would relieve pressure on employers and start to decouple health insurance from the employee-employer relationship. And, done correctly, it would provide all Americans with secure health coverage.

Some of the problems with the do-it-yourself retirement system that has evolved over the past twenty-five years were corrected in

legislation that was quietly passed in 2006. In a striking commitment, business and government agreed to take back some of the
responsibilities they had shifted to individuals because they discovered many individuals were not handling them effectively. Now, employees who go to work for a company that offers a 401(k) plan will
be automatically enrolled in the plan unless they object. Their contributions will be automatically increased over time. And the mix of
their investments will be automatically changed to reflect their need
for more or less risky financial assets as they age. The changes in the
2006 law do nothing to expand the number of companies offering
401(k)s or to ensure that people reach retirement with adequate
funds. And they don't help guide people in managing what funds
they do have once they have left the workforce. Still, the law represents a small but telling admission that many of the developments of
the past quarter century have left people too much on their own and
need to be adjusted.

The same is true of the last of the foundation stones of our material lives—a functioning community. For most of the twenty-five
years before Hurricane Katrina struck New Orleans in 2005, the federal government had been playing a bigger, more organized role in
aiding communities hit by disaster. Implicit in its efforts was a recognition that, in an era when we are all dependent on a national, and in
many cases a global, economy, leaving the job of reconstructing a
community solely to its residents is good neither for the residents
nor for the broader economy. Such thinking was behind the plan to
bring back New Orleans devised by former representative Richard
Baker, the conservative Louisiana Republican. But the plan was rejected out of concern it would inappropriately put Washington into
the real estate business. However, the rejection put Washington into
a seemingly even more inappropriate business of handing out billions of dollars, then leaving it to families to decide one at a time
whether to return to New Orleans. Washington involvement in disaster recovery does not have to mean that the federal government

simply picks up the tab for people caught in the path of a hurricane or earthquake or wildfire. It can involve some tough decisions about where and how rebuilding should be supported. But there is nothing un-American or surprising in the government playing a role in a comeback from disaster. Washington has been doing it for centuries and—until Katrina—seemed to be taking on its responsibilities in a more organized fashion.

AMERICANS TODAY almost reflexively assume that the people of some previous period—the Revolutionary generation that created the nation, for instance, or the Greatest Generation that endured the Great Depression and fought World War II—lived on a more heroic scale, facing more dire threats and achieving more sweeping victories. But most people—even many who engaged in great national undertakings of the past—spend most of their days inside their families and communities, among their belongings, and at their work. Few in previous generations sought out the tests that befell them. Much the same is true of this generation.

For most Americans alive today and for their children, restoring the sense of mutual obligation embodied in the Mayflower Compact nearly 400 years ago is likely to be the defining challenge of our time. It will be a decades-long struggle to reestablish a set of values that lies at the heart of what most of us mean when we say "America."

The task will not be what it is so often described as—the soft job of learning to live with the prosperity that surrounds us. Instead, it will be the difficult and confusing work of doing something about the loss of security amid all of this plenty. This does not mean doing away with markets or personal responsibility. It's not about embracing utopian, collectivist schemes. There is not the remotest chance that the United States will knowingly do any of these things, nor that it will need to do any of them. Rather, the task is to work within our present system to reset the balance point between what's acceptable as good for the individual and what must be recognized as good for the many. It is not feasible to construct a society in which there is no risk for anyone. In the long run, it is also not feasible, or morally tenable, to organize society so that a comparative few enjoy great wealth at almost no risk while the great majority must accept the possibility that any reversal—whether of their own or someone else's making—can destroy a lifetime of endeavor.

Recalibrating the balance and devising ways to achieve it in the face of a rapidly changing world will not be quick or easy. But the challenge is more than noble; it is necessary. And it is possible. What has been damaged by some can be repaired by others. Americans have been proving as much for nearly four centuries.

METHODS

This is intended to address some of the technical issues about the numbers in Chapter 3 without slowing down the argument. There is no reason general readers need to wade through it. But it seems important for the credibility of the book that I lay out some of the major decisions that were made about what data and techniques to use and explain how those decisions were made. Then specialists and journalists can decide for themselves how strong a case I've made.

Let me start with an issue of interpretation that has caused a lot of confusion: how family income volatility and the increase in volatility that I argue has occurred ought to be understood. Like the "beta" of a stock, I treat volatility as a risk measure. Also like a stock "beta," there is a story behind the measure that helps explain why it should be so treated. In the case of a stock, the story is that the more the price of a company's shares fluctuates, the greater the chance that investors could get caught short with the price down when they want or need to sell, and then they could end up losing money. In the case of family income, the story is that the more income swings up and down, the more likely that a family could find itself in a downdraft when a setback such as a job loss, illness, or injury strikes and the family lands in serious financial straits. In each case, the story both illustrates why volatility should be taken as a risk measure and describes part of the very danger that it is measuring. But the primary purpose of both kinds of betas is as a measure. The most important dangers in the case of a stock involve what about its business is causing its share price to bounce up and down so much. And the most important dangers in the case of a family are what changes in the economy, in relations with employers and government and so forth, are causing its income to take increasingly large swings. In interpreting income volatility primarily as a measure, I differ from others, such as Yale political scientist Jacob S. Hacker, who have written on this subject and who appear to treat it primarily as a previously unnoticed danger in its own right.

I have drawn on a broad array of government statistics to tackle the question of how Americans can be leading economically more perilous lives—as many tell pollsters they are doing—even amid prosperity. Among the sources: surveys by the Bureau of Labor Statistics, the U.S. Census, the Bureau of Economic Analysis, and the Federal Reserve. But many of my key findings come from the Panel Study of Income Dynamics.

The panel study has followed a nationally representative sample of 5,000 families and many of their offshoots for nearly 40 years, and as such is the most comprehensive, publicly available source of information about families' earnings and incomes in the world. It is run by the University of Michigan and is principally underwritten by the National Science Foundation.

As with any effort to follow a large number of people over a long period of time, the questions that participants are asked, the ways that their responses are recorded, and the means that are used to code those responses into the computer have all changed, raising questions about the quality and comparability of results. Some of the problems have been extraordinarily basic and comparatively easy to deal with. For example, the NSF chose to reduce funding for the panel study after 1997, forcing its administrators to switch from interviewing families on an annual basis to interviewing them on an every-other-year basis. That has raised questions about how to produce results for years before 1996 (the data for which were gathered in 1997) and afterward that can be compared. On the advice of experts at several major universities and the Urban Institute, a nonpartisan Washington think tank, I used two methods. The first was to examine trends in five-year, overlapping measuring periods and when I got to 1996 to hold myself to the same sample standards, but applied to five-year periods in which some years were missing. The second was to look at trends in seven-year, overlapping periods, but ones that include only every other year so that I could look consistently across the entire thirty-four-year era being examined. The two methods produced income volatility trends that were broadly similar both in the size of their end-to-end increase and in the pattern of change.

Other problems have been more difficult to handle. For example, some economists have raised questions about the accuracy of panel study results for several years during the early 1990s, especially 1993 and 1994 when, using some measuring methods, income volatility appeared to peak. I have handled this problem chiefly by focusing on the end-to-end changes in income fluctuations and not highlighting these peak years.

Still other problems have been raised by economists who are seeking to use powerful new computing techniques to replace, for many purposes, surveys such as the panel study with direct analysis of administrative databases such as for all income-tax filers in America or all participants in Social Security. The experts on whom I have relied and I have tried our best to address the concerns of these administrative database economists, although we have been handicapped by the fact that access to their databases is restricted, because of privacy concerns, to a select group of government officials and economists.

The broadest criticism of the administrative database analysts is that the early 1990s flaws in the panel study were sufficiently serious that they effectively have cut the study in half, making it impossible to compare results from the 1970s and 1980s with those of the late 1990s and this decade. To try to examine this issue, Urban Institute experts and I sought to compare the panel study results on either side of the suspect years with those of the separate Census-administered Survey of Income and Program Participation (SIPP).

We took annual data from the SIPP for three-year periods beginning in 1983–1984, 1990–1993, 1996–1997, and 2001; used the same programs as we used in analyzing the panel study; and came up with broadly similar findings. The similarity suggests that the panel study can be used to examine trends across the suspect years. The SIPP results confirm the finding of an increase in volatility in family income from the early 1980s to the middle of the 2000s, and therefore an increase in the risks families face.

The broad outlines of my look at the panel study were worked out during 2003 and 2004 with the guidance of Robert A. Moffitt, a Johns Hopkins University economist and editor of the *American Economic Review,* and with economists Ann Huff Stevens and Marianne E. Page, both of the University of California-Davis. The techniques I used were subsequently refined in 2007 by an Urban Institute group led by Sheila Zedlewski and including economist Austin Nichols and research associate Seth Zimmerman.

These experts and I took a number of steps to ensure that our examination was not distorted by data problems with the panel study. Besides coping with the early 1990s problem, we eliminated a subsample of Latino families that was added to the panel study in the early 1990s. Independent researchers have concluded that the subsample was poorly designed and that its inclusion could skew the results. We looked at pre-tax income, rather than after-tax income, because some analysts believe that the panel study's after-tax records during the early years are not accurate.

In order to make sure we were looking at working families, we focused on men and women twenty-five to sixty-four years old whose households had some income. To avoid double-counting income in cases where families broke up, we added such payments as alimony and child support to the incomes of receiving households and subtracted them from paying households. We looked at income from all sources, including labor earnings; investments; public transfers such as jobless benefits, food stamps, and cash welfare; and private transfers such as inheritance.

In looking at income-threatening events, I relied on techniques developed during the 1980s by economists Richard Burkhauser of Cornell University and Greg Duncan of Northwestern University. Following the pair, I chose to focus on seven types of events that people can experience during the course of a typical work life. These included: divorce or separation, a major decline in the work hours of a spouse, the death of a spouse, the birth of a child, a major decline in the work hours of the head of the household due to disability or retirement, a major spell of unemployment for the head, and a major decline in work hours of the head due to illness. In every case, "major" is defined as involving at least 320 hours, or 8 weeks. Of families who experienced one or several of these events during a decade, I asked what fraction subsequently saw its annual income drop by 50 percent or more.

In trying to examine these events in a way that makes sense for the current generation of Americans, I faced certain constraints. When the panel study was started in the 1960s, most families had a single male earner. As a result, the study has only limited information about the employment status, earnings, and hours of women during the early years.

In examining family income volatility, I relied on the pathbreaking work of Moffitt and Boston College economist Peter Gottschalk. I looked at overlapping five-year increments from 1970 through 2004 and examined the annual fluctuations in each family's income. For example, for a family whose income rose from $60,000 to $65,000 over a five-year span, I asked how that family's income made the journey from the lower number to the higher one. Did it move in steady, upward, $1,000 increments? Or did the family's income take big jumps in some years and plunges in others? The basic finding of the analysis is that the fluctuations in annual income that individual families have experienced have grown larger over the past three-plus decades. I averaged the results of individual families to get the results I presented.

In looking at volatility, there were a number of choices that I had to make. In some cases, I made ones that differ from those of Gottschalk and Moffitt in their most recent work. For example, I picked a method for calculating income volatility that the pair originally developed in a 1994 paper. They now label this method "descriptive" and generally treat it as simple compared to their more involved current methods. But I chose it precisely because it is descriptive and comparatively simple, and therefore more accessible to me and, I hope, to general readers.

Then there is the matter of making cuts among low-income panel study families. Because of the mathematical nature of calculating volatility, including families with extremely low incomes can drastically alter the results. Gottschalk and Moffitt handled the problem in one recent paper by trimming the bottom one or two percent of income earners. Another group of analysts has proposed rounding upward the incomes of all those who report less than $4,000 annual incomes to $4,000. Instead of making either of these very large alterations to the data, I chose to remove only the several hundred observations (out of several hundred thousand observations of working-age people in the PSID) in which a person reported an annual income of less than $10. The Urban Institute's Zimmerman discovered that this minimal trim yields results that are quite similar to those produced by much larger cuts, while lowering the risk of ignoring people who experienced precipitous income drops. Together with the Urban Institute experts, I ran a series of tests to determine whether my income volatility results were the product of data problems or reflected real changes in the economy, and to address still other concerns about the panel study that have been raised by specialists. We ran our numbers with and without 1 percent and 2 percent bottom and top trims and with and without the $4,000 bottom rounding. We ran them with and without an immigrant subsample that was separate from the troubled Latino subsample, and with and without adjustments for changes in the size of families. In every case where the results with the changes were similar to those without, we chose to add back the removed families on the theory that we wanted to make the fewest possible adjustments to the database and maintain the largest possible sample.

Finally, it seems important to address the views of Peter Orszag, the director of the Congressional Budget Office (CBO), and the results of a paper that Orszag commissioned by Molly Dahl and others mentioned in the endnotes to Chapter 3. Orszag believes that income volatility has not risen since 1980, and may even have declined. This obviously is different from my results going back to the 1970s that suggest volatility has increased. It is important to understand what might account for the difference. This is especially so because although I rely on the PSID for most of my findings, the experts at the Urban Institute and I have examined the data set that Orszag used, the SIPP, and we find that this data set, too, shows that volatility has increased. Indeed, the CBO itself came to a similar conclusion when it looked at the SIPP alone. But in their most recent work, Orszag and his colleagues have handled the SIPP in a different way. The CBO group has sought to match the SIPP data on individuals with data on those same individuals from confidential Social Security records. The team has used the results only when it can come up with a match. But the matching process appears to have produced some unusual results. For example, in 2002 the CBO group found that only 57 percent of the SIPP sample could be matched with the Social Security records. As a result, it threw out the remaining 43 percent. That's a huge fraction of a data set to disregard. Even in instances where the match rate was higher, questions remain about whom the CBO researchers were picking up with the matches and whom they were discarding because of a lack of a match. The most accurate estimate of income volatility most likely lies somewhere between the estimates based on the PSID, which show an increase, and the CBO's matched SIPP–Social Security results, which show no increase. None of the arguments I make about income volatility depends on a particular-size increase, only on the trend being positive.

For a more detailed explanation of the quantitative findings in this book and for a more detailed argument that income volatility is appropriately treated as a risk measure, I encourage the reader to look at a technical paper I coauthored with Seth Zimmerman, "Trends in Income Volatility and Risk, 1970–2004" (Washington, D.C.: Urban Institute, November 2007), available online at either of two websites: www.urban.org/reports/incomevolatility.cmf or www.highwirethe book.com.

ACKNOWLEDGMENTS

Announcing you're writing a book elicits a response similar to what I imagine you'd get by declaring you're moving to the Arctic or joining a monastery; people look at you as if you're out of your mind. At a time when so much is pose and facsimile, books are still considered tough stuff, perhaps ridiculously, wastefully so. But once listeners get over the craziness of the enterprise, a funny thing happens; people—even people you've never met—offer help. It is to these people I owe a great debt.

First and foremost, I am indebted to the hundreds of families of various means and across the country who agreed to be interviewed—often repeatedly—about their economic circumstances. They did so even though there was nothing in it for them and when the interviews involved private matters, personal papers and some of the most painful setbacks of their lives. Each is engaged in a heroic effort to carve out good lives for themselves and their families amid the increasingly confusing cross-currents of the U.S. economy.

I am deeply indebted to the circle of journalists who've comprised my workplace family and whose ranks are being winnowed by economic change and altered tastes. Dean Baquet and John Carroll, each once editor of the *Los Angeles Times*, supported the newspaper series from which much of the book is drawn almost entirely on faith. Equally supportive, Doyle McManus and Tom McCarthy graciously accepted my dashing in and out of my beat even as they struggled to maintain a smooth-running Washington bureau. Rick Wartzman, Deborah Nelson, and Roger Smith served as indispensable mid-wife to one part or another of the project. Beatrice De Gea created beautiful photographs. Paul Duginski, and later my sister, Andrea Haraldsson, managed to turn my numbers into understandable graphics. Dick Cooper steadied me when I discovered that books aren't newspaper stories, only longer. He re-wrote virtually every chapter and was unstintingly cheerful when I re-wrote his re-writes. There would be no book without him. Thanks as well to the newspaper's current leadership, which has given me the time to finish, and to all of my Washington and L.A. colleagues who've carried the ball when I should have been carrying it.

I am indebted to a long line of economists. At its head is Robert Moffitt of Johns Hopkins University, who co-authored the techniques I used in generating the key numbers for the book. Moffitt is a paragon of the academic—quiet, skeptical and very, very careful. Dealing with journalists is not standard fare. But in small ways, he has signaled his interest in my undertaking. I'm also grateful to his graduate students, Xiaoguo Hu and Anubha Dhasmana. I owe similar debts to Richard Burkhauser of Cornell University and Greg Duncan of Northwestern University; to Ann Huff Stevens, Marianne Page and their graduate student, Sami Kitmitto, all at the UC-Davis; to Robert Schoeni of University of Michigan, Henry Farber of Princeton University, Sanford Jacoby of UCLA, and Alicia Munnell and Steven Sass of Boston College.

When it came time to do a book, I was lucky enough to attract the attention of the Rockefeller Foundation. I owe thanks to the foundation's president, Judith Rodin, for agreeing to financially supporting the effort. I'm grateful to Katherine McFate, formerly with Rockefeller, now with the Ford Foundation; and to Darren Walker and Janice Nittoli, both of Rockefeller, for taking a personal and continuing interest in the work.

The Rockefeller support gained me access to the Urban Institute, where my debts run in all sorts of directions. Its president, Robert D. Reischauer, plowed the bureaucratic path to my being a visiting fellow. He and his wife, Charlotte, have been family friends in a city famously devoid of friends. Gregory Acs, Olivia Golden, Edward Gramlich before his untimely death, and Robert Lerman have all served as crucial sounding boards. Eugene Steuerle has long been an inspiration. But my deepest debts go to a group headed by Sheila Zedlewski and especially to two of its members, economist Austin Nichols and research associate Seth Zimmerman. Without their expertise and, perhaps as importantly, their easy confidence in the push and shove of debate over the numbers, the book would never have been completed.

For breaking me into the book business—and getting me a contract with Basic Books—I am indebted to Wendy Strothman and Dan O'Connell. At Basic, I'm grateful to my editor, Bill Frucht.

There are a few people who don't fit neatly into any category. David Moss of Harvard Business School was extraordinarily generous with his time and ideas. Peter L. Bernstein was equally an inspiration and equally generous with his thinking. Mary Ellen Signorille, Mark DeBefosky, and especially James Wooten of SUNY-Buffalo were unbelievably patient in explaining key ERISA court rulings. Jared Bernstein of the Economic Policy Institute was equally patient in reminding me of economic trends I should already have known about. My friend

John Aloysius Farrell helped guide the writing and has provided my family with crucial support at a difficult time.

Finally, there is my family.

My father, Dr. Robert E. Gosselin, taught me about the importance of work and the thrill of ideas. He and his wife, Patricia, put up with endless telephoned complaints about various aspects of the project.

More immediately, during the several years I devoted to the series and subsequent stories and the year and a half plus I poured into the book, Nora and Jacob, now both 11, came to take it as a given that their father would vanish to his study most weekend days, and either work or not show up at all for summer vacations. Jake was always willing to talk, although he favors politics over economics. Nora once delivered a note informing me that I was the most "on task" father she knew. Blessedly, she never explained whether this was a compliment or complaint.

As for my wife, Robin, I cannot write as other authors do about her unconditional support and happy participation in every phase of the undertaking. Robin endured the series, but came to abhor the book because it stole from family time. As a reporter, she believes that if you have something to say, say it in a daily or a one- or two-week developed piece, preferably on Page 1, and get on with it. But she is still in every page. That's because she taught me what I knew abstractly, but now know viscerally—that we are here to love and help each other; that our common activities, including government, can be forces for big, good things as well as bad; and that whenever cutbacks are floated either by business or government, there's somebody out there on the receiving end, somebody whose life is about to get tipped over.

We may ultimately have to accept the cutbacks in the safety nets we enjoyed during much of the second half of the 20th century, and may have to cut still more. But if we do, we must to do so together, fairly and as minimally as possible. Robin has taught me this in the way she conducts herself as a reporter, wife, and mother; in the way she is bravely confronting the disease that now threatens her; and in giving me Jake and Nora. And for this, I'll be forever grateful.

Washington, D.C., March, 2008

NOTES

Chapter 1: Introduction

1   **The gross domestic product:** Bureau of Economic Analysis, Department of Commerce, http://www.bea.gov/national/xls/gdplev.xls. All dollar amounts are adjusted to constant 2007 dollars using the Consumer Price Index-U-RS, unless otherwise specified. For inflation adjustment, see http://www.bls.gov/cpi/#data.

2   **And behind these questions:** There is a great deal of polling on economic insecurity, and almost all of it finds a growth of insecurity over time. Some of the longest-running is by Towers Perrin-ISR. ISR has regularly asked tens of thousands of people whether they worry "frequently" about being laid off. During the depth of the 1980s recession, only 12 percent answered yes. But by the height of the 1990s boom, the number had topped 40 percent. The number has come down somewhat since then, but still remains well above 30 percent, or more than double its early 1980s level. Other work includes Karlyn Bowman, *Economic Insecurity* (Washington, D.C.: American Enterprise Institute, April 2007), http://www.aei.org/research/politicalCorner/subjectAreas/pageID.912,projectID.14/default.asp; Andrew Kohut, various polls, Pew Research Center, 2006–2007, http://pewresearch.org/topics/economics/; and Janice Nittoli, "American Workers Economic Security Survey Reveals Pervasive Anxiety" (New York: Yankelovich Research and the Rockefeller Foundation, May 2007), http://www.rockfound.org/initiatives/initiatives_dev/amer_workers.shtml.

3   **In that year, as the small sailing ship:** Nathaniel Philbrick, *Mayflower: A Story of Courage, Community, and War* (New York: Penguin, 2007), 40–47.

6   **And almost everybody applauded:** There is a rich literature of economic optimism, some of it technical, some of it popular. An extreme version of the popular argument appears in Gregg Easterbrook, *The Progress Paradox: How Life Gets Better While People Feel Worse* (New York: Random House, 2003). A technical work that is similarly optimistic is Clair Brown, John Haltiwanger, and Julia Lane, *Economic Turbulence: Is a Volatile Economy Good for America?* (Chicago: University of Chicago Press, 2006). Other recent versions of the popular case can be found in Anne Kim et al., "The New Rules Economy: A Policy Framework for the 21st Century," in *Third Way* (Washington, D.C.: Third Way, 2007), http://www.thirdway .org/data/product/file/71/Third_Way_New_Rules_Economy_Report .pdf; and, as part of a larger argument, in Brink Lindsey, *The Age of Abundance: How Prosperity Transformed America's Politics and Culture* (New York: HarperCollins, 2007). For more technical arguments, see, for example, Martin Feldstein, ed., *American Economic Policy in the 1980s* (Chicago: University of Chicago Press, 1994); and Alan B. Krueger and Robert Solow, eds., *The Roaring Nineties: Can Full Employment Be Sustained?* (New York: Russell Sage and Century Foundations, 2001).

6   **And the American economy returned:** Ben S. Bernanke, "The Great Moderation," paper presented at the Eastern Economic Association meetings, Washington, D.C., February 20, 2004, http://www.federalreserve .gov/BOARDDOCS/SPEECHES/2004/20040220/default.htm.

6   **I was interviewing him for a story:** The account of the Cosses, both Jr. and Sr., is based on interviews with them and their families off and on since 2002.

7   **Indeed, in the past twenty-five years:** Thomas Piketty and Emmanuel Saez, "Income Inequality in the United States," *Quarterly Journal of Economics* 118, no. 1 (February 2003): 1–39, and updating of their figures on Saez's website, http://elsa.berkeley.edu/~saez.

8   **But focusing on income inequality:** Karlyn Bowman, *Attitudes about the American Dream* (Washington, D.C.: American Enterprise Institute, 2007), final version forthcoming.

8   **Equalizing institutions that used to ensure:** Frank Levy and Peter Temin, *Inequality and Institutions in 20th Century America*, Working Paper no. 13106 (Cambridge, Mass.: National Bureau of Economic Research, 2007), 1–54, http://www.nber.org.

9   **For all of the seeming promise of the Great Moderation:** Interviews with Robert A. Moffitt and personal correspondence.

13   **The latest figures from the Federal Reserve's Survey of Consumer Finances:** Arthur B. Kennickell, *Currents and Undercurrents: Changes in the Distribution of Wealth, 1989–2004,* SCF Working Papers (Washington, D.C.: Federal Reserve, January 2006), http://www.federalreserve.gov/pubs/oss/oss2/papers/concentration.2004.5.pdf.

14   **It's a bit of a math game:** Figures for stock and home equity come from the Federal Reserve, Flow of Funds report, http://www.federalreserve .gov/release/z1/zlr-5.pdf. Figures for the face value of all personal lines of insurance are estimates based on interviews with major insurance-industry trade associations and research organizations, among them the American Insurance Association in Washington and the Insurance Information Institute in New York.

Of course, in this comparison the deck is stacked in favor of insurance because the insurance figure assumes that everybody with a life policy drops dead, everybody who is covered by health insurance gets sick, and essentially every house and car in America is destroyed simultaneously. But that's precisely what insurers can be all but certain will not happen and therefore why they don't have to collect the exorbitant amount that it would cost to, in effect, replace America all at once. Instead, they can charge large numbers of people comparatively moderate premiums to cover the losses of the few who actually are struck by the setback during the course of a year, and in this way spread the risk and cost of the danger across the entire group. Nevertheless, the face-value number has an important meaning; you can think of it as the figure you'd come up with if you asked everybody with a policy how much coverage they have and tallied the results. It's the protection all of us get in return for each of us paying a relatively modest amount. And it is this quality that gives insurance its kinship with the Mayflower Compact.

15   **"All insurance, indeed all of modern finance:** Interview with Robert J. Shiller. Shiller's book *The New Financial Order: Risk in the 21st Century* (Princeton, N.J.: Princeton University Press, 2003) may be the most optimistic book in print both about people's ability to deal with the risks that have been shifted to them and about financial markets' ability to provide them with the means of doing so. The markets have yet to show their readiness to deal with these dangers.

20   **Despite all the talk of greater opportunities:** Interview with Paul Osterman. I relied on Osterman, *Securing Prosperity: The American Labor*

Market—How It Has Changed and What to Do about It (Princeton, N.J.: Princeton University Press, 1999).

26   For example, George Gilder, whose 1981 book: George Gilder, *Wealth and Poverty* (New York: Basic Books, 1981), 110.

28   Virtually all advocates of moral hazard: Interviews with David A. Moss, an economic historian and professor at Harvard Business School. I have relied heavily on Moss's thinking throughout this book. His book, *When All Else Fails: Government as the Ultimate Risk Manager* (Cambridge: Harvard University Press, 2002), is a sweeping reinterpretation of the history of American domestic policy as an effort to lift risk from individuals and businesses and shift, spread, or reduce it. Its account ends in 1980. Moss believes that despite efforts to reduce the government's risk-managing role, that role remains essentially intact, and the biggest changes in who shoulders risk have occurred in the private sector.

29   "It turns out that people can scramble: Joseph Nocera, *A Piece of the Action: How the Middle Class Joined the Money Class* (New York: Touchstone, 1995), 187.

29   "We've finally gotten a piece of the action: Ibid., 34.

30   Investors may demand more choices: The argument that a substantial fraction of retirement investors falters at each stage of the investment process was first convincingly made by Alicia H. Munnell and Annika Sundén in *Coming Up Short: The Challenge of 401(k) Plans* (Washington, D.C.: Brookings Institution, 2004), and has been updated in the publications of the Center for Retirement Research at Boston College, which Munnell leads. Center publications discuss the effects of the 2006 Pension Protection Act, which solves some but not all of the problems.

30   One study found that the chief reason: Interviews with David Laibson and Brigitte C. Madrian, both economists at Harvard University. Information is from James J. Choi, David Laibson, and Brigitte C. Madrian, *$100 Bills on the Sidewalk: Sub-optimal Saving in 401(k) Plans,* Working Paper no. 11554 (Cambridge, Mass.: National Bureau of Economic Research, August 2005).

31   In a recent column assessing the career: Joe Nocera, "Bullish, Sure, but There Was More to Say," *The New York Times*, May 6, 2006, C1.

32   Burkhauser and Duncan concluded that: Richard V. Burkhauser and Greg J. Duncan, "Economic Risk of Gender Roles: Income Loss and Life Events over the Life Course," *Social Science Quarterly* 70, no. 1 (March 1989): 3–23.

CHAPTER 2: BENEFITS

35   **On Labor Day, 1974:** James A. Wooten, *The Employee Retirement Income Security Act of 1974: A Political History* (Berkeley and Los Angeles: University of California Press, 2004). Much of this chapter relies on Wooten's book and on extensive conversations with Wooten, a law professor and historian at the State University of New York-Buffalo. It also relies on conversations with Mark D. DeBofsky, a lawyer with Daley, DeBofsky, & Bryant in Chicago; and with Mary Ellen Signorille, a senior attorney with the AARP Foundation.

37   **"People who try to claim:** Interview with William M. Acker Jr. Acker is no liberal. In 2005, he made news by announcing he would refuse to accept law clerks from Yale Law School, his alma mater, because the university refused to permit military recruiting on campus.

37   **Or as California's Democratic lieutenant governor:** Interviews with John Garamendi.

37   **Employer-sponsored health insurance:** For health insurance, see Paul Fronstin, *Employment-Based Health Benefits: Access and Coverage, 1988–2005* (Washington, D.C.: Employee Benefit Research Institute, March 2007), http://www.ebri.org/pdf/briefspdf/EBRI_IB_03-20071.pdf. For disability and employer-provided life insurance and for retirement provisions, see Employee Benefit Research Institute, *Databook on Employee Benefits,* online publication found at http://www.ebri.org/publications/books/index.cfm?fa=databook.

38   **But when Studebaker Corporation shut:** Steven A. Sass, *The Promise of Private Pensions: The First Hundred Years* (Cambridge, Mass.: Harvard University Press, 1997), 184–186.

38   **The reformers' view was:** Interviews with Wooten.

39   **In other words, they came to reject:** Thomas Hobbes, *Leviathan* (Oxford, U.K.: Oxford University Press, 1957).

39   **The seemingly simple shift:** Peter L. Bernstein, *Against the Gods: The Remarkable Story of Risk* (New York: Wiley, 1998). I have relied heavily on Bernstein, a financial theorist and prolific author.

40   **But in his book on government risk policy:** Interview with Moss. See also, Moss, *When All Else Fails,* 1–21. The historical developments described in the following pages are drawn from Moss's book.

42   **Moss described the situation:** Moss, *When All Else Fails,* 6.

42   **As late as the 1970s:** Richard Nixon, "Special Message to the Congress Proposing Job Security Assistance," April 12, 1973, from John Woolley

and Gerhard Peters, American Presidency Project (online), University of California-Santa Barbara, http://www.presidency.ucsb.edu/ws/index.php ?pid=3806.

43   **Debra May (soon to be Potter) ended up:** As with all of the people whose personal stories appear here, Potter's story is based on extensive interviews with her and her family starting in 2004, as well as a review of her voluminous medical records. These conversations were cut short in 2007, when Potter signed an agreement that gave Focus Films exclusive rights to make a movie about her story. Focus Films executives refused to grant the author permission to continue his conversations with Potter to update his story.

46   **Under the terms of Diane's:** Travelers subsequently sold its health business to MetraHealth Insurance Company, a private company formed through the combination of the group health business of Metropolitan Life Insurance Company and Travelers. MetraHealth was then bought by health insurance giant United Health Care.

49   **In May 2004, J. D. and Linda sued Aetna:** *Lind et al. v. Aetna Health Inc.,* Tulsa County District Court, Okla., CJ-2003-2071.

51   **LaRue figured that the delay cost him:** *LaRue v. DeWolff Boberg et al.,* 2:04-cv-1747-18 (D., S.C., 2004).

51   **For many years, from the end of World War II**: For example, in the nearly thirty years from 1947 through 1973, the real after-inflation incomes of families in the middle of the economic spectrum climbed nearly 100 percent. By contrast, in the nearly thirty years between 1973 and 2000, they grew less than one-third of that amount, and in the past few years, they have shrunk. See Lawrence Mishel, Jared Bernstein, and Sylvia Allegretto, *The State of Working America, 2006–2007* (Ithaca, N.Y.: Cornell University Press, 2007), 57.

52   **Businesses must find ways "of protecting:** Francis X. Sutton et al., *The American Business Creed* (Cambridge, Mass.: Harvard University Press, 1956), 220. The quote was pointed out to me by Sanford M. Jacoby, on whose writings I relied, especially *Modern Manors: Welfare Capitalism since the New Deal* (Princeton, N.J.: Princeton University Press, 1997).

53   **"With costs through the roof:** Interview with Sylvester Scheiber. Until he retired in 2007, Scheiber was the head of research for Watson Wyatt Worldwide, one of the nation's most influential benefits-consulting firms. His views on health care are mirrored in his views on pensions. See Scheiber, *Pension Aspirations and Realizations: A Perspective on Yesterday, Today, and Tomorrow* (Arlington, Va.: Watson Wyatt, 2007), http://www

.watsonwyatt.com/research/whitepapers/wprender.asp?id=2006-US-0103.

55   **"We . . . have done what government policy:** Quoted from Alex Taylor III, "Looking Out for No. 1," *Fortune,* November 24, 2003, 169.

56   **"Recent predictions of the pension:** Interview with Ron Gebhardtsbauer, a senior fellow at the American Academy of Actuaries in Washington.

56   **How quickly and effectively this group's:** Conference Board survey results from Peter Cappelli, *The New Deal at Work: Managing the Market-Based Employment Relationship* (Boston: Harvard Business School Press, 1999), 34.

57   **According to ERISA's preamble, its intent:** A copy of the full preamble can be found at http://www.law.cornell.edu/uscode/html/uscode29/usc_sec_29_00001001—-000-.html.

57   **But starting with a 1985 case:** *Mass Mutual v. Russell,* 473 U.S. 134, 138 (1985); John H. Langbein, "What ERISA Means by 'Equitable': The Supreme Court's Trail of Error in Russell, Mertens, and Great-West," *Columbia Law Review* 103, no. 1317 (October 2003).

57   **The high court has interpreted:** *Pilot Life v. Dedeaux,* 481 U.S. 41 (1987).

57   **And it has invited insurers and others:** *Firestone v. Bruch* 489 U.S. 101 (1989).

58   **"It has allowed companies and unions:** Interview with Steven J. Sacher. Sacher helped draft ERISA as a young Labor Department lawyer and now represents insurers as an attorney in Washington with the law firm Jones Day.

59   **In one 1995 memo, Ralph W. Mohney Jr.:** *Hangarter v. Provident Life and Accident Insurance Company and Paul Revere Life Insurance Company; UnumProvident Corporation,* 236 F.Supp. 2d (2004) at 1083–1086; May 22, 1995, memorandum from Mohney to company chief executive Harold Chandler.

59   **In another 1995 memo, Jeffrey G. McCall:** *Schneider v. Provident Life and Accident Insurance Co.,* United States District Court, Northern District of California, C-97-4646 SC; October 2, 1995, memorandum from McCall to "IOC Management Group" and Glenn Felton.

59   **In 2004, regulators representing all fifty states:** "Report of the Targeted Multistate Market Conduct Examination for Maine . . . Massachusetts . . . Tennessee and 49 Participating Jurisdictions of Unum Life Insurance Company of America et al.," November 18, 2004, http://www.maine

.gov/pfr/insurance/unum/UNUM_Provident_Regulatory_Settlement_A greement.htm.

60   **In a 2005 probe, California regulators:** State of California, Department of Insurance, "Public Report of the Market Conduct Examination of the Claims Practices of Unum Life Insurance Company of America et al., Oct. 3, 2005," http://64.233.169.104/search?q=cache:JIz_szT3vQEJ: 208.56.213.85/archives/CSA-Market%2520Conduct.pdf+California +Insurance+Public+Report+Market+Conduct+Examination+Claims+ Practices+Unum+Life+Insurance+Company+America&hl=en&ct=clnk &cd=2&gl=us.

60   **John Garamendi, then California's:** Interview with John Garamendi.

60   **According to court papers in a subsequent lawsuit:** *Andrews-Clarke v. Travelers et al.,* 984 F.Supp. 49 (D., Mass., 1997).

61   **Writing in one recent case, Justice Ruth Bader Ginsburg:** *Aetna Health Inc. v. Davila,* 542 U.S. 200, 222 (2004).

63   **As one senior congressional staffer:** Wooten, *Employee Retirement Income Security Act of 1974,* 264–270. More generally, the discussion of how the law's structure allowed its purpose to be so dramatically shifted comes from Wooten.

63   **Among other things, the court used the decision:** *Mass Mutual v. Russell,* 142.

64   **The status also has meant:** *Firestone v. Bruch.* Yale law professor John H. Langbein discusses what he believes is the Supreme Court's flawed interpretation in *Bruch* and the UnumProvident case in "Trust Law as Regulatory Law: The Unum/Provident Scandal and Judicial Review of Benefit Denials under ERISA," *Northwestern University Law Review* 101, no. 3 (Spring 2007).

65   **"Under traditional notions of justice:** *Andrews-Clarke v. Travelers et al.,* 52.

68   **Potter's search for an answer:** All of the quotes from Capone and from UnumProvident in the account that follows come from documents that UnumProvident sent Potter when it denied her claim and closed her case. The documents were provided to me by the family.

72   **UnumProvident CEO Thomas R. Watjen refused:** Interview with Watjen.

72   **James Sabourin, UnumProvident's communications vice president:** Multiple interviews with Sabourin.

73   **It ruled that the federal benefits law:** *Verity v. Howe,* 516 U.S. 489 (1996).

73 **In other decisions, the court appeared:** *New York State Conference of Blue Cross & Blue Shield Plans v. Travelers,* 514 U.S. 645 (1995); *Pegram v. Herdrich,* 530 U.S. 211 (2000).

73 **The justices suggested that states:** *Pegram v. Herdrich.*

74 **They also appeared to authorize states:** *Rush v. Moran,* 536 U.S. 355 (2002).

74 **The high court even seemed to signal:** Ibid.

74 **Writing about one of the rulings:** Peter J. Hammer, "*Pegram v. Herdrich:* On Peritonitis, Preemption, and the Elusive Goal of Managed Care Accountability," *Journal of Health Politics, Policy, and Law* 26, no. 4 (2001): 767–788, http://jhppl.dukejournals.org/cgi/content/abstract/26/4/767.

74 **In one case, the justices issued:** *Great-West v. Knudson,* 534 U.S. 204 (2002).

74 **And in its June 2004 ruling:** *Aetna v. Davila.*

74 **"The cases have been greeted with despair:** Interview with John H. Langbein. Langbein, a Yale law professor, is the nation's leading scholar on employee-benefits laws.

75 **Aetna's lawyers used the Supreme Court's:** *Lind v. Aetna Health,* 04-cv-492-K (D., Okla., 2004).

76 **In 2005, federal judge Terence Kern:** *Lind v. Aetna Health,* Order, March 2005.

76 **On Halloween of 2006:** *Lind v. Aetna,* 466 F.3d 1195 (10th Cir., 2006).

77 **In LaRue's case, a three-judge:** *LaRue v. DeWolff Boberg,* 450 F.3d 570 (2006).

77 **The brief warned that the judges' decision:** *LaRue v. DeWolff Boberg,* "Secretary of Labor's Amicus Curiae Brief in Support of Petition for Rehearing and Rehearing En Banc," July 2006.

77 **On February 20, 2008, the high court:** *LaRue v. DeWolff, Boberg & Associates, Inc.* Bench opinion, 552 U.S. (2008).

Chapter 3: The Numbers

80 **I have not been the only one:** Jacob S. Hacker, *The Great Risk Shift: The Assault on American Jobs, Families, Health Care, and Retirement—and How You Can Fight Back* (Oxford, U.K.: Oxford University Press, 2006).

80 **Most of the numbers in this chapter:** Panel Study of Income Dynamics, http://psidonline.isr.umich.edu.

81   **All of this can affect data quality:** PSID officials have conducted a series of studies to test the accuracy of their database and compare the
results to other databases such as the Census's Survey of Income and Program Participation, to see if they generally match up. Some of the resulting papers can be found at http://psidonline.isr.umich.edu/Publications/
Papers.

81   **There are different ways to perform:** Austin Nichols and Seth Zimmerman, *Estimating Trends in Income Variability* (Washington, D.C.: Urban
Institute, forthcoming).

82   **Recently, government statisticians began:** Examples include the development by the Census Bureau's Longitudinal Employer-Household Dynamics Program and the recent use by researchers including those at the
Congressional Budget Office, Congress's numbers-crunching arm, of Social Security earnings records and Social Security and matched Internal
Revenue Service records.

84   **"Big Losses" and "Big Gains" charts:** The data in these charts were developed as follows: For each year during the measuring periods—
1970–1979, 1980–1989, 1990–1999, and 2000–2002—Seth Zimmerman
of the Urban Institute and I looked at PSID sample families that experienced 50 percent or greater income gains or losses during the subsequent
two years. We had to use two years to cope with the fact that the PSID
went from an annual to an every-other-year survey after 1996. We averaged our results across each of the years in the measuring period and calculated the fraction of the sample the average constituted.

84   **Because of the nature of the PSID:** Because of funding cutbacks, the
panel study switched from annual data collection to an every-other-year
schedule after 1997. This meant I could examine events and their subsequent income effects on an annual basis before 1997. I did so by contrast-
ing comparable periods in the 1970s, 1980s, and 1990s. But I couldn't
look at events annually after 1996. To bring my examination up-to-date
and to be able to compare trends before and after 1996 on a consistent
basis, I had to take a separate look of events and income consequences in
two-year intervals. I compared the mid-1970s to the mid-1980s, the mid-
1980s to the mid-1990s, and the mid-1990s to the mid-2000s.

85   **And while the 1-in-20 chance:** The Congressional Budget Office, using a
different database than the PSID and looking at earnings rather than
family income, came up with about the same odds of suffering a 50
percent–plus income drop in the current period. But the agency found no
evidence of an increase in the odds of a steep drop in earnings between
1980 and 2003. Peter R. Orszag, "Economic Volatility," testimony before

the Joint Economic Committee of the Congress, February 2007; *Trends in Earnings Variability over the Past 20 Years* (Washington, D.C.: Congressional Budget Office, April 2007). More recently, the CBO has looked at both earnings and incomes and said that, although it finds that the volatility of both has been high since 1980, it does not find an increase in income volatility over time. See, for example, Molly Dahl, Thomas DeLeire, and Jonathan A. Schwabish, *Trends in Individual Earnings Variability and Household Income Variability over the Past 20 Years* (Washington, D.C.: Congressional Budget Office, January 2008), 1–35. For a critique of the CBO findings, see Austin Nichols, *Discussion of* "Trends" . . . (Washington, D.C.: Urban Institute, January 2008), unpublished.

86 **In looking at these families, I applied:** Richard V. Burkhauser and Greg J. Duncan, "Economic Risks of Gender Roles: Income Loss and Life Events over the Life Course," *Social Science Quarterly* 70, no. 1 (March 1989).

88 **"Declining Incidence" and "Rising Consequence" charts:** "Incidence": For each year during the measuring periods—1973–1983, 1983–1993, and 1993–2003—and for each of the seven income-threatening events, Zimmerman and I looked for instances of PSID sample families experiencing one of the events in the following two years, then averaged the number of families for each year across the years of that measuring period and calculated the percentage of the sample that that average constituted. "Consequence": For each of the years in the measuring periods, we looked at PSID sample families that experienced one of the threatening events and examined how many of those families had a 50 percent or greater income fall in the subsequent two years, and then averaged and calculated a percentage as above. In doing this, we followed Burkhauser and Duncan, "Economic Risks." For detailed definitions of the events and the techniques, see Peter Gosselin and Seth Zimmerman, *Trends in Income Volatility and Risk, 1970–2004* (Washington, D.C.: Urban Institute, November 2007), 1–37.

90 **"Managing risk is really what finance:** Interview with Robert J. Shiller, a Yale finance theorist and economist who gained substantial fame by predicting in advance both the 2000 tech stock bust and the 2005 housing bust.

91 **The most widely used risk measure:** John Downes and Jordan E. Goodman, *Barron's Finance & Investment,* 7th ed. (New York: Barron's, 2007), 227.

91 **The groundwork for using betas:** Peter Gottschalk and Robert A. Moffitt, "The Growth of Earnings Instability in the U.S. Labor Market," *Brookings Papers on Economic Activity* 2 (1994).

93   **As with a stock beta, the idea behind using:** There has been considerable confusion in recent discussion of income volatility about whether the growth in income swings represents a new and previously unrecognized danger to American families or, like a stock beta, simply provides a means of gauging dangers that are being caused by economic conditions outside the swings themselves. The distinction is more than academic. If you think that the swings are the danger, then you are apt to emphasize their large size and how the dollar amounts could destabilize a family's finances. By contrast, if you treat income volatility, as I do, as a sort of beta for family income and a measuring stick of change, then what's important is the general increase over time—and the rising risk that I believe it signals—rather than the specific size of the swings. See Hacker, *The Great Risk Shift.*

93   **"The long-run trend in the volatility:** Interviews and correspondence with Robert Moffitt. Although Moffitt agrees with one of the central tenets of this book—that the volatility of family income has risen over the past several decades—both he and his colleague Gottschalk believe that the trend is more mild than my results indicate. In discussing the issue, Moffitt has been at pains to make clear he is not endorsing my particular volatility numbers.

94   **The Census figures for the same median families:** For comparison, see http://www.census.gov/prod/2004pubs/p60-226.pdf. As with all of the PSID income figures in the book, these were adjusted to 2007 dollars using the Consumer Price Index-U-RS.

94   **"Rising Volatility" chart:** In calculating the rising volatility of the entire PSID sample and the various subgroups described in the following pages, I followed Gottschalk and Moffitt, "Growth of Earnings Instability." For details of the techniques used and a description of the ways in which what I have done differs from Gottschalk and Moffitt, see the Methods appendix and Gosselin and Zimmerman, *Trends in Income Volatility,* 6–8.

It's important for readers to understand the scale by which volatility is being measured in this chart and in the ones to follow. The percentages on the y axis represent the maximum swing in annual income that the majority of PSID sample families experience. Rather than being an average, which is the way many things economic are measured, this represents an outer bound, the outer bound of the income swings that sample families—and therefore Americans generally—experience. Some families experience larger swings, but most experience up to and including this level of income swing. The important thing to notice is that the outer bound is getting bigger and, as I show later on, this is not simply because of a few outliers. One more thing: The reason I say the "majority" rather than all sample families is because if I were to pick an outer bound that included every single family, it would be so large as to be meaningless for practical purposes. So I picked an outer bound that includes the majority, but not everybody.

95 **"Across the Board" chart:** See references and explanations for the "Rising Volatility" chart.

98 **"Across Generations" chart:** Ibid.

100 **"Deep into America" chart:** Ibid. The differences in how this chart was made as compared with the ones that immediately precede it are explained in the text.

101 **"The main reason incomes have grown:** David Brooks, "Who's Afraid of the New Economy," *The New York Times*, "Week in Review," February 11, 2007, 13.

102 **"Men and Women" chart:** See references and explanations for the "Rising Volatility" chart.

103 **The volatility numbers drawn from the panel study:** For figures from the Census Current Population Survey that reinforce this point, see Lawrence Mishel, Jared Bernstein, and Sylvia Allegretto, *The State of Working America, 2006–2007* (Ithaca, N.Y.: Cornell University Press, 2007), Table 1.8, 55.

103 **"Only One Way Out" chart:** For this chart, Zimmerman and I sorted PSID sample families into four categories: those who were two-earner and one-earner families who took no breaks from this pattern of income earning, those who switched from two-earner to one-earner status once, and those who switched back and forth repeatedly. Otherwise, the chart follows the pattern of the other volatility charts. Ibid.

104 **It's that you shouldn't measure how well:** Dirk Krueger and Fabrizio Perri, "Does Income Inequality Lead to Consumption Inequality? Evidence and Theory," *Review of Economic Studies* 73, no. 1 (2006): 163–193.

105 **"On the whole, we have moved toward a freer market:** Interview with Gary S. Becker.

Chapter 4: Jobs

109 **On a typical morning in America:** Estimates based on Bureau of Labor Statistics, "Workers on Flexible and Shift Schedules in May 2004," Table 7, http://www.bls.gov/news.release/flex.nr0.htm. Updated for full-time

wage and salary workers, twenty and older, May 2007, using Bureau of Labor Statistics, "The Employment Situation, May 2007," http://www .bls.gov/news.release/archives/empsit_06012007.pdf.

109   **With the exception of a tiny sliver:** Lawrence Mishel, Jared Bernstein, and Sylvia Allegretto, *The State of Working America, 2006–2007* (Ithaca, N.Y.: Cornell University Press, 2007), 79.

110   **As signs that something new was happening:** Barry Bluestone and Bennett Harrison, *The Deindustrialization of America* (New York: Basic Books, 1982); Ira C. Magaziner and Robert B. Reich, *Minding America's Business: The Decline and Rise of the American Economy* (New York: HarcourtBraceJovanovich, 1982).

110   **When the economy confounded these prophets of trouble:** Kevin Kelly, *New Rules for the New Economy* (New York: Penguin, 1999).

110   **By most conventional measures, Fredo is:** Interviews with E. Paul Fredo from 2002 through 2007.

111   **From his perch several rungs down:** Interviews with Ron Burtless from 2004 through 2008.

113   **In both instances, the increases were the products:** Bureau of Labor Statistics, "Job Openings and Labor Turnover Survey," http://www.bls.gov/ jlt/home.htm; Bureau of Labor Statistics, "Business Employment Dynamics," http://www.bls.gov/bdm/home.htm. Compare to the net numbers that appear in the BLS's "Current Employment Statistics," http://www.bls.gov/ces/home.htm.

114   **But even as sunny an observer:** President George W. Bush in an interview with Maria Bartiromo, CNBC-TV, October 11, 2007.

115   **Moreover, the rush of new technology represented:** "Because [China, India, and the former Soviet bloc] had approximately half of the world's population, their entry into the global economy effectively doubled the number of workers in the world's labor pool . . . I have called this 'The Great Doubling'" from Richard B. Freeman, *America Works: Critical Thoughts on the Exceptional U.S. Labor Market* (New York: Russell Sage Foundation, 2007), 128–129.

116   **By 2006 . . . BLS statistics show that number:** Bureau of Labor Statistics, "Employee Tenure in 2006," http://www.bls.gov/news.release/pdf/ tenure.pdf.

116   **Even when Farber adjusted for such factors:** Henry S. Farber, *Is the Company Man an Anachronism? Trends in Long-term Employment in the U.S.,*

1973–2005, Working Paper no. 518 (Princeton, N.J.: Princeton University, Industrial Relations Section, September 2007), 7–18.

116 **Farber also found that women's tenure:** Of course, not all analysts are convinced that job tenure is declining. University of California-Davis economist Ann Huff Stevens compared surveys that asked men near the ends of their work lives, aged 58 to 62, how long their longest-running job had been. She found that those asked in 1969 and those asked in 2002 gave almost identical answers of a little more than 21 years. Her conclusion, and the title of her academic paper on the subject: "The More Things Change, the More They Stay the Same," *NBER* (December 2005). But there are reasons to think that Stevens's 1969 results may have been a fluke since similar-aged men in 1975 and 1980 reported much longer job tenures than those either before or after them. The longest-running job of those asked in 1980 was typically 24.1 years. The longest-running job of those asked in 2002, the latest year in Stevens's study, was 21.4, more than a 10 percent drop.

Stevens's paper is representative of a generation of books and academic papers by economists who are deeply reluctant to conclude that anything fundamental about the nature of work has changed until the change has unambiguously shown itself in the headline statistics or huge surveys such as the one Stevens used for this paper. In part, this reluctance reflects an admirable desire on the part of economists not to be hustled into making snap judgments. But it also is the product of a profession so mathematized that its practitioners are reluctant to look beyond the numbers to consider the reports of both ordinary working people and human resource executives that the nature of the employer-employee relationship, and therefore the nature of work, has substantially changed.

116 **"Analysis of the best data on job tenure:** Interview with Henry Farber, a Princeton economist.

117 **"Falling Tenure" chart:** From Farber, *Is the Company Man an Anachronism?* Table 7, 18. Farber measures the tenure of workers born at different times, or the lengths of time that they have hung onto their jobs, and compares them to the tenure of those born in 1914. He sets the tenure of the 1914 group as equal to zero and measures the tenure of groups born in more recent periods compared to that.

117 **"Over time [workers'] job changes result:** Clair Brown, John Haltiwanger, and Julia Lane, *Economic Turbulence: Is a Volatile Economy Good for America?* (Chicago: University of Chicago Press, 2006), 52. *Economic Turbulence* can be read as a sustained argument in favor of "creative destruction" and one that outstrips even the claims of the phrase's originator, conservative

economist Joseph Schumpeter. Brown, Haltiwanger, and Lane assert not only, as Schumpeter did, that upheaval is good for the economy as a whole but additionally something that Schumpeter did not argue—that it is also good for the very people whose lives it scrambles because it results in most moving to better jobs and careers. Such a claim, if supported, would represent a powerful endorsement for letting the economy continue along its current arc, even if that meant leaving many Americans increasingly prone to steep financial falls. It would be an argument that people are being more than compensated for taking greater risks by the reward of higher incomes and more fulfilling jobs. But the book has several serious shortcomings. It is based on a look at just five industries in six states. It does not measure whether turbulence is rising, falling, or staying the same, and it can't say whether turbulence is responsible for the job and career improvements that it says have occurred. And, beyond a passing mention, it does not examine the costs to individual families in uncertainty and unemployment.

119   **He'd been granted six months of pay:** Typical severance-pay estimates are from WorldatWork, a trade association of compensation executives based in Scottsdale, Arizona, http://www.worldatwork.org/waw/home/html/home.jsp.

120   **There, the group's director, Charlie Beck:** Interview with Beck, who introduced me to the world of unemployment support groups that I write about here and in the next chapter.

123   **Economists have a name for the former:** Bureau of Labor Statistics, "Worker Displacement, 2003–2005," http://www.bls.gov/news.release/disp.nr0.htm.

123   **They call the latter long-term unemployment:** Bureau of Labor Statistics, www.bls.gov. Under "Get Detailed Statistics," under "Access to Historical Data for the 'A' Tables of the Employment Situation Release," click on Table A-9, then on "27 Weeks and Over."

124   **"Greater Chance" chart:** From ibid., Table 10, 26. Farber uses the government's "Displaced Workers" surveys to calculate a job-loss rate. The surveys estimate the number of workers who have lost their jobs to plant closings, layoffs, and other reasons that are no fault of their own over the three years preceding the survey. Farber calculates a job-loss rate by dividing the number of job losers over the three years by the number of workers who were employed at the survey date or who reported a job loss. See ibid., 25.

125   **What that means is that the odds of losing your job:** Henry S. Farber, *Job Loss and the Decline in Job Security in the United States,* Working Paper

no. 520 (Princeton, N.J.: Princeton University, Industrial Relations Section, September 2007).

125 **"Out Longer" chart:** Based on statistics from the Bureau of Labor Statistics, "Employment Situation" reports, Table A-9, "Unemployed Persons by Duration of Unemployment." See percentage distribution, 27 weeks and over, seasonally unadjusted, http://www.bls.gov/cps/cpsatabs.htm.

126 **But with each passing business cycle:** See long-term unemployment statistics. For a discussion of the trend, see Bureau of Labor Statistics, "A Glance at Long-Term Unemployment in Recent Recessions," *Issues in Labor Statistics* 6, no. 1 (January 2006), http://www.bls.gov/opub/ils/pdf/opbils53.pdf.

127 **On average, college graduates who lost their jobs:** Henry S. Farber, *What Do We Know about Job Loss in the United States? Evidence from the Displaced Workers Survey, 1984–2004,* Working Paper no. 498 (Princeton, N.J.: Princeton University, Industrial Relations Section, January 2005), http://www.irs.princeton.edu/pubs/pdfs/498.pdf.

128 **Reading it today, you can experience:** *Work in America: Report of a Special Task Force to the Secretary of Health, Education, and Welfare* (Cambridge, Mass.: MIT Press, 1973).

128 **"Work," the report's authors wrote:** Ibid., xv.

130 **"Housekeeping may still be the main occupation:** Ibid., 57.

130 **"This element of the American Dream:** Ibid., 21.

132 **The size of these so-called consumption commitments:** Raj Chetty and Adam Szeidl, "Consumption Commitments and Risk Preferences," *Quarterly Journal of Economics* 122, no. 2 (2007): 831–877; interview with Chetty.

138 **What "most American workers have in common:** James O'Toole and Edward E. Lawler III, *The New American Workplace* (New York: Palgrave Macmillan, 2006), 15.

138 **"What has emerged," O'Toole and Lawler wrote:** Ibid., 66.

Chapter 5: Unjobs

141 **Onstage, a middle-aged business executive:** Based on interviews with Bruce Meyer from 2004 through 2007. Also based on interviews with friends and business associates.

142 **But on this night in 2006, Meyer's swan song:** Presented by the directors of the Atlanta Dogwood Festival, Inc. on April 7, 2006.

146   The labor participation rate for men has dropped: Bureau of Labor Statistics, "Historical Data for 'A' Tables of the Employment Situation Release, Men 20 and Over, Participation Rate, 1978–2007," http://www.bls.gov/webapps/legacy/cpsatab1.htm.

146   The rate for women climbed substantially: Bureau of Labor Statistics, "Historical Data for 'A' Tables of the Employment Situation Release, Women 20 Years and Over, Participation Rate, 1978–2007," http://www.bls.gov/webapps/legacy/cpsatab1.htm.

146   When the question is put to employers, however: Lawrence Mishel, Jared Bernstein, and Sylvia Allegretto, *The State of Working America, 2006–2007* (Ithaca, N.Y.: Cornell University Press, 2007), 238–239.

147   The fraction of company employees classified: Ibid., 241.

147   From Priority Two and Joseph's People in slow-growing Pittsburgh: Whatever the numbers of people stuck in job networking, there are two elements of the trend that suggest—if only suggest—a future very different from that of the past. The first is the notion of unemployment with assets. The people you are meeting in this chapter are not unemployed in the way we have been taught to think of unemployment. They are not without means and so in need of a weekly jobless benefit to tide them over. But those means have limits, and they can be quickly tested by the big expenses in life, like medical care. That suggests that policymakers might want to think about a different kind of unemployment benefit for people over certain prejobless income levels, one that might not provide the weekly paycheck that families with fewer resources need, but would promise coverage if something catastrophic—like a major illness—occurred. The second is the idea of affluent "survivalism." Networkers leads lives that have the look and feel of something from an era that predates the modern, highly interdependent economy. The texture of their lives may not have any policy implications. But it suggests how out of sync with the mainstream economy we've allowed some of the nation's most trained and experienced working people to become.

147   The rise of this self-help movement for people: Barbara Ehrenreich, *Bait and Switch: The (Futile) Pursuit of the American Dream* (New York: Metropolitan, 2005), 67.

148   "Hard times have a way of making people: PBS, *Frontline,* "The Jesus Factor," Raney Aronson, producer (Boston: WGBH, aired April 29, 2004), transcript available at http://www.pbs.org/wgbh/pages/frontline/shows/jesus/etc/script.html.

151 **The company's effort culminated in a 1998 book:** Brian Friedman, James Hatch, and David M. Walker, *Delivering on the Promise: How to Attract, Manage, and Retain Human Capital* (New York: Free Press, 1998).

153 **There's a nationwide "Employment Service":** This is one of the many of state-federal programs overseen by the U.S. Department of Labor's Employment and Training Administration. See, for example, http://www.dol.gov/21cw/resources.htm.

153 **There's something called "America's Workforce Network":** U.S. Department of Labor, *Workforce Tool Kit: The Resource for Employers* (Washington, D.C.: Department of Labor Employment and Training Administration, 2001), 2, http://www.doleta.gov/whatsnew/insidebind.pdf.

153 **"At this point, our spending on training:** Interview with Anthony Carnevale, an authority on education, training, and employment who has served as vice president of the Educational Testing Service and was appointed to commissions on training and employment by both Presidents Ronald Reagan and Bill Clinton. He is now a research professor at Georgetown University in Washington, D.C.

154 **From all outward appearances, Allan Hess's life:** Based on interviews with Hess from 2004 through 2008.

159 **"The employment security system is obsolete:** Interview with Michael L. Thurmond.

160 **"We decided to add a certain exclusivity:** Interview with Chip Schuneman.

160 **In a May 2000 issue of *Fortune*:** Devin Leonard, "They're Coming to Take You Away . . . ," *Fortune*, May 29, 2000, cover story; interview with Barry Trout.

162 **Or as Vonderhorst put it:** Interview with Robert Vonderhorst.

Chapter 6: The Poor

165 **"The poor are not like everyone else:** Michael Harrington, *The Other America: Poverty in the United States* (New York: Scribner, 1997), 138.

166 **When Rojas and Maldonado escaped the Salvadoran civil war:** Interviews with Elvira Rojas and José Maldonado from 2004 through 2006, translated by Susana Enriquez and Leslie A. Ortiz.

166 **And they were stuck:** The 1989 poverty threshold for a family of four was $12,575. In 2007 dollars, that amounts to $20,390.

167 **"We've won the War on Poverty:** Interview with Robert Rector.

170 **"The only way to improve your life if you're poor today:** Interview with Christopher Jencks.

172 **"We've produced tens of thousands of units:** Interview with Jan Breidenbach.

173 **Political scientist Francis Fukuyama:** Francis Fukuyama, "Immigrants and Family Values," *Commentary* 95, no. 5 (May 1993), http://heather .cs.ucdavis.edu/pub/Immigration/ImmAndTheFamily/Fukuyama.html.

174 **Consider Albert Grimes:** Interviews with Grimes from 2004 through 2007. Also interviews with his sister, Yvonne, in 2004 and 2006.

175 **"Steady, year-round employment:** Quote provided by David A. Moss. Also see Davis Dyer et al., *Rising Tide: Lessons from 165 Years of Brand Building at Procter & Gamble* (Boston: Harvard Business School Press, 2004), 187.

175 **"There is a close correlation between firm size:** Interview with Sanford Jacoby, an economist and economic historian who is vice chairman and a professor at the Anderson School of Management at the University of California-Los Angeles.

176 **According to Census data:** Based on U.S. Census Bureau, "2002 Economic Census," http://www.census.gov/econ/census02. The bureau performs such a census every five years.

180 **By now, the 1996 law has reduced:** U.S. Department of Health and Human Services, *Indicators of Welfare Dependence: Annual Report to Congress, 2007* (Washington, D.C.: Government Printing Office, September 2007), A12. See also Ron Haskins, *Work over Welfare: The Inside Story of the 1996 Welfare Reform Law* (Washington, D.C.: Brookings Institution, 2006), 1–428.

181 **A 2004 study:** Laura Wheaton, *Cost Avoidance and Cost Recovery in California's Child Support System* (Washington, D.C.: Urban Institute, 2004), 1–28.

181 **"The system was largely about:** Interview with Curtis L. Child.

182 **Betty Furness, President Lyndon Johnson's:** Quoted in Joseph Nocera, *A Piece of the Action: How the Middle Class Joined the Money Class* (New York: Touchstone, 1995), 34.

182 **Federal Reserve figures show:** Comparison of the 1989 and 2004 Surveys of Consumer Finances. See Arthur B. Kennickell and Janice Shack-Marquez, "Changes in Family Finances from 1983 to 1989: Evidence from the Survey of Consumer Finances," *Federal Reserve Bulletin* 78 (January 1992): 13, Table 9. See also: Brian K. Bucks et al., "Recent Changes in U.S.

Family Finances: Evidence from the 2001 and 2004 Survey of Consumer Finances," *Federal Reserve Bulletin* 92 (February 2006): A28, Table 11.

183 **Gregory Elliehausen, a finance expert:** Interview with Elliehausen, who is now an associate professor at George Washington University.

183 **They borrow their way through the bad patches:** Dirk Krueger and Fabrizio Perri, "Does Income Inequality Lead to Consumption Inequality? Evidence and Theory," *Review of Economic Studies* 73, no. 1 (2006): 163–193.

CHAPTER 7: HOUSING

187 **On average, 60 percent of the value:** Based on 2004 Federal Reserve Survey of Consumer Finances. Estimates by Desmond Toohey of the Urban Institute, Washington, D.C.

187 **For the least-wealthy half of homeowners:** In having so much of the value of our belongings tied up in our homes, most Americans differ from the rich minority that has plenty of financial room for yachts, planes, and giant investment accounts. Primary homes account for only 12.5 percent of the assets of the richest 1 percent of the country. Based on ibid.

188 **That's because the financial industry invented:** For a prescient account of the dangers of subprime mortgages, see Edward M. Gramlich, *Subprime Mortgages: America's Latest Boom and Bust* (Washington, D.C.: Urban Institute Press, 2007). Gramlich, a former Federal Reserve governor who died in the fall of 2007, tried to warn federal bank regulators that subprime lending was getting out of hand, but went largely unheard.

190 **According to one recent estimate by former:** Alan Greenspan and James Kennedy, *Sources and Uses of Equity Extracted from Homes*, Working Papers (Washington, D.C.: Federal Reserve, April 2007).

191 **Two hills over, the Scott-Ferguson family:** Much of the account of the Oakland Hills fire is based on interviews in 2006 with Peter Scott and his wife, Teresa Ferguson.

191 **Sometime around nine o'clock the next morning:** Alameda County Grand Jury, *Final Report, 1992–1993*, Alameda County, California.

193 **"Insurers think of what they're doing:** Interview with Rade T. Musulin.

194 **Despite Katrina and a string of other big storms in 2005:** Annual profit figures are based on financial records filed by the property casualty insurance companies with the National Association of Insurance Commissioners,

as well as information from the industry-funded Insurance Information Institute and the insurance trade press.

194   **"Because of the adoption of these techniques:** Interview with Robert P. Hartwig.

195   **As the industry refines its computerized techniques:** Interview with Mike Geeslin.

196   **Over the course of that time, police and fire officials:** Interviews with Don Pearman, construction expert and authority on the Oakland Hills fire. Pearman was indispensable in confirming details of Scott's and Ferguson's account and helping assemble the chronology of events.

199   **Besides the twenty-five dead, the final tally:** Alameda County Grand Jury, *Final Report, 1992–1993.*

200   **By one reputable estimate, almost 60 percent of Americans:** Interview with Peter M. Wells, president of MSB, the largest building-cost data provider for the U.S. real estate and insurance industries.

201   **Terry and Julie Tunnell and their son Brian:** Account based on several days of interviews with the Tunnells in 2006.

202   **"The fire spread three times faster:** Interview with Rich Hawkins.

203   **Asked why the company would clutter:** Interview with Dick Luedke.

204   **Strahm accepted the company's $300,000 claims payment:** Account based on interviews with Erik Strahm.

205   **"I asked for a replacement-cost policy:** Interview with Karen Reimus.

206   **"We think we offer an alternative:** Interview with Paul VanderMarck, executive vice president of Risk Management Solutions, Inc.

206   **Hemant Shah is in the business of creating catastrophes:** This account of RMS's operations relies heavily on extensive interviews with Shah and the firm's top experts. Although he disagrees with the notion that the firm's work may be contributing to the undoing of insurance, Shah and his executives were extraordinarily generous with their time and frank in their views during interviews in 2006.

207   **"Between hurricanes along the East and Gulf coasts:** Interview with Howard Kunreuther.

210   **In 2006, ten of the nation's top climate experts:** Kerry Emanuel et al., "Statement on the U.S. Hurricane Problem, July 25, 2006," http://wind .mit.edu/~emanuel/Hurricane_threat.htm.

210   **Former Allstate chief executive Edward M. Liddy:** From Liddy's Commonwealth Club speech, April 2006.

211   "You simply cannot make the case: Interview with Judith T. Kildow. Statistics from National Ocean Economics Program, http://noep.mbari.org.

212   Harvey Ryland, a former deputy director: Interview with Ryland.

212   From its base in Northbrook, Illinois: Classification numbers for policies from interviews with the executives of various insurance companies.

213   "If I have a lot of house fires: Interview with Mike Kreidler.

214   "Insurers are squeezing subsidies: Interview with Bruce Greenwald.

215   "I don't think you're ever going to get: Interview with Greg Heidrich.

215   "When you begin to tailor or refine policies: Interview with Alessandro A. Iuppa.

215   "It means the story of under-insurance: Quoted in Jeannette Steele, "Some Rebuild, Others Wait: Scripps Ranch Owners See Benefits in Building Bigger," *San Diego Union-Tribune*, October 24, 2005, B1.

216   But they were able to do so only because: Interview with Bob Cave. Cave is a local legend in the Scripps Ranch area for his willingness to offer burned-out homeowners a low package rate for rebuilding.

CHAPTER 8: EDUCATION

217   If it's one of the premier colleges: U.S. News and World Report, *Ultimate College Guide, 2008* (Naperville, Ill.: Sourcebooks, 2007).

217   What Americans believe they are getting: John Immerwahr et al., "Squeeze Play: How Parents and the Public Look at Higher Education Today," *National Center Report* 7, no. 4 (San Jose, Calif.: National Center for Public Policy and Higher Education, 2007), 8–9.

218   To begin to understand both how things have changed: Lawrence Mishel, Jared Bernstein, and Sylvia Allegretto, *The State of Working America, 2006–2007* (Ithaca, N.Y.: Cornell University Press, 2007), Table 3.17, 150.

219   In 1970, the United States accounted for 30 percent: Richard B. Freeman, *America Works: Critical Thoughts on the Exceptional U.S. Labor Market* (New York: Russell Sage Foundation, 2007), 133.

220   "What we're seeing in science and engineering: Interview with Richard B. Freeman, Harvard University.

220   Leah Bryner, thirty, has tried just about every: Interviews with Bryner during 2007.

223   The fraction of high school seniors in vocational education programs has steadily dropped: Personal communication with Anthony Carnevale.

223 And of those who do finish, only one-quarter: Robert J. LaLonde, Louis Jacobson, and Daniel Sullivan, *Do Displaced Workers Benefit from Community College Courses? Findings from Administrative Data and Directions for Future Research,* Working Paper no. 051 (Washington, D.C.: Hudson Institute, October 2005); Daniel G. Sullivan, Louis Jacobson, and Robert J. LaLonde, *Estimating the Returns to Community College Schooling for Displaced Workers,* Working Paper no. 2002-31 (Chicago: Federal Reserve Bank of Chicago, December 2002).

223 "You can't assume college and community college: Interview with Louis Jacobson, CNA Corporation.

224 We earned our special privileges: Anthony Carnevale, "Discounting Education's Value," *Chronicle of Higher Education* 53, no. 5 (September 22, 2006): B6.

224 "We Americans welcome our increasing reliance on education: Interview with Anthony Carnevale, Georgetown University.

224 One recent calculation by Princeton economist: Lisa Barrow and Cecilia E. Rouse, "Does College Still Pay?" *Economist's Voice* 2, no. 4 (2005), http://www.bepress.com/ev.

224 The sticker price of an average private four-year school: *Trends in College Pricing* (New York: College Board, 2007), 11, http://www.collegeboard.com/prod_downloads/about/news_info/trends/trends_pricing_07.pdf.

225 This, at a time: From our analysis of the Panel Study of Income Dynamics.

225 Loans accounted for: From analysis by Sandy Baum, senior policy analyst at the College Board, based on *Trends in Earnings Variability over the Past 20 Years* (Washington, D.C.: Congressional Budget Office, April 2007).

226 As college budget authority Jane Wellman put it: Interview with Wellman, executive director, Delta Project on Postsecondary Costs, Washington, D.C.

229 During the early and mid-1970s, generally no more than 2 percent: The statistics here come from personal communication with Elisabeth Jacobs and part of the work for her doctorate at Harvard. The techniques that Jacobs used in her work are similar, but not identical, to those I used in Chapter 3.

229 "A college education certainly provides some insurance: Interview with Elisabeth Jacobs, the Brookings Institution and Harvard University.

230   **"Education no guarantee" chart:** For this chart, Seth Zimmerman and I
      sorted PSID sample families by the educational attainment of the head or
      spouse, whichever was higher, and examined the pattern of income
      volatility over time of the subgroups.

CHAPTER 9: HEALTH

234   **About 162 million other Americans:** Employee Benefit Research Insti-
      tute, *EBRI Databook on Employee Benefits*, Chapter 26, Table 26.3; *Sources
      of Health Insurance and Characteristics of the Uninsured: Analysis of the
      March 2007 Current Population Survey,* EBRI Issue Brief no. 310 (Wash-
      ington, D.C.: Employee Benefit Research Institute, October 2007), Fig. 1,
      5; and conversations with Paul Fronstin, EBRI's health research director.

235   **Statistics show that people with insurance:** Kaiser Family Founda-
      tion/Health Research and Education Trust, *Employer Health Benefits,
      2007: Annual Survey*, 89; Kaiser Family Foundation, *Distribution of Out-
      of-Pocket Spending for Health Care Services* (May 2006), Fig. 4, 3.

235   **The fraction of the working Americans and their families:** *Sources of
      Health Insurance,* Fig. 3, 7; and interviews with Fronstin.

235   **The fraction of large employers offering retirees:** Kaiser Family Foun-
      dation/Health Research and Education Trust, *Employer Health Benefits,
      2007*, 154; and conversations with Fronstin.

235   **Surveys show that even big, financially healthy companies:** *The Future
      of Employment-Based Health Benefits: Have Employers Reached a Tipping
      Point?* EBRI Issue Brief no. 312 (Washington, D.C.: Employee Benefit Re-
      search Institute, October 2007), 1–20.

236   **Statistics show that about 40 percent of small firms:** Ibid.

238   **As recounted by Jonathan Cohn in his recent book:** Jonathan Cohn,
      *Sick: The Untold Story of America's Health Care Crisis—and the People
      Who Pay the Price* (New York: HarperCollins, 2007), 7–11.

239   **And it was reinforced immediately after the war:** U.S. Government,
      Budget of the United States, Fiscal Year 2008: Analytical Perspectives
      (Washington, D.C.: Government Printing Office, 2007), Table 19-1, 287.

240   **"Just as cheap health premiums:** Cohn, *Sick,* 10.

242   **Rebecca J. Rowlands started her work life managing an almond farm:**
      Interviews with Rowlands, July 24–25, 2007.

244 **But recent reporting by *Los Angeles Times* reporter Lisa Girion:** Reporting in 2006 and 2007, including "Health Insurer Tied Bonuses to Dropping Sick Policyholders," *Los Angeles Times*, November 9, 2007, A1.

245 **"People pay insurance companies:** Interview with Cindy Ehnes.

246 **"We were seeing a lot of abuses:** Interview with Burt Margolin.

246 **It read, "No insurer issuing or providing:** California Assembly Bill 1100, 1993. As filed March 2, 1993.

246 **"This may not have been the intent:** Michael Arnold, "Request for Opposition—AB 1100," memorandum from Blue Shield of California to members of the California Senate Insurance, Claims and Corporations Committee, July 13, 1993.

246 **As it finally emerged from the legislature:** California state law, Chapter 1210 of the Statutes of 1993, signed by the governor, October 11, 1993.

248 **But as a subsequent court case would reveal:** Case No. 356-634, *Rebecca J. Rowlands v. Blue Shield Life & Health Insurance Co., Blue Shield of California et al.,* "Plaintiff's Notice of Motion and Motion for Summary Adjudication of Issues . . . , October 15, 2007, Exhibit 12, Application Dated Mar. 30, 2000."

248 **Hunt says that Rowlands and Adler met:** Interview with Lili Pope Hunt.

249 **Whatever was said, the result was an application:** *Rebecca J. Rowlands v. Blue Shield,* "Complaint for Damages and Injunctive Relief . . . Filed August 8, 2006, Application Dated Apr. 6, 2005."

249 **She immediately put the coverage to use:** Ibid.

250 **When Rowlands underwent the operation:** Rowlands provided me with many of her medical records. This diagnosis comes from Yuki Takasumi, "Pathology Report for Rebecca J. Rowlands," based on results of an operation on November 14, 2005, St. John's Health Center, Santa Monica, California, November 17, 2005, 3.

250 **Blue Shield dashed off an "URGENT MEDICAL RECORDS REQUEST":** This comes from one of the records Rowlands provided, titled "To: Medical Record, Dr. Jane Spiegel's Office . . . From: Blue Shield of Calif./Admin Review," November 17, 2005.

252 **Blue Shield executives discussed Rowlands's case:** Interview with Tom Epstein and David Seldin.

252 **Blue Shield, although a nonprofit, has amassed:** Financial report filed by Blue Shield of California with the California Department of Managed Health Care, 2002–2006.

253 **"Blue Shield committed serious violations:** California Department of Insurance, press release, December 13, 2007.

Chapter 10: Retirement

255 **As a twenty-five-year-old graduate student:** Peter L. Bernstein, *Capital Ideas: The Improbable Origins of Modern Wall Street* (New York: Wiley, 1992), 41.

257 **Mastering the art of long-term money management:** Alicia H. Munnell and Annika Sundén, *Coming Up Short: The Challenge of 401(k) Plans* (Washington, D.C.: Brookings Institution, 2004). I rely heavily in this chapter on the work of Munnell, a Boston College economist and head of its Center for Retirement Research, and her associates, including Steven Sass.

258 **"I either had in my head:** Interviews with Harry Markowitz.

259 **Essentially, we don't save in any other way:** Alicia H. Munnell, Francesca Golub-Sass, and Andrew Varani, *How Much Are Workers Saving?* Issue in Brief no. 34 (Boston: Center for Retirement Research, Boston College, October 2005).

259 **When it comes to nonfinancial house wealth:** National Association of Realtors, median tenure data, http://www.realtor.org/press_room/ news_releases/2006/survey_shows_buyers_and_sellers.html.

259 **As for our business acumen, there is a:** Alicia H. Munnell and Annika Sundén, *401(k) Plans Are Still Coming Up Short,* Issue in Brief no. 43 (Boston: Center for Retirement Research, Boston College, March 2006).

260 **"Employers are no longer interested:** Alicia H. Munnell, Storrs Lectures, Yale Law School, March 5–6, 2007.

261 **By 2005, that number had dropped to just 10 percent:** "Retirement Trends in the United States Over the Past Quarter Century," in *Facts from EBRI* (Washington, D.C.: Employee Benefit Research Institute, June 2007), Fig. 1, 1, http://www.ebri.org/pdf/publications/facts/0607fact.pdf.

263 **"By the year 2000, employees will be managing:** Earl C. Gottschalk Jr., "On Your Own: Companies Are Giving Employees Investment Control of Their Retirement Money; That Can Be Good—or Bad," *Wall Street Journal,* December 9, 1994, A1.

264 **In 2004, the last year for which figures are available:** Brian K. Bucks, et al., "Recent Changes in U.S. Family Finances: Evidence from the 2001 and 2004 Survey of Consumer Finances," *Federal Reserve Bulletin* 92 (February 2006): A1–38.

264   **That may seem like a reasonable amount:** Calculated using http://www.immediateannuities.com.

264   **As a result, he said:** Interview with Douglass C. North.

265   **"If I'd only listened to myself:** Interview with Joseph E. Stiglitz.

265   **George Akerlof, who shared the prize with Stiglitz:** Interview with Akerlof.

265   **In a survey of several premier universities:** Interviews with retirement administrators at the schools.

265   **One study suggested almost three-quarters failed to make:** John Ameriks and Stephen P. Zeldes, *How Do Household Portfolio Shares Vary with Age?* Working Papers (New York: Graduate School of Business, Columbia University, September 2004), 31, http://www1.gsb.columbia .edu/mygsb/faculty/research/pubfiles/16/Ameriks_Zeldes_age_Sept_ 2004d.pdf.

266   **"I think very little about my retirement savings:** Interview with Daniel Kahneman.

266   **"Investment is not something you can do:** Interview with Robert M. Solow.

266   **"I would rather spend my time:** Interview with Clive W. J. Granger.

267   **"The problem of vision was especially acute:** Steven Sass, *The Promise of Private Pensions: The First Hundred Years* (Cambridge, Mass.: Harvard University Press, 1997), 9. This section relies heavily on Sass's work.

268   **"People say they want more choice:** Interview with Sheena S. Iyengar.

268   **"It's astounding:** Interview with David Laibson; James Choi, David Laibson, and Brigitte Madrian, *$100 Bills on the Sidewalk: Sub-optimal Saving in 401(k) Plans,* Working Paper no. 11554 (Cambridge, Mass.: National Bureau of Economic Research, August 2005).

268   **"The law that created Section 401(k):** Interview with Daniel Halperin.

269   **"The idea was that you could educate people:** Interview with David C. John.

269   **What this study found was that those who retired at the peak:** Gary Burtless, "What Do We Know about the Risk of Individual Account Pensions . . . ?" *AEA Papers and Proceedings* 93, no. 2 (May 2003): 354–359.

270   **"This is the free market on cruise control:** Interview with Ann L. Combs.

271   **Markowitz and his successors invented:** Bernstein, *Capital Ideas.*

272   **Wall Street broker and pundit Gerald Loeb:** Ibid., 48.

276   **For more than two decades, Lowell Seibert:** Interviews with Seibert and his wife, Christine Ferranti.

CHAPTER 11: NEW ORLEANS

283   **Laurie Vignaud and Nicole Mackie face double dilemmas:** Interviews with Vignaud and Mackie.

284   **"All of a sudden, time sped up:** Interview with Reed Kroloff. .

285   **Michael Chertoff, the secretary of the Department of Homeland Security:** Chertoff interview on *Fox News Sunday,* September 4, 2005.

287   **"There are classes of problems that free markets:** Interviews with Thomas C. Schelling.

287   **Prospects for a speedy, publicly led comeback:** Bush's speech can be found at http://www.whitehouse.gov/news/releases/2005/09/20050915-8 .html.

288   **In place of these approaches:** Interview with David A. Moss; Moss, *When All Else Fails: Government as the Ultimate Risk Manager* (Cambridge: Harvard University Press, 2002), 257.

288   **A House report on a 1970 law:** Ibid.; Disaster Assistance Legislation: Hearings before the Subcommittee on Flood Control . . . House of Representatives, 91st Cong., July 1970, 20.

288   **When the Mississippi River jumped its banks in 1993:** Stephen P. Dinnen, "In Illinois, a Town Turns Tide on Disaster . . . ," *Washington Post,* March 26, 1994, E1; Robert L. Koenig, "Flood Aid Swells with Vote . . . ," *St. Louis Post-Dispatch,* November 10, 1993, A1.

289   **The only problem is that none of these aid efforts:** Ann M. Simmons et al., "Katrina Aid Far from Flowing . . . ," *Los Angeles Times,* August 27, 2006, A1; Congressional Budget Office, *The Federal Government's Spending and Tax Actions in Response to the 2005 Gulf Coast Hurricanes* (Washington, D.C.: Congressional Budget Office, August 2007), Fig. 1, 5; United States House of Representatives, House Budget Committee, Hearing on the budgetary effects of Hurricanes Katrina and Rita, August 2, 2007; United States Senate, Senate Homeland Security and Governmental Affairs Committee, Ad-Hoc Subcommittee on Disaster Recovery, hearing on the Louisiana housing recovery program, May 24, 2007.

290   **When asked why the Lower Ninth Ward had failed to come back:** Gwen Filosa, "The Lonely Lower 9: 16 Months after Hurricane Katrina Hope Is as Rare as People . . . ," *New Orleans Times-Picayune,* December 18, 2006, 1.

290 **"What's missed [by the market advocates]:** Interviews with Richard H. Baker.

290 **Baker's idea was gaining considerable momentum:** Spencer S. Hsu, "Post-Katrina Promises Unfulfilled . . . ," *Washington Post*, January 28, 2006, 1; Adam Nossiter, "Rejection of Building Plan Causes Dismay in Louisiana," *The New York Times*, January 26, 2006, 16; Greg Allen, "Bush, Louisiana at Odds over Reconstruction Plan," National Public Radio, *Morning Edition*, January 24, 2006.

291 **"I busted some ground there:** Interview with Leroy Vignaud.

293 **To get some sense of what greeted:** I visited Vignaud's ruined house during a week spent in post-Katrina New Orleans in November 2005.

293 **"Conditions are optimal for the fungi:** Interview with Mervi Hjelmroos-Koski.

295 **"New Orleans is the biggest through-put port:** Interview with Gary P. LaGrange.

296 **But as New Orleans descended into chaos:** Daryn Kagan et al., "Office Building Burns in Downtown New Orleans . . . ," CNN, *Live from . . .* , September 2, 2005; Mark Babineck, "Troopers Roll into Chaotic New Orleans . . . ," Reuters, September 1, 2005.

296 **He told the *Los Angeles Times* that without a clear plan:** Interview with C. Ray Nagin.

296 **"I'm a property-rights person:** Gwen Filosa, "Nagin Says He'll Oppose Building Moratorium . . . ," *New Orleans Times-Picayune*, January 22, 2006, 1.

298 **"The flooding caused a breakdown:** John Schwartz, "Army Builders Accept Blame over Flooding," *The New York Times*, June 2, 2006, 1.

298 **The extra money appears never:** Mark Schleifstein, "For the First Time, the Army Corps of Engineers Proposes Voluntary Buyouts . . . ," *New Orleans Times-Picayune,* January 28, 2008, 1.

299 **"They're taking complete flyers:** Interview with Robert G. Bea, now a University of California-Berkeley engineering professor.

300 **As Craig Colton, a Louisiana State University geographer:** Interview with Colton.

301 **"We organized everything:** Interview with John P. Georges.

301 **Fr. Anthony Stratis worked the phones:** Interview with Stratis.

301 **Dr. Nick Moustoukas followed up by wiring money:** Interview with Moustoukas.

302   **"We're doing government's job for them:** Interview with Denise Thornton.

304   **"It used to be [before the hurricane]:** Interview with Earl Mackie.

Chapter 12: Conclusion

309   **The change is apparent in a simple set:** Frank Levy and Peter Temin, *Inequality and Institutions in Twentieth Century America*, Working Paper no. 13106 (Cambridge, Mass.: National Bureau of Economic Research, May 2007), 2.

309   **"It's hard for me to believe:** Interview with Frank Levy, an economist at the Massachusetts Institute of Technology.

319   **First, one of the biggest debt burdens:** The Project on Student Debt, *Student Debt and the Class of 2006* (Berkeley, Calif.: Institute for College Access and Success, September 2007), 3, http://projectonstudentdebt.org/files/pub/State_by_State_report_FINAL.pdf.

INDEX